CLIMB

Leaving Safe and Finding Strength on 100 Summits in Japan

Susan Spann

Prometheus Books

Guilford, Connecticut

℗Prometheus Books

An imprint of The Rowman & Littlefield Publishing Group, Inc.
4501 Forbes Boulevard, Suite 200
Lanham, Maryland 20706
www.rowman.com

Distributed by NATIONAL BOOK NETWORK

British Library Cataloguing in Publication Information Available

Library of Congress Cataloging-in-Publication Data

Name: Spann, Susan, author.
Title: Climb : leaving safe and finding strength on 100 summits in Japan / Susan Spann.
Description: Guilford, Connecticut : Prometheus, 2020. | Includes bibliographical references. | Summary: "After more than forty years of living 'safe and scared,' California attorney and mystery author Susan Spann decided to break free by climbing one hundred of Japan's most famous mountains, inspired by a classic list of hyakumeizan peaks. But when an unexpected cancer diagnosis forced her to confront her deepest fears, the mountains of Japan became the setting for an even more transformative journey from pain and fear to a new life fueled by hope, confidence, and strength. This immersive, inspiring, and witty page-turner captures the terrifying lows and breathtaking highs of a woman's journey from timidity to confidence, cancer to healing, and regret to joy, as she breaks the mental and physical chains that once prevented her from living out her dreams. Susan chronicles her journey with an insightful, often humorous eye for not only her travels across Japan, but the culture, food, nature, and obstacles she encountered along the way, and complements her honest and vivid prose with breathtaking personal photographs"— Provided by publisher.
Identifiers: LCCN 2019054679 (print) | LCCN 2019054680 (ebook) | ISBN 9781633885929 (cloth) | ISBN 9781633885936 (epub)
Subjects: LCSH: Spann, Susan. | Mountaineering—Japan. | Mountaineering—Psychological aspects. | Cancer—Patients—Biography. | Japan—Description and travel.
Classification: LCC GV199.44.J3 S73 2020 (print) | LCC GV199.44.J3 (ebook) | DDC 915.2—dc23
LC record available at https://lccn.loc.gov/2019054679
LC ebook record available at https://lccn.loc.gov/2019054680

♾™ The paper used in this publication meets the minimum requirements of American National Standard for Information Sciences Permanence of Paper for Printed Library Materials, ANSI/NISO Z39.48-1992.

This book is for everyone with a dream

May you find the strength you need to make it real

日々旅にして旅を栖とす
[Every day is a journey, and the journey itself is home]

—Matsuo Basho

CONTENTS

ACKNOWLEDGMENTS

I may have hiked most of these mountains solo, but I could not have written this book alone. It would be impossible for me to thank everyone involved in making *Climb* a reality—the list would run longer than the book itself. However, there are a few individuals who require special mention. In roughly chronological order:

Thank you to Dr. Daniel Herron for finding my cancer early enough that I had a chance for a real cure, not just remission; to Dr. Joelle Jakobsen for scheduling my surgery on a moment's notice and performing it so skillfully; and to Dr. Gurvinder Shaheed for believing in my ability to tolerate dose-dense chemotherapy and for guiding me through it with skill and compassion. I am alive today because of each of you.

Thank you to Marie, my nurse navigator, for walking me through the process and for holding my hand (literally and figuratively) when I needed support. Thanks to my nurses Jaime and Vickie, for the infusions of love and laughter (along with chemotherapy) and for cheering me on even after my treatments ended. Thank you to Ashley, the biopsy nurse at Mercy San Juan, to JJ, the recovery nurse—and to all nurses, everywhere, who care for those of us facing this horrific disease. You are my heroes, and I do not say that lightly.

On the publishing side, thank you to my fabulous literary agent, Sandra Bond, for believing in this project, finding it a publishing home, and all the million other things—large and small—that you do on my behalf. I am so grateful to have you in my life, and to have you as a friend as well as a business partner.

Thank you to Jill Maxick, for loving this book immediately, and to Jon Kurtz, for seeing the promise in the story of a middle-aged woman breaking free from fear to live her dreams. And thanks to my editor, Jake Bonar, for helping me cram a year-long journey (and 56,000 photographs) into 100,000 words and 14 images.

Thank you to Ido Gabay, Takuto, the Yamabushi (D), and Hokkaido Nature Tours, not only for introducing me to your spectacular island and guiding me up its peaks, but also for teaching me to reach beyond my perceived boundaries and discover capabilities I didn't realize I had. You are indeed "Hokkaido Strong," and my time with you created memories I will cherish—and skills I will use—for a lifetime.

Thank you to Nishiguchi Sensei, for your patience and careful instruction in traditional Japanese calligraphy. *Shodō* lies at the heart of Japanese culture and tradition, and I am honored to have the opportunity to learn this ancient art from you.

Thank you to Kaitlyn and Laurie Bolland, Paula Ross-Jones (a.k.a. Mom), Spencer Jones, Claire Youmans, Annamaria Alfieri, Corinne O'Flynn, and Laura VanArendonk Baugh, not only for your love and support, but for putting your money—and your feet—where your mouths are and flying halfway around the world to climb with me. I love you all very, very much.

Thank you to Ron and Joan, David and Yoko, Ron and Linda, Karen, and everyone else I met and hiked with in Kyoto, on the Kumano Kodo, and elsewhere on my 100 Summits journey.

Thank you to my friends and Tokyo officemates: Greg, Ellen, and Kira. I am fortunate indeed to have the opportunity to work, and laugh, with each of you.

Thank you to Kerry Schaffer (a.k.a. Kerry Ann King), Heather Webb, Rae James (R. F. James), Kathy Owen, Jenny Hansen, Wing Ng (and Peter Ultsch), and all the many, many fellow authors and friends I do not have room to list by name. I love you, and miss you, and hope to see you soon.

Thank you to my family: Marcie, Gene, Robert, Lola, Anna, Matteo, and Spencer III; it is not easy to see someone you love move halfway around the world, and I treasure the fact that you supported me and my journey.

Thank you to my son, Christopher, for so many things and reasons that I could not possibly list them all—from acting as my translator in those early days to so many wonderful conversations over coffee and choco-cro at the St. Marc.

Thank you to my husband, Michael. Your love, and your belief in me and in this journey, carried me through the times when I could not see the trail on my own.

* * *

And finally, thank you, reader, for joining me on the journey through these pages. I hope this book inspires you to find the strength to face your challenges and the courage to pursue your dreams.

INTRODUCTION

Hyakumeizan

I have always been afraid of the things I love.

Afraid I wasn't good enough. Afraid I would fail. Afraid my failure would disappoint the people I love and that they wouldn't love me anymore.

From childhood, I always chose the safest path to any destination. I followed every rule to the letter. I feared the consequences of rebellion. As an adult, I clung to safety, terrified that pursuing my dreams would only leave me broke and brokenhearted.

I loved the mountains but lived in the city. I loved to write, but my fear that it wouldn't provide a stable income drove me onto the path my father chose (and for similar reasons): I became a lawyer and practiced law.

I had wanted to climb Mount Fuji since I first saw a photograph of the mountain when I was a pudgy, nearsighted, clumsy child. But I knew, despite the siren song of Fuji's snowcapped cone, that such an iconic mountain lay impossibly far beyond my abilities.

Instead, I devoured every issue of *National Geographic* magazine, fingers caressing the vivid photographs of glowing glaciers and snowy peaks. In college, I blew my entertainment budget on mountaineering books and travelogues. My friends fawned over movie stars, but my heroes were Reinhold Messner, Tenzing Norgay, and Junko Tabei (the first woman to stand on the summit of Mount Everest).

Yet even as I imagined the exhilaration of standing atop Denali or K2, I always knew I would never dare to climb them . . . until a nearly-disastrous trip to Japan in 2015 inspired a burning desire to see what would happen if, just for once, I listened to my hopes and not my fears.

* * *

After that trip in 2015, I remembered a mountaineering book called *Nihon Hyakumeizan* (*One Hundred Famous Mountains of Japan*), written by Japanese mountaineer Kyūya Fukada. The book became an instant classic in Japan, and since its original release in 1964, it has inspired generations of hikers to climb the 100 mountains on Fukada's list. The mountains are not difficult by mountaineering standards—many can be climbed in a single day—but for serious Japanese hikers, climbing the *hyakumeizan* is a major life achievement.

I originally read Fukada's book in college, but bought a new copy in 2015. As I read about the beautiful, wild mountains he described, my lifelong love of reading about adventure ripened into a compelling need to climb these mountains for myself.

My emotions vacillated between excitement and abject terror.

What was I thinking? I had a job. I had *responsibilities*. I was wildly out of shape.

And yet, something inside me believed that I could do it. Not just climb, but face my fears. Rise to the physical challenges and finally answer the siren song of the mountains I loved so dearly.

My father let his need for safety and security cage him in. He lived, and died, without ever breaking past his fears.

I did not want to spend my life in my father's chains.

In June of 2017, I made the decision: I was going to climb the *hyaku-meizan*—but not the way Japanese hikers do, as a long-term rite of passage.

I would climb them all in a single year.

The physical and logistical challenges were daunting. Few people—and no Western woman over 45—had ever climbed the *hyakumeizan* in a year, and I was a middle-aged, overweight woman who courted disaster even hiking *down* a single mountain. To make it happen, I would need to suspend my law practice (which paid my family's bills), obtain notorious-ly tricky visas for myself and my husband Michael, move to Japan, and execute a year-long expedition in a country whose language I barely spoke. That, in addition to climbing 100 mountains, more than 30 of which are active volcanoes and several of which kill hikers every year.

"Terrifying" didn't begin to describe the emotions this inspired.

And yet, it was also a chance to shatter the shackles of my old, "safe" life, to overcome my fears of risk and failure, and to experience the incredible sights that had made my heart sing since that awkward child first fell in love with Mount Fuji in the pages of *National Geographic* magazine.

Terrified or not, I was going to try.

I

VICTORY—AND MISERY—ON MISEN

June 2015

I fell in love with climbing mountains the day one almost killed me.

In June 2015, my son Christopher was a university sophomore majoring in Japanese language and completing a three-month study abroad in Kyoto, the former capital of Japan. He invited me to visit him in the country he had grown to love, where he also planned to live after graduation.

I loved Japan myself—I majored in Asian studies at Tufts University before attending law school and pursuing a "safe" career in law. By 2015 I had also written three critically acclaimed mystery novels set in 16th-century Kyoto, even though I had never been to Asia. Too scared to make the 10-hour flight, I did my extensive research in books and through interviews with contacts in Japan.

Only when Christopher asked me to visit did I finally summon the courage to white-knuckle my way across the Pacific to the country I had studied, and adored, for more than three decades.

Near the end of my time in Japan, we spent the night on Miyajima, an island off the coast of Hiroshima that I'd wanted to visit since seeing a picture of Itsukushima Shrine's Great Torii in *National Geographic* magazine when I was nine years old. The enormous vermilion Shintō gate stands 15 meters high. When the tide comes in around its base, the "floating gate" is among Japan's most memorable and iconic sights.

The shrine sits directly in front of sacred Mount Misen (弥山) (535 meters), Miyajima's highest mountain. In 806, a Japanese priest named Kōbō Daishi (also known as Kūkai) spent 100 days meditating on Mount Misen and lit a sacred eternal flame in a temple near the summit. This sacred fire was later used to kindle the eternal flame at the World War II memorial in Hiroshima Park. I desperately wanted to see Kōbō Daishi's flame, which had burned for more than 1,000 years, but knew my middle-aged, overweight body couldn't handle a two-kilometer climb up ancient steps to the temple near the mountain's peak.

However, the Miyajima Ropeway carried visitors from the base of Mount Misen to Shishiiwa Observatory, just half an hour's hike below the summit—and a half-hour climb, I thought I might just manage.

At the ropeway, Christopher and I faced a decision: Should we ride the gondola round-trip or buy a one-way ticket up and hike back down? My son suggested the round-trip ride, but riding most of the way to the top struck me as "cheating" on the climb, so I persuaded him to ride one way and hike back down the mountain on the trail.

"It will be fun," I promised. "An adventure."

He glanced at the overcast sky but didn't argue.

We started up a well-marked earthen trail punctuated by flights of steep stone stairs. Shifting mist obscured the path ahead. The smell of the surrounding pines, combined with the scents of earth and mist, made my spirit sing despite the way my thighs burned from the unaccustomed exercise.

Signs on the path informed us that the trip to the summit would take about 30 minutes, but I suspected we would need a little more. In fact, it took me 35 minutes just to reach the Eternal Fire Hall, which sits in a clearing on the mountain's shoulder. Swirls of mist drifted through the clearing as I approached the wooden worship hall. I felt the mountain's holiness—a peace and stillness in my spirit that, for once, had silenced all my fears.

The eternal flame burned on an altar at the back of the tiny hall. Around it, rows of candles flickered, kindled from the holy fire by worshippers who climbed Mount Misen's slopes.

After viewing the sacred flame, we continued toward the summit. The roughhewn steps were slick with mist. The lack of handrails and the dizzying drop-off to my right made me cautious. My feet slipped more than once, sending bursts of adrenaline through my limbs.

Every couple of minutes, I was passed by one of the many Japanese octogenarians who moved up and down the mountain with confident speed. Under any other circumstances, I would have found the experience mortifying. As it was, I simply wanted to reach the top without plummeting to my death.

Twenty minutes later, we reached the summit.

Thick mist swirled past the boulders that ringed the peak. Three stone Buddhas peered benevolently down from their perch atop a rock that rose a meter higher than my head. Silver coins that visitors tossed up as offerings lay around the statues' feet; Christopher pitched a coin at one of the Buddhas until it settled without rolling off.

I tried too, without success, so Christopher tossed my offering up as well.

Stomachs rumbling, we investigated the building at the center of the summit. It had no restaurant but did have toilets (an initially unexpected, but delightful, feature of most Japanese hiking trails: nothing improves an outdoor experience like an indoor loo).

At that time, I lived my life with an undercurrent of fear—a constant, background-level worry about failure, loss, or making a mistake—but as I stood taking pictures on Misen's misty summit, I felt my fear withdraw.

In that moment, I felt only joy.

I didn't understand how, or why, the mountain replaced my fear with a peace that radiated outward from my chest and filled me with energy like nothing I had felt before. I suspected this was a shadow of the euphoria mountaineers reported feeling on the summit of real peaks, like Everest. I'd read about that feeling many times but never thought I would experience it. I didn't tell Christopher—after all, we hadn't even really *climbed* the mountain—but I felt a true sense of accomplishment.

The slippery mist and lack of handrails made the stone steps even scarier on the descent. I turned sideways and moved at a pace that would have made an arthritic tortoise sneer. Even then, I barely avoided the ignominy of a seated scoot down the mist-soaked stairs.

My son soon disappeared from view, but I found him waiting at the Eternal Fire Hall.

"You're sure you want to climb back down, instead of taking the cable car?" he asked.

I was sure. "It will be an adventure!"

Truer words were never spoken.

The 2.5-kilometer Momijidani (Maple Valley) Trail winds down the forested slopes of Mount Misen along the course of the Momiji River. Posted signs suggested the hike would take about 90 minutes.

"You're sure about this?" Christopher looked doubtful.

I was still sure, so down we went.

For the first 20 minutes, the trail alternated between gently sloping earthen paths and old stone stairs. To my relief, the steeper sections all had handrails. My legs ached, but I didn't want to ask for a break so soon, since I'd insisted on the hike.

We passed a marker saying we had 2.3 kilometers to go.

I converted the distance in my head. "That must be wrong. We've walked more than a tenth of a mile."

"I doubt it's wrong." Christopher paused. "Want to go back and take the ropeway?"

I looked back the way we came. "I think down is easier."

His expression suggested he thought otherwise.

"We're through the steepest part," I insisted (with no factual basis for my opinion—which later proved to be wildly wrong). "Let's keep going."

The mist remained, but the temperature slowly rose to a sweltering 29 degrees Celsius (85 Fahrenheit). Humidity and exertion made me sweat in places I didn't even realize I had pores. We hadn't brought anything to drink. My mouth grew pasty, and I felt a dehydration headache coming on. My feet ached and my thighs burned painfully with every step.

Then, as if on cue, it started raining.

Fortunately, we had brought umbrellas. As we opened them, Christopher said, "You know, I'm really glad we didn't take the ropeway."

(Have I mentioned that sarcasm runs in the family?)

"It's an adventure," I replied, though less enthusiastically than before.

Ten minutes later, while descending another set of uneven steps, my foot slipped out from under me. As I flailed my arms for balance, my other foot slipped, and I felt myself fall.

In that instant, I realized *this could kill me.*

After a lifetime of avoiding risk, I was about to die on a mountain so small it barely deserved the name.

The steps were carved from stone, and more than capable of breaking my limbs or neck. Three meters down, the stairs curved sharply left, and only a narrow bamboo rail separated me from a 15-meter fall to the rocks below. Even if I survived the fall, we were kilometers from help.

I bounced down three stone steps and into a thorn bush at the side of the trail, which arrested my fall and likely saved my life. It also left a dozen inch-deep, bleeding punctures in my butt and hands.

A massive jolt of adrenaline coursed through me.

"Mom!"

I heard Christopher's terrified shout and wanted to reassure him.

I took a deep breath. "I'm okay."

He hurried toward me. "Are you hurt?"

I was sitting in a thorn bush. Every part of my body screamed with pain, and I may have wet myself a little when I fell. (With all the sweat, I really wasn't sure.) I had shooting pains in my hips and back that registered at least an 8.5 on the *you'll regret this later* scale—but I wasn't dead and had no broken bones.

Gritting my teeth against the pain, I extracted myself from the bush and forced a smile. "I'll be fine."

Within two steps I knew I'd escaped the fall with only minor injuries, but also that I had to reach the bottom before the adrenaline wore off and the true pain set in. I didn't want to frighten Christopher by telling him how much the fall had hurt me, so I sucked it up and hiked on through the pain.

Farther down the slope, the trail moved closer to the river, which cascaded over rocks and filled the air with the sound of waterfalls. At first, this seemed like a great distraction.

However, the river was also home to swarms of enormous biting flies—for which my son and I were the Blue Plate Special.

These flies do not sneak up on you. They buzz your head like fighter jets with a bite that feels like daggers in your neck. The bites swell up immediately, and they bleed and hurt long after the flies have drunk their fill and gone their merry way.

Wild flailing scares them—temporarily—so every time I heard one roaring in, I raised my arms and did my best impression of an overexcited Muppet. This redirected the flies to Christopher, whose flailing sent them back to me again. This unplanned game of insect-pickle worked all right on flatter bits of trail, but when we came to a flight of stairs—of which there were many—I had to clutch the railing, leaving myself at the mercy of the flies.

For the record, these flies have no mercy.

Two hours, five enormous bruises, many puncture wounds, and count-less fly-bites later, we reached the base of the mountain—just as the sun broke through the clouds, transforming the sky to a brilliant summer blue.

"That wasn't so bad," I told Christopher, "and now we can always say we had an adventure on Mount Misen."

"I don't think we need any more adventures," Christopher said drily.

Despite the bites and injuries, I really had enjoyed the hike (in retrospect, at least), although I decided I would try to skip the falling bit on future climbs. Because, to my surprise, I knew right then there *would* be future climbs.

The joy I felt on Misen's summit coursed through my memory like a drug. My fear of risk had not diminished—the potential consequences of my fall made my knees go weak each time they sprang to mind—but the desire to feel that "summit high" again made me willing to accept a little risk.

Even so, I did not imagine the magnitude of the adventure that lay ahead.

2

ONE HUNDRED AND ONE

November 2017

It sounds cliché to say I came home "changed" in 2015, but it's also true. My body returned to California but, in a very real sense, my heart remained in the mountains of Japan. Each time I thought about that summer trip or looked at the photographs, my throat felt tight with longing.

I had to return.

And I did—in the autumn of 2016, and again in 2017 to celebrate Christopher's college graduation. Shortly after the graduation trip, I made the decision to take a sabbatical from law practice, travel to Japan, and attempt to become the first American woman over 45 to climb the *hyakumeizan* in a year.

My family supported this wild decision. Christopher was already searching for employment in Japan, and my husband Michael (a stay-at-home dad) agreed to sell our house and trade California suburban life for a year in Tokyo. His knees would not allow him to join me on any of the mountains, but he understood and supported my need to climb.

It was exactly the kind of thing I read about other people doing but would *never* do myself . . . and yet, I started making plans.

I wanted to begin the climbs on March 26, 2018, my father's birthday and the 10th anniversary of his death. He had taught me many important lessons, some of which had made me strong while others—including my abiding fears of risk and change—had enslaved me all my life. I hoped that climbing the *hyakumeizan* would help me break the cycle of fear that governed my father's entire life and the first half of my own.

In early November 2017, a month before I was scheduled to leave for Tokyo to sign my visa application (which I had to do in person because I had no Japanese sponsor), I went in for a routine mammogram.

* * *

Afterward, I had barely reached the changing room when the tech knocked on the door. "Don't get dressed. The doctor would like more images."

My stomach dropped. "Is something wrong?"

"It happens. Sometimes the images aren't clear."

The tech took two more images and asked me to wait in the changing room for an ultrasound tech, who would come and get me soon. I didn't worry—much. A lump I'd found in my right breast the year before had turned out to be merely a duct exposed by the 50-pound weight loss I achieved through a year of diet and exercise. I expected this would turn out to be something similar.

The ultrasound tech spent less than a minute scanning my right breast and only a little longer on the left. Then, to my horror, she moved the wand into my armpit.

I started shaking.

She paused the exam and looked at me. "Are you okay?"

"We both know I'm not," I said, "because you're looking at my lymph nodes."

She stammered an apology and stood up. As she left the room, she said the doctor would be in momentarily.

Those two minutes were the longest of my life.

Please, God, I prayed, *don't let me have cancer.*

I had lived my life with many fears, but cancer terrified me more than all the others put together.

Breast cancer was a specter that had shadowed my life since it stole my beloved grandmother, Peggy, when I was twelve years old. I still remember visiting her at St. John's hospital in Santa Monica, California. The night before the visit, I finished a needlepoint of a dog that I'd been working on for months. Mama Peggy had taught me to needlepoint, and I wanted her to see this one, complete, before she died. I needed her to know the skill she taught me would live on after she was gone.

My parents tried to prepare me, but when I entered the hospital room, with its sharp smell of antiseptic, I saw that cancer had transformed my pleasantly loaf-shaped grandmother into a hairless, withered shadow of the woman I remembered. Fighting tears, I showed her my needlepoint. She praised it, and her smile made me proud.

Mama Peggy died a short time later, and I miss her to this day.

Her death was my first experience with cancer, but not my last. In the years that followed, cancer stole my paternal grandfather, two aunts, my father's brother, and, possibly, my father too (his official cause of death was a massive cardiac arrest, but the evidence suggested he had undiagnosed cancer at the time).

Peggy's death had another impact on me, too: from the moment I developed breasts, I believed that someday they would try to kill me.

On November 2, 2017, that fear came true.

The radiologist, Dr. H., said he saw an unusual spot on my mammogram, which the ultrasound confirmed. He couldn't diagnose cancer without a biopsy but warned me to expect that diagnosis. He felt so certain that he scheduled not only a biopsy on the following day but also an appointment with a cancer surgeon early the next week.

I held my terrified tears in check until I left Dr. H.'s office, but the moment I reached my car, I lost control. Sobbing, I called my friend Kerry Schafer, a breast cancer survivor who was diagnosed several years before, shortly before the release of her debut fantasy novel. I begged her to tell me that I could survive breast cancer too. I was drowning in terror and clung to her survival like a lifeline.

Five days later, while I was sitting in the surgeon's waiting room, my phone rang with the biopsy results: *infiltrating ductal carcinoma*.

I had cancer.

The medical group had already assigned me a nurse navigator named Marie, who met with me before I saw the surgeon. Marie became my anchor, on that day and in the weeks that followed. I don't remember our first conversation well, but I clearly remember her saying that I had the legal right to choose any surgery I wanted, from a lumpectomy to a double mastectomy, with or without reconstruction, and that the insurance company would have to pay for it.

When the surgeon entered the room, I stood up and extended my hand.

"I'm Susan," I said, "and I'm having a double mastectomy. How does tomorrow work for you?"

To her credit, she barely blinked before answering, "Can I examine you first?"

By the time I left the office, the surgeon's staff was already contacting my insurance and the hospital to schedule my double mastectomy.

I also opted not to undergo breast reconstruction. For almost 30 years, the sight of my breasts had made me worry that I would die of cancer. I hoped removing them completely would help me shed my other fears as well.

On Friday, November 10, eight days and six hours after that fateful mammogram, I showed my breasts what happens when you try to kill a mystery novelist.

The novelist kills you first.

When I woke up in the recovery room, my anesthesiologist—a doctor so young and talented the hospital staff apparently called him "Doogie"—asked me how I felt.

"I feel like someone cut my boobs off," I replied, "but otherwise, I'm fine."

The nurses stared at me, wide-eyed, but the doctor burst out laughing.

"Well, she's fine."

That moment, and many others in the difficult weeks that followed, demonstrated laughter's power to transform sorrow into something positive and strong.

* * *

Twenty-eight days later, I flew to Tokyo with Christopher—not to sign my visa application, as originally planned, but to enjoy Japan at Christmas while my son attended interviews for jobs. On December 26, I left him in Tokyo and returned to California to begin four months of intensive chemotherapy. The surgical pathology report had classified my cancer as stage 1a, with no lymph or vascular involvement, but it was also "triple negative" (not fueled by hormones) and highly aggressive, making chemotherapy my best chance to prevent its return.

I had met my oncologist, Dr. S., before my December trip to Japan. As a fellow cancer survivor, he understood my fears, and I respected his experience and candor.

That said, I didn't like his initial treatment timeline very much.

Due to my diagnosis, he recommended the most aggressive chemotherapy available: A/C (a combination of Adriamycin and cyclophosphamide) followed by Taxol. The standard course of treatment ran six months, with infusions at three-week intervals.

To give me a chance of reaching Japan in time to complete my climbs on a one-year deadline, Dr. S. gave me the option of attempting a "dose dense" chemotherapy regimen, under which I would receive an infusion every other week, beginning December 27, 2017, and—assuming I tolerated the drugs well enough to receive every treatment on schedule—finishing on April 10, 2018.

Dr. S. described chemotherapy as my first and most difficult mountain, "making your total one hundred and one." He encouraged me to write about the experience, because my story could inspire and strengthen others if I chose to share it honestly. It scared me to think about sharing pictures of myself as my hair fell out and, even more, to consider acknowledging my weakness (and my fears) so publicly.

Even so, I believed that he was right.

The day after that conversation, I revealed my cancer diagnosis on my blog and social media feeds. In the weeks that followed, I posted photographs of myself in chemotherapy and my "bald baby bird" head when my hair fell out. I blogged about chemo and posted daily updates on my Facebook page, encouraging everyone who read the posts to share their struggles and achievements in the comments too. The outpouring of love and support those posts received sustained me through the crushing pain of chemotherapy. As friends and strangers shared their struggles, all of us felt less alone.

That process changed the horror of cancer treatment into a meaningful experience. It was the first—though not the last—of many lessons I would learn in the coming year: With the proper attitude, shared weakness can become a source of communal strength.

Speaking up had made a difference, and I was grateful Dr. S. encouraged me to be as public with that first mountain as I would be with the ones to come.

3

CHERRY BLOSSOMS AND LIVER SPOTS

March–May 2018

I continued training for the mountains during cancer treatment, to the best of my ability. I couldn't walk 12,000 steps a day as I had before, but I tried to walk 1,000 steps the day after each infusion, and to increase my total by 2,000 steps each day until I worked my way back to 10,000 daily steps. When I reached that goal—usually by day seven—I continued to walk that distance every day until the next infusion.

At which point I began the painful cycle again from scratch.

My chemotherapy nurses, Jaime and Vickie, made my treatments as enjoyable as chemotherapy could ever be. Except for infusions and doctor's appointments, I spent my time on self-imposed house arrest to protect my weakened immune system, so—as strange as it sounds—chemotherapy days were the highlights of my month. I looked forward to visiting Jaime and Vickie at the infusion center where, in addition to chemotherapy drugs, I got a healthy dose of funny stories, cat photos, and talks about everything from bicycling to writing books and my plan to climb the *hyakumeizan*.

After chemo treatments, I felt so sick that I went to bed for the rest of the afternoon. In the days that followed, I set multiple alarms to ensure I didn't forget to take the dozens of pills I needed to combat nausea during the first few post-infusion days. I had no appetite and struggled to keep from losing weight. The surgical sites on my chest, though healed, often hurt so much I couldn't sleep.

Most days, I felt like I was dying.

My muscles ached. I was always cold. Reading and writing—formerly the pillars of my life—now gave me vertigo. Many nights I crumpled to the floor and sobbed.

I no longer even remembered what "healthy" felt like.

But through it all, I walked. Each morning I forced myself out of bed to begin the hours of pacing forward and backward across the cold tile floor until I hit my daily goal. If nothing else, I was determined to maintain the strength to climb when this ordeal was through.

I found daily inspiration in an itinerary I received at the end of February from Hokkaido Nature Tours, the company I hired to guide me on the isolated, dangerous *hyakumeizan* peaks of Hokkaido (Japan's northernmost major island). When reading made me nauseous, I stared at the photographs of smoking volcanoes, fields of lavender, and bears. I tried to imagine myself in Hokkaido, strong and healthy, but most days it felt like a distant dream that would not come true.

Halfway through chemotherapy, I flew to Japan to finally apply for the one-year visa I would need to climb the *hyakumeizan*. My mother went along to help and, for the first time in my life, I rode a wheelchair through an airport. On a good day I could have reached the plane on foot, but we had scheduled the trip to thread the gap between my chemo treatments, which meant I departed for Tokyo 48 hours after receiving a massive dose of chemotherapy.

It was not a good day.

Dr. S. approved the trip, but wanted me to take extra precautions; I agreed to wear a surgical mask in public and booked tickets in the first-class cabin to minimize my exposure to other people. Aboard the plane, I was also supposed to clean my entire seating area with antibacterial wipes. My cheeks burned with embarrassment behind my mask as the first-class flight attendant approached and asked if I needed help.

She thinks I'm a germaphobe.

I explained I was undergoing chemotherapy, and inwardly cringed at the sympathy that clouded her face. When she asked about my trip, I told her about my visa and my plan to climb the *hyakumeizan* after finishing cancer treatment.

Word got around, and several other flight attendants came to chat with me during the flight to Tokyo. They seemed equally curious and amazed by my planned adventure, and while I'd known my decision to break free from "safe" and face my fears was unusual, I hadn't expected other people to find it so compelling.

In Japan, Mom and I traveled by taxi and ate in the hotel restaurant at odd hours to avoid the crowds. Dr. S. deemed outdoor activities reasonably safe, so one sunny morning Mom and I took a trip to the Imperial Palace gardens in central Tokyo. In addition to the ruins of Edo Castle, the gardens feature many different flowering plants and trees, including a collection of cherry trees that draw enormous crowds each spring when the *sakura* (cherry blossoms) bloom.

Mom and I had arrived too early to see the *sakura*—the official "cherry blossom" forecast called for the blooms to begin the following week— but as the taxi carried us through the streets of downtown Tokyo, I wished I could have seen even a single tree in bloom.

I still remembered the kindergarten art project that introduced me to *sakura*. We blew brown paint through drinking straws to create the branches of a tree, which we decorated with pink and white tissue paper crinkled into three-dimensional puffy blooms. My kindergarten class had a visiting student from Japan, a girl named Yoko whose father was on sabbatical in Southern California. Despite her limited English, Yoko and I became close friends. She returned to Japan at the end of the year, and I never saw or heard from her again, but our friendship doubtless played a role in my love of the country she called home.

Mom and I strolled through the Imperial Palace gardens, enjoying the sunshine.

Near the famous cherry trees, I stopped in shock.

A single tree at the front of the garden was in bloom, its branches covered in a riot of delicate, puffy blossoms. From a distance, the tree looked like an enormous fluffy popcorn ball.

The other trees stood stark and bare, without a single bud on their empty branches.

My vision blurred as my eyes filled up with tears. I didn't know why one tree bloomed and the rest were barren, but I took it as a sign that everything was going to be okay.

When I returned to California, Michael and I put our house on the market, culled our worldly possessions down to nine suitcases' worth of items (and a few pieces of furniture, which went into a storage unit), and moved to a small apartment near the infusion center, where we would live while I finished chemotherapy.

We purchased airplane tickets for our May departure to Japan and arranged for a six-week rental on a furnished apartment in central Tokyo's Shinjuku Ward (a necessity, because we could not legally enter into a year-long lease until our visas were approved). I prepared the immigration paperwork for Oobie, our tortoiseshell cat—the final step in a complicated nine-month process that would allow her to enter Japan without quarantine.

I finished chemotherapy on April 10, and on April 21 I went for my follow-up CT scan with a happy heart. In three more weeks I would move to Japan to live my dream.

But three days later the dream became a nightmare, when the CT scan revealed a spot on my liver that the doctors could not identify.

It could be benign.

It could also be a metastasis.

I burst into tears when I heard the results, fear and frustration boiling up in heaving sobs that offered no relief. My body felt like an aging automobile, doomed to fall apart a little at a time as I spent the rest of my days in the medical equivalent of the mechanic's shop.

Dr. S. arranged an immediate biopsy, and my mother flew up from Los Angeles to accompany me to what I hoped would be a routine procedure.

By that point I should have known better.

Due to the spot's small size and tricky location, and because I needed to follow instructions during the procedure, the doctor (whom I had never met) chose to perform the biopsy under a local anesthetic. The injection numbed my skin but didn't penetrate into my abdomen, a fact I discovered only when the doctor stuck the biopsy needle—which looked like something you'd use to euthanize a Tyrannosaurus Rex—into my gut.

I felt it enter my side and pierce my liver.

I felt my liver *crunch* as the doctor carved away a sample.

And I felt pain on a level that nothing—including a double mastectomy and the birth of a child—had prepared me to handle.

Before he started the procedure, the doctor explained that if I moved *at all* he might not get a useful sample. He made sure I understood that I *Absolutely. Could. Not. Move.*

So when that unspeakable pain arced through me like a fiery electric shock, I did as instructed. I did not move.

The doctor finished the biopsy and took the sample to the lab. The nurse injected me with morphine, but it didn't help. In fact, the pain grew worse.

My vision narrowed and I couldn't breathe.

I heard an alarm but couldn't focus well enough to process what it meant or where it came from.

The nurse called for the doctor and they raced me down the hall for an emergency CT scan. As they rolled my gurney into the room, I saw them wheeling another patient out—they had interrupted his CT scan to determine as quickly as possible if I was hemorrhaging internally. Ultimately, the CT scan revealed no internal bleeding, and a second dose of morphine reduced my pain. (Technically, I did still hurt, but I no longer cared.) Before I left the recovery room, the doctor sent me excellent news: the CT scan confirmed that he had biopsied the proper spot, and Dr. S. would call me when they had results.

Less than ten days remained until our flight to Japan, but I couldn't bring myself to pack the suitcases that lined the wall like soldiers on review, or to schedule a shipping date for the ones we weren't taking on the plane. I couldn't face the possibility of unpacking if the biopsy revealed I still had cancer.

I did not want to die. I felt as if I hadn't even lived. More accurately, I felt as if I hadn't lived *enough*.

Seven days before our scheduled departure for Japan, the biopsy came back benign. I cried again, this time from joy, and started packing.

Later that night, I received an email from my immigration consultant in Tokyo.

My visa application had been denied.

I had applied for a one-year visa as a journalist, but the Japanese government did not agree that my plan to write a nonfiction book about climbing the *hyakumeizan* was "journalism." I spent a terrified, sleepless night convinced that I had ruined not only my life but Michael's too. We had sold our house and given much of what we owned to charity. I closed my practice and told my clients I was taking a sabbatical in Japan. And, because I hoped to inspire others with what I was now calling the "100 Summits Project," I had done it all on a highly public stage.

At dawn I asked Michael if he wanted to pull the plug on the whole endeavor.

"And do what?" he asked.

"Re-rent this apartment, find a job." *Stay here, where it's safe,* my instincts screamed. *If you go, you will end up broke in a foreign land.*

He stared at me for what seemed like an eternity. "We didn't get rid of everything we own, sell the house, and go through all the rest of this to give up. We'll go to Japan on a tourist visa and we'll figure it out from there. Even if we come back in three months' time, we will have tried."

For at least the 20th time in as many hours, I burst into tears.

Michael's faith and trust gave me the courage to go forward. I'd like to say the fear receded at that point, but my worries fed on uncertainty like a pack of velociraptors at an all-you-can-eat brontosaur buffet.

However, as I was beginning to learn, "brave" is not the absence of fear, it's feeling fear and moving forward anyway.

And so, despite my many fears, I packed my bags and prepared to fly.

BASE CAMP: TOKYO
MOUNTAIN TOTAL: 0

Michael and I landed at Tokyo's Narita Airport on May 15, 2018, with Oobie and four large suitcases in tow. We filled out paperwork to request the 90-day tourist visa customarily granted to US citizens upon arrival in Japan. An immigration official took our pictures and scanned our finger-prints, but instead of stamping visas in our passports, he asked us to step aside.

Two other officials escorted us to a nearby room, where they asked me why my fingerprints didn't match the ones they had on record from my visit to Japan in March.

I knew the answer. "Chemotherapy makes your fingers peel."

They stared at me blankly.

"I had cancer." I removed my hat to reveal my head, which was now completely bald.

Five minutes later, we left immigration with 90-day tourist visas in our passports.

We passed through animal import just as quickly, and two hours after our plane touched down, Michael and I wheeled four large suitcases and a yowling carrier out of the airport and into the Tokyo Metro.

Our adventure had begun.

4

YOU ARE NOT PREPARED

May 20, 2018

From the moment I landed in Japan, I felt overwhelming pressure to start the climbs. I worried about the schedule—which had no wiggle room for delays or injuries—and about the winter snow that would close the peaks for several months. I worried about our savings holding out, with neither Michael nor me working for a year.

Most of all, I worried about my visa. I had no assurance that immigration would grant me another tourist visa, even if I left the country and returned when the initial 90 days ran out, and Oobie could not leave and return at all. Unless I resolved the visa issue fast, my *hyakumeizan* plan was doomed to fail.

A friend and fellow author named Claire Youmans, who was living in Japan on a writer's visa, put me in touch with her immigration lawyer. I exchanged emails with him when I arrived in Tokyo, but his schedule made it hard to arrange a meeting.

With worries closing in from every side, I did what any mature adult would do:

I ran off to the mountains.

At 4:30 a.m. on May 20, 2018, as dawn bleached the Tokyo sky from black to gray, I filled the water reservoir in my brand-new, bright blue day pack, laced up my hiking boots, and caught an early train to Gunma.

Mount Akagi (赤城山) rises 1,828 meters above the northern end of the Kantō Plain—the largest agricultural area in Japan. The mountain sits about an hour by bus from Maebashi, the capital city of Gunma Prefecture, which also bears the distinction of sitting farther inland than any other prefectural capital in Japan. Although Maebashi is only an hour from Tokyo by *shinkansen* (the high-speed rail system also known as the "bullet train"), I made the stingier choice to take a local train, which made the journey three times as long (but at less than half the price).

On the train, an elderly woman sitting across the aisle opened a pale pink bakery bag and withdrew a trio of puffy, bite-sized rolls filled with a sweet bean paste called *an*. I had skipped breakfast, on the theory that I could find a local specialty to eat in Maebashi before the climb. Like so many other bad decisions I would make in the months to come, it seemed like a good idea at the time.

I looked out the window as my stomach growled.

By the time I reached Maebashi, I was so hungry that my standards had fallen from "find the most exciting regional delicacy available" to "I'll eat anything that isn't poisonous." The tiny station had only a single shop that offered food, and the shop had only a single tandoori chicken sandwich on the shelf. I grabbed the sandwich, along with a tiny raspberry Danish.

I devoured the pastry on the two-minute walk to the bus stop near the station, and barely resisted eating the sandwich too.

Five minutes before the bus was due to leave, a crowd of people in colorful hiking gear emerged from the station and queued up behind me in groups of two and three. Their floppy sun hats made me remember I didn't have one of my own. I'd also forgotten sunscreen and a sweater.

You are not prepared for this, my anxiety said. *Go home. Come back another day.*

Just then, the bus arrived. I climbed aboard before my fears could change my mind.

The forecast called for sun in Maebara, but as the bus drove toward the mountain, threatening clouds blocked out the sky. By the time we reached the visitor center at the base of Mount Akagi, the sky had grown so dark that I considered turning back. If it got any colder, if it rained, or if I failed to complete the hike before the last bus left for Maebara that afternoon, I could end up in serious trouble.

What made you think you could climb a mountain anyway?

As the Japanese hikers trooped past me off the bus, I almost gave in to fear, but I reminded myself that I'd come to break that cycle.

I forced myself to heft my pack and follow them out the door.

After studying the colorful trail map at the visitor center, I hiked down the asphalt road in the direction of the trailhead. Ten minutes later, I reached a wooden sign with an arrow pointing to an earthen path that did lead upward into the forest, but didn't look anything like my mental image of a hiking trail. It looked more like a steep embankment covered in rocks that someone labeled "hiking course" as a cruel joke.

I saw no trace of other hikers. Somehow, the crowd from the bus had completely vanished.

Forget this. Let's go climb an ice cream sundae back in Maebara instead.

Just then, three college-aged Japanese girls appeared around a bend in the road, approached, and—after asking me to take their picture standing by the trailhead—started up the rock-strewn trail.

I screwed my courage to the sticking point and followed.

The miles I'd walked during chemo didn't pay quite the dividends I expected. I puffed for breath and my thighs began to burn, even though I moved at roughly the speed of a garden slug.

After cutting several switchback turns across the mountainside, the trail ended at the base of a huge metal staircase that zig-zagged upward like Picasso's version of a giant zipper. The steep, narrow stairs disappeared into the trees above, and I wondered if they went all the way to the summit. I hoped they did. A staircase seemed much easier, and more familiar, than the rocky trail I'd been ascending.

It took less than a minute for those stairs to change my mind. The freezing metal railing burned my hands. My thighs and calves ached even worse than they had before. When the clang of boots on metal announced the approach of descending hikers, I froze in fear. The staircase wasn't wide enough for anyone to pass, and its narrow railings offered scant protection against the 15-meter drop on either side.

I closed my eyes and clung to the railing as the other hikers passed. They didn't even slow their pace, and—to my shock—our bodies didn't touch.

Afterward, I opened my eyes in more ways than one. Chemotherapy had dropped my weight to its lowest point in 30 years, but I still saw myself as the overweight woman I had been two years before. The realization that I was a stranger in my body made me eager to learn what other surprises this year would have in store.

At the top of the metal stairs (which, mercifully, ended after a rise of only 100 meters), I unhooked the drinking tube from the strap of my pack, feeling smug that I didn't have to stop to hydrate, and sucked up a mouthful of water that tasted like melted plastic.

In addition to overlooking my sweater, hat, and sunscreen, I'd forgotten to wash the silicone reservoir in my pack before I filled it up for its initial use.

I spit the foul-tasting liquid on the ground, pulled out my mobile phone, and quickly searched the connection between unwashed plastic reservoirs, chemical poisoning, and cancer.

The search revealed that, on the internet, everything causes cancer.

I reminded myself that millions of people across the world drink far more dangerous water than what comes out of an unwashed plastic reservoir.

They die of horrible diseases too, my inner voice replied.

My plan to climb a hundred mountains was a fool's errand for which I was not prepared.

And yet, I had spent my entire life using fear as a reason not to try.

In second grade, as I stood in line for the inflatable bounce house at the Franklin Elementary School carnival, I saw a sign beside the entrance that read "Enter At Your Own Risk." I stepped out of line immediately, frightened and confused. What risk would I take if I went inside? Would the house collapse? Would I suffocate? Would it pop, or possibly explode?

I walked away from the bounce house. To this day I've never been inside one. By the time I understood the sign was a standard warning, and that bounce houses were not deathtraps waiting to murder unsuspecting children, I was too big to jump around inside them.

That morning on Mount Akagi, I knew—with absolute clarity—that if I let the tainted water in my pack excuse my turning back, I would not climb a hundred mountains.

Fear would win.

I returned the tube to my mouth, sucked up a mouthful of disgusting water, and swallowed it.

Then I continued up the trail.

An hour later I emerged onto a ridge and stared in awe at the mountains, hills, and cities of Gunma Prefecture spreading out below me—far below, and as far as I could see. Looking down on the world from such a

YOU ARE NOT PREPARED

height made me feel I had accomplished something *real*. I had seen the world from heights before, but this time I had earned the bird's-eye view.

I turned around, and the view in the other direction revealed that I still had a long, long way to go to reach the summit.

From that point on, the route wound steeply upward between long-limbed trees and leggy wild azaleas covered in vibrant purple and fuchsia blooms, along a trail that alternated between hard-packed earthen paths and wooden stairs.

Ninety minutes after I left the ridge, I was hungry, sweaty, sore, and had no idea how much trail remained between my current position and the summit marker, but I didn't care. I was going to reach it, if I had to crawl.

A mere 15 minutes later, I crested a rise and found myself on top of Mount Akagi.

As I snapped my first-ever selfie with a summit marker, I burst into tears. I tried (almost successfully) to hide them from the dozens of Japanese climbers all around me and retreated to a nearby rock, where I wiped my eyes with a handkerchief and regained my self-control. With the waterworks contained, I devoured my sandwich and a box of "smoked cheese"–flavored potato sticks, washed down with tepid, plastic-flavored water from my pack.

Nearby, a pair of Japanese women prepared a meal of tea and ramen on a camp stove they had carried with them. In fact, every one of the Japanese hikers had better fare than a half-eaten chicken sandwich and potato sticks.

Next time, I would bring a better lunch.

I planned to hike Akagi as a loop, descending by a shorter route than the one I used on the ascent. However, I hadn't considered the fact that in mountaineering, "shorter" means "steeper"—a fact that made itself painfully clear as I started down the mountain.

This is a rock slide, not a trail. You'll be lucky not to break your neck.

I had no time to retrace my steps if I wanted to catch the final bus to Maebara, so I tried to focus on the trail and not my fears. At times, I hugged the trunks of trees to keep myself from falling. Given the pitch of the slope and the jagged boulders that covered the trail, I would have hugged poison ivy if it got me down the mountain in one piece.

Just as my legs began to feel like overstretched rubber bands that had lost their spring, I reached the road and the trailhead sign. I walked to the visitor center, and even had time to buy a commemorative "Mount Aka-gi" pin before my bus arrived.

On the train ride back to Tokyo, I questioned whether I could do this 99 more times. Mount Akagi was supposed to be an easy climb, but my legs and feet were aching and my chest felt raw where the straps of my pack had rested.

If this was an easy mountain, I wasn't sure I wanted to experience a hard one.

Somehow, I had fooled myself into believing Japan would change me, miraculously and without effort, into the person I aspired to be.

I now realized that wasn't going to happen.

However, I did feel I had accomplished something important on Mount Akagi, and learned some valuable lessons too.

A journey of 1,000 miles—or 100 mountains—starts with a single step.

I had taken that step.

Now it was time to take step two.

STATION 1:[1] TRAILHEAD TOKYO
MOUNTAIN TOTAL: 1

I headed home from Mount Akagi with my urgent housing situation pressing on my mind. Our short-term apartment lease expired at the end of June, and the visa denial left us scrambling for a place to stay. Michael had never been to Japan before our move and spoke no Japanese; I spoke only a little more than he did, but I knew the country and its customs, so it fell to me to take the lead.

Tokyo has thousands of short-term furnished rentals, but most don't welcome pets. Worse, we had to move in early summer, when most of the short-term apartments in the city were already leased. The company that owned our Shinjuku apartment had no vacancies in any of its buildings until August. A dozen inquiries to other companies yielded no better results: the ones with vacancies all had no-pet policies, and the ones that allowed a cat were fully booked.

Increasingly desperate, I scoured the internet and emailed the owners of all the available listings, asking them to make an exception for one small cat.

The Hail Mary pass connected. I secured a furnished apartment in Sumida Ward, not far from the famous Tokyo Skytree. It was available only until mid-August, and the rent went up because of Oobie, but I sent the deposit without complaint.

With homelessness prevented (at least until August), I was free to climb.

---

1. Many Japanese mountains have station markers at intervals along the trail, numbered 1 through 10 (for unknown reasons, Fuji also has a Station 9.5) to mark a climber's progress toward the summit. In this book, the Stations act as progress markers and as windows on the changes happening off the mountains.

5

DON'T FORGET THE BUG SPRAY

May 27, 2018

A week after climbing Mount Akagi, I once again woke before 5 a.m., filled the (well-rinsed) reservoir in my day pack, and set the pack—which I'd christened "Blue" for its brilliant color—on the bed while I dressed to climb.

Five minutes later, I hefted Blue—and was promptly drenched by a rush of water that poured from the day pack onto the bed, the floor, and my hiking pants. I hadn't closed the mouth of the reservoir properly, so water had leaked out and filled the pack while Blue was resting on the bed.

Two towels and many curse words later, I'd mopped the floor, but my pack and pants were soaked. The delay also meant I missed my train; I took a later one, but it didn't arrive in Enzan until 7:45 a.m.—too late for me to catch the first bus to the Daibosatsu trailhead.

At 8:20, I found myself once again in a line of senior citizens clad in high-end hiking gear. When the bus arrived, we trooped aboard for the 90-minute ride. I was so excited that I felt like bouncing in my seat. Mount Daibosatsu (大菩薩岳) (2,057 meters) is known for its stunning views of Mount Fuji, and despite more than 30 previous excursions to places where Fuji was supposedly visible, I had never actually seen Japan's most famous peak except in photographs.

When we reached the trailhead stop, I was the only one who left the crowded bus.

I watched it pull away.

What do they know that I don't know?

A consultation of the trailhead map revealed a second bus stop farther up the mountain, for hikers who preferred a shorter trek.

I puffed out my chest, proud to have chosen the toughest route, and started up the trail through a forest of small-leafed Japanese maple trees. Sunlight filtered through the branches. Birds chirped and cicadas rattled. The thump of my hiking boots on the packed earth trail blended with the other sounds, and I took a deep breath, feeling my tension fade away as the final signs of civilization disappeared behind me.

Refreshing breezes cooled the sweat that beaded on my face. I removed my cap and, for the first time since my hair fell out, enjoyed the way it felt to expose my head to the open air.

Two minutes later I put the cap back on, having learned that my hairless, sweaty scalp was irresistible to the swarms of Enormous Winged Biting Things that lived in the forest on Mount Daibosatsu.

Rivulets of sweat ran down my head and soaked my cap, which clung to my head and itched, but every time I tried to expose my scalp, the Biting Things moved in.

So much for "I won't need repellent this early in the year."

Three itchy, sweat-soaked hours later, I emerged from the forest and followed the trail across a highland meadow filled with brilliant pink azaleas. There, I caught my first glimpse of the forested summit rising high above me.

Far too high, given how far I thought I'd come.

I collapsed on a nearby log and checked the map. I was 45 minutes behind the "standard hiking time" from the trailhead to the meadow and still several kilometers from the mountaintop. At that pace, I couldn't reach the summit and descend in time to catch the 4 p.m. bus back to the train, but since I'd planned to be off the mountain by four o'clock, I hadn't noticed whether or not there was a later bus that day.

I stared at the summit as I weighed my options.

I'd planned to hike the mountain in a loop, returning to the bus by a different trail, and I didn't know how long that trail would take. The Daibosatsu trailhead was almost a 90-minute drive from the city of Enzan, where I had to catch the train. I had a mobile phone, but didn't think my Japanese was good enough to explain my situation to a taxi company if I missed the final bus—assuming a taxi would even come to the mountain to pick me up.

If you give up and go back now, you'll make the bus.

The Enormous Winged Biting Things whined around my head. The sound they made reminded me of Mount Misen.

I had not sold my house, closed my business, and moved to Japan to make another downhill walk of shame through a gauntlet of Enormous Winged Biting Things.

I stood up and followed the trail toward the summit.

An hour later, I was higher on the mountain but still hiking through an endless forest, besieged by Biting Things, and even more convinced that I would miss the final bus and end up stranded overnight. My legs hurt. I felt stabbing pains in my chest along my surgical scars. Every time I tried to stop and rest, the Biting Things zoomed in.

I hadn't seen another hiker on the trail, and worried about what would happen if I didn't have the strength to reach the summit. I had long since given up on the four o'clock bus; I simply hoped I could reach the top in the next 40 minutes—if not, I would have to give up and turn around to ensure I returned to the trailhead by dark.

Thirty minutes later—almost five hours to the minute after I began the climb—I stopped at the bottom of yet another rocky slope and thought I heard voices through the trees. I hurried upward, hoping against hope that I had reached the top.

As I crested the rise, I saw the summit marker and hikers picnicking among the trees. Overwhelming joy rose in my chest. I made an Enormous-Winged-Biting-Thing-line (trust me, they fly much straighter than bees) to the marker, where I encountered a trio of men in their 60s who had just arrived from the opposite direction. They seemed surprised to see a foreigner on the summit and were delighted to hear I was climbing the *hyakumeizan.*

They asked how many I had climbed so far.

"Two."

They found this answer hilarious—as did I—and yet I felt a genuine sense of achievement too. Seven weeks after finishing chemotherapy, I had climbed two mountains—more than I had climbed in the 46 years I'd lived before.

I'd planned to stop for lunch on the summit, but when I tried, the Biting Things declared all-out war, so I started down the far side of the mountain with a sandwich in my hand.

The trail, though steep, was far less rocky than the one I used on the ascent. The sky grew overcast, the temperature dropped to a comfortable level, and I increased my pace. I began to suspect I might even catch the four o'clock bus.

Halfway down the mountain, a two-lane asphalt road bisected the trail. On the far side of the road, a pair of trails diverged; each one led down the mountain, but in different directions.

I couldn't decide which one to take, and I had no time to double back if I chose poorly.

I swatted Biting Things with one hand as I used the other to open the GPS app on my mobile phone. It didn't help me choose a trail but did reveal that the curving asphalt road continued all the way down to the base of the mountain. Walking on the road would add an extra four kilometers (about two miles) to my hike but guaranteed I'd eventually reach the bus stop.

I decided to take the road.

Five minutes later, it began to rain.

I stopped to stretch a yellow plastic rain cover over Blue, feeling proud that I'd remembered to bring it with me. I had no jacket, but it wasn't cold and the rain felt good on my sweaty skin.

A half hour later, it was clear I wouldn't make the bus at 4 p.m. My back and hips were throbbing. Every impact of my boots felt like a hammer on the soles of my aching feet. I was drenched in a foul combination of sweat and rain, and besieged by Enormous Winged Biting Things that followed me like bloodhounds on the trail of a wanted criminal. I killed them by the dozens, but their numbers only seemed to grow.

They even tried to crawl inside my ears.

I wanted to cry, but crying wouldn't help. Instead, I pushed myself as hard as my pain tolerance allowed. An hour later, I reached the trailhead bus stop—just four minutes before the final bus of the day pulled in.

I had made it, and I felt proud of myself for persevering, although I wished I hadn't wasted so much of the afternoon worrying. In my distress, I had even forgotten to look for Mount Fuji at the summit.

By the time I fell into bed that night, I had walked 24 kilometers—a personal record. I felt no closer to overcoming fear, but believed I would make true progress when I undertook my next big challenge: back-to-back hikes in the Tōhōku region, north of Tokyo.

6

HOPE FOR THE BEST, GORE-TEX FOR THE WORST

May 31 to June 1, 2018

On the morning of May 31, I finally met with the immigration lawyer and signed the paperwork for my second attempt at a visa—this time, in the "cultural activities" category. That afternoon, I boarded a *shinkansen* for the three-hour and 20-minute, 577-kilometer ride to Aomori City on the northern tip of Honshu (Japan's largest major island, which is also home to Tokyo and Kyoto).

I could barely contain my excitement over my first trip to the Tōhōku region. I couldn't wait to see the mountains, taste the regional specialties, and add more summit pins to my collection (which currently numbered two).

The morning after I arrived, I went to the visitor center at Aomori Station to buy a round-trip "Skyline bus" ticket to Mount Iwaki (岩木山), a 1,625-meter stratovolcano whose yawning summit crater measures two kilometers in diameter (making the mountain broader than it is tall).

The woman behind the counter greeted my request with concern. "*Iwaki-san?* But it might rain!"

I, too, had seen the low, gray clouds, but my plans did not allow for rain delays. I had adopted a philosophy of "hope for the best and Gore-Tex for the worst." Besides, Mount Iwaki had a "sightseeing lift" (a repurposed skiing chairlift) that carried visitors almost to the top.

What harm could a little rain do?

After my desire to visit the mountain persisted through three choruses of "it might rain," the clerk sold me the bus pass—but she looked at me like a doctor watching a critical patient leave the hospital against medical advice.

When the Skyline bus left Aomori, I was the only person on it. I tried to persuade myself that this was not cause for concern. For once, my inner critic did not disagree—but only because it was too busy calling me out for planning to take the lift.

The lift is cheating. The summit doesn't count if you don't climb all the way.

A number of popular Japanese mountains feature gondolas, cable cars, or chairlifts that let hikers skip a portion of the climb. Every Japanese person I consulted said "of course the summit counts if you take the lift" (and my friends and family agreed) but after a lifetime of reading about serious mountaineering expeditions, where people spent days or weeks ascending difficult peaks, riding a lift (even part of the way) felt less than sporting.

It also opened up an Everest-sized can of mental worms.

From the time I was old enough to understand there was an easy way to do some things, I had always refused to take it.

The first time I remember taking the hard way was—again—in elementary school. I had written my first essay, and my mother—a former English teacher—offered to review it, and offer comments, before I turned it in.

To my eight-year-old mind, accepting help was cheating. It never occurred to me that my scrupulously honest mother would never let me cheat, or that other kids might also be getting help. I refused to let her see it, and I took my lumps when the grade came back.

I continued to take the hardest possible routes through high school, college, law school, and my working life. I refused to ask for or accept assistance and took pride in my ability to succeed alone. But it wasn't only pride that made me do it.

I was afraid that if I needed help, it meant that I was weak, and, by extension, unworthy of being loved.

If you ride the lift, it's proof you couldn't hack the climb.

The continuing, unsolicited input from my inner voice put me over the edge in a new direction: I made a personal rule that I would ride not only the lift on Mount Iwaki but every other ropeway, gondola, and chairlift I encountered on my climbs.

It was time for me to learn that I didn't always have to take the hardest path to my destination.

Decision made, I turned my attention to the scenery outside the bus—or, more accurately, the lack of it. On clear days, the curving "Skyline" offers expansive views of Aomori's famous forests, but thick white clouds and fog obscured the mountains and the rolling hills beyond.

At the Mount Iwaki visitor center, I made careful note of the fact that I had six hours until the final bus departed for Aomori City. I felt confident that I could reach the top and return in time—after all, I was taking a chairlift to the summit.

The cable for the sightseeing lift disappeared into the heavy mist that enveloped the mountain's upper slopes. Red bench-style seats hung down at regular intervals, like giant Christmas lights on a massive wire—but they weren't moving.

Maybe that's why there was no one on the bus.

I crossed the parking lot toward the lower station, unsure what I would do if the lift was closed. When I approached, the chairs began to move. (As it turned out, the operator turned the chairlift off to conserve energy when no one was around.) Three minutes later I was riding up the misty slope with Blue in my lap and my feet dangling less than a meter off the ground.

The lower station disappeared behind me, swallowed by the mist. The world consisted of nothing but me, the surrounding empty lift chairs, and the cloudy, shrub-covered mountainside. The cable creaked as it carried me slowly upward. For an instant, it seemed as if everyone and every-thing had disappeared and that I was the only person left on earth.

Although I knew that wasn't true, I felt a rush of relief when the upper station—and its safety-vested worker—appeared through the fog a couple of minutes later.

I disembarked in front of a wooden sign that read "Mount Iwaki Cra-ter, 1,470m."

All well and good, but Mount Iwaki was 1,625 meters high, which left me quite a bit more trail to climb—significantly more than I expected.

Between the lift and the summit, the trail wound up and down along a rocky route that looked more like a series of boulder piles than a hiking path. Heavy, shifting mist reduced visibility to less than a dozen meters. I couldn't see—or even estimate—how far I had to go.

At times, the trail became so steep that I had to use my hands and truly climb. The experience reminded me how much I loved exploring the boulder-strewn inlets of Catalina Island, off the California coast, when I was young. I hadn't thought about those coastal rocks in decades, but the memory calmed my nerves. I used it to remind myself that I had climbed on rocks before, even though the trail up Mount Iwaki looked more like Frodo's ascent into Mordor than the California coast.

Later on, the trail grew steeper still, and I began to feel afraid. I didn't think I was scared of heights, but the higher I climbed, the harder it was to continue moving upward.

You are not afraid of heights. You're terrified of falling to your death.

I considered this, and realized my inner voice was right. I wasn't scared of going up. I was afraid I'd fall when I came back down. I told myself that "down" was a bridge I didn't have to cross just yet. To my surprise, it helped.

A few minutes later, I felt unexpected warmth on my shoulders. I kept climbing, and the sun appeared, along with the summit.

Beneath me, the mountain disappeared into a sea of clouds—a sight I'd never seen except from an airplane or in photographs of someone else's life.

The puffy white blanket of clouds stretched all the way to the pale blue horizon. A breeze blew gently across my face, and sunshine warmed my mist-chilled cheeks.

In that moment, I forgot about my fear. This was the reason I came to the mountains. *This* was why I chose to climb.

The summit was still a 30-minute hike away, but the rocky trail—by which I mean a trail made *entirely of rocks*—did flatten out enough to let me walk upright.

I reached the mountaintop just after noon and rang the large bronze summit bell. Its peal reverberated through the empty air. After taking pictures of the summit and the bell, I walked to the little Shintō shrine that stood on the far side of the summit area. There, I prayed for peace and health for every person who had ever stood on Iwaki's summit, for my friends and family, and, finally, for myself. I prayed that my cancer would not return and that I would complete my 100 Summits project.

When I finished, I turned and stared at the sea of clouds once more, almost unable to believe that I had finally made it to this place. For years I had imagined what it must be like to climb a real mountain, stand on its peak, and see what mountain climbers saw.

Now, I was actually doing it—and the reality was even better and more beautiful than I expected.

The descent was not as terrifying as expected either. I retraced my path back through the clouds and down the misty slopes of my personal Mordor. As I did, I contemplated Kyūya Fukada's reason for creating the *hyakumeizan* list: to assemble a group of mountains that, when climbed, would reveal "the essence of Japanese mountains."

I suspected they would also reveal the essence of the people who tried to climb them, and I hoped they would show me who I was inside. More accurately, I hoped they would change me into a stronger and more confident version of myself before the year was through.

When I returned to my hotel, I treated myself to a freshly baked "Aomori apple pie," a local specialty made from the apples of which Aomori is justifiably proud. Although it bore a suspicious resemblance to the small, rectangular pies sold by some US fast-food chains, the first bite of tender, flaky crust bursting with juicy apples revealed that Aomori apple pies are to drive-thru food what diamonds are to pebbles. I could have spent the entire evening gorging myself on celebratory pies (and did consider it) but decided to forgo gluttony in favor of a good night's sleep.

I would need it, because my next climb upped the ante to three peaks in a single day.

7

FEAR IS A LIAR

June 2, 2018

"Mount Hakkōda (八甲田山)" is a volcanic range that encompasses more than a dozen mountain peaks. For *hyakumeizan* purposes, however, it counts as only one—and the one is Mount Ōdake (1,585 meters), the highest peak in the Hakkōda range. To get there by the normal route, a hiker must also climb up and over (and down, and up, and over) Mount Akakura (1,548 meters) and Mount Ido (1,550 meters). Since my goal was to climb the *hyakumeizan*, I couldn't count Ido or Akakura toward my 100 summits, but that didn't change the fact that I had to climb them.

I took a bus from Aomori City to the lower gondola station on Hakkōda. On the way, I struggled once again with my choice to take the lift. As I stared out the window, feeling guilty, Christopher texted me to check my progress.

"Made it up Iwaki, and heading for Hakkōda," I texted back. "Still concerned people will think I cheated because I took the gondola."

"Doesn't matter what anyone thinks," he replied. "This is your journey. The mountains have no rules but the ones you impose."

He was right. What's more, most hikers used the gondolas.

Why did I still feel inclined to take the hard way?

I didn't undertake the *hyakumeizan* as a feat of strength. They weren't technically difficult mountains, and fighting cancer had proven more about my strength than mountains ever could. I came to Japan to break away from "safe," to face my fears, and to accomplish something I spent decades believing I could never do.

I looked at Christopher's text again. *"No rules but the ones you impose."*

The rule I had imposed was "You Have to Take the Lift."

* * *

The upper gondola station on Mount Hakkōda sits at the edge of an alpine plateau, at the entrance to a wetlands park. An elevated boardwalk made of wooden planks runs through the wetland area, preventing hikers from trampling on the delicate plants and offering unimpeded views of snowcapped peaks in all directions.

The morning sun felt warm on my face, but the breeze still carried a winter chill, picked up as it crossed the beds of snow that remained on many of the mountains. At the far end of the wetland park, the boardwalk disappeared beneath a blanket of snow the size of a football field and two feet deep. Pink tape flashes fluttered on the trees to mark the boot-churned route. Grateful for my hiking poles and boots, I followed the prints across the snow, which made a satisfying crunch beneath my feet.

All too soon, I left the snow behind and began a long, steep climb up the seemingly countless earthen steps that led to the summit of Mount Akakura. A forest of pine trees mixed with *sasa*—dense, broad-leafed bamboo—grew on both sides of the narrow trail.

The trees grew shorter as I climbed, until I hiked past stunted shrubs whose tops were barely shoulder-high. I stopped to look across them. On the far side of Hakkōda's peaks, more snowcapped mountains rose in saw-toothed lines, like the spines of sleeping dragons. I tried to memorize each detail, from the songs of cuckoos calling in the twisted pines to the spicy scent of the air and the way the sunlight made the fields of snow glow brightly against the deep green mountainsides.

Winds howled across the summit of Mount Akakura like angry spirits. I clutched my cap, concerned the gusts would blow it off, and stopped just long enough to take a photo with the summit marker before I hurried on. The winds abated as I reached the relative safety of the trail that connected Mount Akakura with neighboring Mount Ido.

On top of Ido, I added a stone to the summit cairn on behalf of everyone who felt as trapped in their lives as I had felt in the life I'd left behind. I hadn't broken free completely yet, myself, but I'd begun the journey. I wished everyone could have the chance to break their shackles too.

The deep-green, snowcapped peaks beyond Ido's crater made me feel as if someone had dropped me into *The Sound of Music*. I had known Japan had Alps, but I hadn't expected them to look so . . . alpine. I even started singing as I hiked along the trail.

The music stopped abruptly when I rounded the crater rim and saw the steep descent ahead and the steeper climb beyond it. Far below, a mountain hut nestled in a saddle between Mount Ido and Mount Ōdake. To its left, the final stretch of trail ascended along the side of a massive snowfield on Ōdake's upper slope.

You'll never make it there and back in time to catch the gondola.

I reminded myself the trail was a loop and that the return was shorter than the approach across the summits. Even so, it wasn't reassuring. I hurried down to the mountain hut and sat outside it on a wooden bench to eat my lunch in a tiny clearing that proved blessedly free of Biting Things (Enormous, Winged, or otherwise).

While eating, I watched a group of hikers moving slowly toward Ōdake's summit. It dawned on me, equally slowly, that they weren't climbing up the side of the giant snowfield. They were hiking directly up the impossibly steep, snow-covered face.

A second set of hikers lurched and skidded down the slippery slope. One woman fell and tumbled several meters down the mountainside before she used a pole to self-arrest.

You can't climb that. You will fall. You'll slide the length of the slope and hit a tree and break a leg—or worse.

The loop trail back to the gondola ran past the benches to my right, safely away from Ōdake's snowy flank. I considered ending the climb right there and abandoning the summit altogether. I did not believe I could get up that snowy slope, let alone back down.

I wanted to cry. I had come so far, and this mountain was supposed to be an easy one.

It would be easy in midsummer, when the snow was gone. I could come back and climb it then—and decided I would, if I needed to, but also decided to take a closer look before I called it quits.

The slope was even scarier up close.

The snow was more than four feet deep and steeper than it looked from the mountain hut. Admittedly, a dozen hikers were moving up and down the face with no apparent trouble—even the woman I saw fall appeared unhurt—but that didn't mean *I* could do it without injury.

I avoided just this kind of situation at all costs. As a child, I wore a motorcycle helmet during horseback riding lessons, because my dad said equestrian helmets weren't safe. The fear his attitude inspired made me switch from stadium jumping to dressage because I lost my nerve to ride over fences higher than three feet.

All my life, my fears had been greater than my courage.

My vision blurred as my eyes filled up with tears.

I had come to climb. I wanted to succeed. And so, with everything inside me screaming that I must turn back, I raised my boot and stepped onto the snow.

The midday sun had melted the upper inch of the snow to slush, but there was hard-packed snow beneath. I took a second step and then a third. I moved up slowly, using my hiking poles for balance.

Twenty yards from the bottom, my foot slipped out from under me. I panicked, clutched my poles, and gasped for breath as I regained my balance.

I had no crampons, no ice axe, no experience climbing snow.

This is scarier than cancer.

I blinked. My inner voice was right.

Cancer, I could fight. A person cannot fight a mountain.

You did not come to fight, I reminded myself. *You came to find your courage and reclaim your life.*

I took a cautious step.

You trained for this.

I took another step.

You're going to die, my inner voice protested.

Someday that will happen, I acknowledged, *but it will not be today.*

All the way up that icy slope, my fear kept telling me that I would fail.

Yet as I climbed, I discovered that beneath my fear, something deeper and more primal wanted to succeed. Step by step, I climbed the snowy face and then the final stretch of trail to the summit. The reddish soil crunched underfoot. I sat beside the summit sign and stared at the snow-capped peaks that stretched as far as I could see in all directions.

I had faced my fear and won.

Not yet, hotshot. You still have to get back down.

As I descended through the snowfield, I tried to use the techniques I had read about in mountaineering travelogues. I sidestepped downward, keeping my shoulders perpendicular to the fall line. With each step, I kicked my heel into the snow and created a solid place to stand. My speed would have mortified a sloth, but I did not slip or fall.

When I reached the bottom, I fought back tears—but this time, they were tears of joy. I wasn't foolish enough to believe I had "conquered" my fears, any more than I could conquer a peak that had stood for millennia before I came and that would exist long after I turned to dust. But I had learned an important lesson.

Fear is a liar.

I could succeed, when fear said I could not.

The hike from Mount Ōdake to the visitor center was a slippery, sweaty adventure (and I use that term in the Misen sense) across an overgrown, partially snowy trail. Gnats and Enormous Winged Biting Things swarmed out of the bamboo grass to hold impromptu raves around my head, completely unrepelled by my repellent. By the time I reached the wetland park, I was sunburned, wrinkled, and covered in mud. My arms hung limp, and my filthy boots scuffed over the wooden boardwalk like I'd walked 100 kilometers instead of only 12.

On the bus ride back to Aomori, I decided to ditch the next day's scheduled climb, to rest my aching muscles and ensure I had the strength to summit back-to-back mountains in the days that followed.

I felt a surprising lack of guilt over this decision. In fact, my only real concern was finding something fun to do in Morioka City on my unexpected holiday.

8

HORSES' BELLS AND DRAGONS' EYES

June 3–4, 2018

At Morioka Station, dozens of orange traffic cones blocked off all traffic to surrounding streets. Before I could figure out if this was business as usual or not, a Japanese woman in khakis and a Day-Glo vest approached me, wearing a hesitant but hopeful smile that signaled her intention to engage.

As a middle-aged, foreign woman, I make an attractive target for the surveys Japanese tourism bureaus often conduct at railway station exits. As a person in search of an interesting way to spend the day in Morioka, I considered the clipboard-wielding woman an unusual boon. I wouldn't need to look for the visitor center; the visitor center had come to me.

"Hello," she said in English. "May I ask you some questions about what brought you to the Kizuna Festival today?"

"Of course." (I had no intention of admitting I had never heard of the Kizuna Festival.)

She asked the usual questions about my country of origin, job, and where I learned about the festival (my only lie: I said, "I don't remember"). When we finished the survey, she handed me a six-page newspaper "program"—apologizing for the fact that it was written only in Japanese—and pointed up the street. "The parade is starting. You can make it if you go right now!"

I joined the stream of pedestrians and quickly found a shady spot to stand on the parade route. Groups of early arrivals had spread blankets on the sidewalks and were having festive picnics in the shade. Carts and vendors lined the street, selling festival food and adding to the carnival atmosphere. The scent of grilling frankfurters and *yakitori* filled the air, along with the calls of barkers hawking soda and *nama-beeru* (Japanese draft beer, which was apparently legal to drink on the street, at least that day).

While I waited for the parade to start, I read about the festival's history in my program. Originally known as the *Tōhōku Rokkonsai* (Tōhōku Six Festivals), the Kizuna Festival was established to celebrate the Tōhōku region and comfort the souls of the people who died in the Great Tōhōku Earthquake. The 9.0 temblor struck northern Honshu on March 11, 2011, and was the strongest earthquake ever recorded in Japan (the fourth-strongest in the world since modern record keeping started). It triggered a tsunami that killed almost 16,000 people, displaced more than 250,000, and caused a disaster at the Fukushima Daiichi Nuclear Power Plant. Since the festival's inception in 2011, it has become a celebration of regional unity and diversity. Entirely by accident, I had picked the best day of the entire year to visit Morioka.

The rhythmic sounds of drums and cymbals announced the parade, and for the hour that followed I watched, transfixed, as hundreds of singers, dancers, musicians, and martial artists exhibited their skills at intervals along the road. Each group represented one of Tōhōku's major annual festivals. Lines of chanting men carried enormous braided sandals—each one measuring 12 meters long—to commemorate the *Fukushima Waraji Matsuri* (Sandal Festival), where celebrants parade through the streets carrying the largest sandals in Japan. Behind them, a platoon of female drummers in colorful costumes marched and played in honor of the Morioka Sansa Odori, a traditional dance that holds the Guinness World Record for the largest concurrent performance of Japanese drums. The groups flowed by in a stream of vibrant sights and sounds that made parades in the United States seem pale and quiet by comparison.

Later I walked to a nearby park to see a few of the hundred horses that would participate in the *Chagu Chagu Umakko Matsuri* the following weekend. The festival celebrates the working horses of Iwate Prefecture, whose owners dress them in elaborate ceremonial costumes and parade them through the streets to a shrine, where a Shintō priest bestows a blessing on the animals.

Half a dozen enormous horses stood beneath the trees, dressed nose to tail in jingling, hand-embroidered finery (*chagu chagu* is an onomatopoeic word derived from the sound of the bells on the horses' costumes). I even saw a jet-black colt who was just being trained to wear the ceremonial attire. He lay in the shade, wearing only a harness and a hand-embroidered headpiece with small pom-poms dangling from his ears.

Enormous, snowcapped Mount Iwate (岩手山) (2,038 meters) rose up beyond the city limits. The snowcapped peak reminded me that I was supposed to be climbing—not watching parades and eating apple-flavored snow cones at a festival.

"I will return," I promised. "We will dance another day."

* * *

The morning after the Kizuna Festival, I caught the early bus to Mount Hachimantai (八幡平) (1,613 meters), the third-highest peak in Towada-Hachimantai National Park. My online trail guide said the hike would be short and easy, but I no longer trusted the judgment of the superhuman trekkers who wrote online trail guides.

As the bus drove up the mountain to the trailhead, patches of snow appeared beneath the trees. They increased in size and depth as we gained altitude, despite the sunny day. At the visitor center, everything—including the trail—was buried under several feet of snow. A map near the bus stop claimed the summit was only a 40-minute hike from the visitor center, and the distance between the topographical lines made it appear as if the trail was almost flat.

The vast majority of visitors had come in jeans and sneakers, and were unprepared to walk on slippery snow. They slid and skidded along in unsteady groups of two and three, clinging to one another and to the pines that lined the trail.

A fur-collared woman clutched at one of the pink-topped wands that marked the route and quickly learned that half-inch bamboo wands are no match for either snow or gravity. The wand bent double and she landed in the snow, to the ill-concealed amusement of her boyfriend—who slipped, and joined her on the snow, a moment later.

Twenty minutes from the visitor center, I reached the famous Kagami-Numa, or Dragon's Eye Pond. It lived up to its name: the ring of cerulean water surrounding a central circle of ice that looked exactly like the eye of a giant dragon hiding beneath the snow.

I hiked around the tree-ringed lake, blinking in the glare of sunlight off the fresh, clean snow, and found it hard to believe that it was June. The perfect winter wonderland of pristine snow and deep-green pines made my heart sing with joy.

Two months before I was lying in bed, so sick and weak and poisoned that I understood how it felt to die. Now I marched with confidence over fluffy snow beneath a deep blue sky, inhaling air that smelled impossibly fresh and clean. My chest, though often sensitive and achy, felt as if it had mostly healed, and I loved the way my shirts fit so much better than they had before my surgery. The dramatic reversal of fortune seemed impossible, but it was real.

I stared at the rows of snowcapped peaks rising up on the horizon and wanted to shout with happiness and gratitude. I felt as if I might explode if I didn't let the emotions out, but also knew a screaming foreigner might cause a panic—so I kept my joy inside.

At the summit, an older Japanese couple offered to use my phone to take my picture with the enormous marker pole. I offered to reciprocate, but the husband pulled a full-sized tripod from his backpack, grinned, and set it up.

These two had come prepared.

My respect for their preparedness increased five minutes later, when they joined me on the observation platform and broke out a four-course lunch, complete with twenty-ounce cans of Asahi beer.

I suddenly felt far less satisfied with my *croque monsieur* and apple Danish.

Another couple arrived at the summit and handed out celebratory honey-lemon candies to everyone, including me. As we exchanged the customary greetings and commentary on the weather ("Very nice!") and the view ("So lovely! Wow!"), we were joined by a silver-haired man wearing business slacks and black leather loafers. He had a large, expensive camera around his neck. Anywhere else, this might have raised some eyebrows. In Japan, it merely triggered another chorus of "Where are you from?" and "Wow, the weather is so nice today."

The man in the loafers asked how I heard about Mount Hachimantai, and I told him I was climbing the *hyakumeizan*. As usual, I omitted "in a year" because Japanese hikers regard the 100 Famous Mountains as more than just a physical challenge and did not understand my compulsion to finish them within a stated time.

"Wonderful!" he exclaimed. "How many have you climbed so far?"

I raised my right hand, fingers splayed. "Today is number five."

As usual, my answer caused hilarity, but when the laughter ended, the man in the loafers told me, earnestly, that the *hyakumeizan* were difficult, important mountains, and that he wished me great success with all my climbs.

After lunch, I hiked back to the visitor center and arrived two hours before the bus was scheduled to depart. I wandered slowly through the gift shop, killing time. Near the back, I found a rack of large-brimmed, floppy hats with adjustable chinstraps and the words "Over the Mountain" embroidered on the front. I bought a tan one, put it on, and went outside to wait for the bus, feeling snazzy in my new hiking hat.

A few minutes later I received a text from my good friend Laurie, saying her beloved elderly cat Louise had died. My heart—so light with joy from the snow and summit—felt a painful tug toward the place I'd once called home. For the first time on my journey, I felt lonely, severed from the friends I'd left behind. I didn't miss California, but it hurt that I couldn't jump in my car and race to Laurie's house to give her a hug and share her grief.

Before I moved to Japan, I hadn't spent much time considering what my life would look like when I finished the hundred climbs. Now I wondered if the friends I loved would be my friends at all when the year was through.

As I texted with Laurie, doing my best to share her pain despite the miles between us, I had no answers for the greater questions: who I would be and what my life would look like in a year. I also knew that fretting would not help. The answers to my questions lay on the far side of 11 months and 95 more mountains.

And the only way to get there was to climb.

9

NO RAISINS ON THE SUMMIT

June 5, 2018

The morning after Hachimantai, I left the hotel at 6 a.m. to catch the earliest *shinkansen* to Sendai, the largest city in the Tōhōku region. As the train left Morioka and picked up speed, I realized the first few climbs had already run together in my memory. I didn't want this year to devolve into a series of "check the box" achievements, devoid of meaning beyond a scoreboard tally. No matter how many mountains I climbed, or who I was, or where I ended up when the year was through, I would have failed completely if I had no lasting memories of the places I had been.

As Morioka shrank into the distance, I resolved to climb in a way that would imprint each mountain on my heart and mind. I would treat this year like a treasure box and fill it with a wealth of memories—wealth that no one and nothing could take away.

From Sendai, I took an express train west into neighboring Yamagata Prefecture and then a bus to Mount Zaō (蔵王山), a volcanic mountain group whose highest summit, Mount Kumano (1,841 meters), was my target for the day. Like Hakkōda, the climb to Zaō's high point also required a secondary climb, in this case, 1,736-meter Mount Jizō.

As the Zaō Ropeway whisked me to the trailhead, I noted that the slopes—a popular ski resort in winter—were completely free of snow.

The climb from the upper ropeway station to the top of Mount Jizō took less than half an hour, up a trail of wooden steps with scrubby pines on either side. I took a photo with the marker even though the summit didn't "count" toward my overall total. Jizō was a mountain, and I had climbed it, and I wanted proof.

While walking along the rocky alpine ridge that connected Mount Jizō with Mount Kumano, I wondered how many total mountains I would climb before my year was up. When I made my plans, I thought each *hyakumeizan* climb would involve a single mountain. Since I had to climb extras, I wanted to count them all, but that wasn't the way the *hyakumeizan* worked.

Cairns of carefully balanced stones rose up at intervals along the trail to Mount Kumano. As I reached each one, I added a stone to the pile and said a prayer for someone I knew and loved. I felt so grateful that I had the chance to live and the strength to climb; I wished everyone was similarly blessed.

A weathered, wooden Shintō shrine stands on the top of Mount Kumano, along with a summit marker and a tall stone obelisk engraved with Japanese calligraphy. When I arrived, a group of Japanese women in colorful hiking gear were clustered around the obelisk, debating the proper pronunciation of the characters running down the charcoal-colored stone.

When I said hello, one of the women turned and spoke to me in Japanese. *"Hello! Are you a student?"*

I shook my head. *"A novelist."*

We chatted in a combination of Japanese and charades as the rest of her group began walking down the trail. A few minutes later she said goodbye and hurried off to join them.

Alone on the summit, I sat on a dusty stone and looked across the valley toward the rows of snowcapped mountains in the distance. I opened Blue and searched for the bag of trail mix my mother bought in the hospital the night I had my biopsy. I hadn't wanted it that night, but had brought it with me to Japan. I hadn't eaten it because I worried that I would miss my mom even more when it was gone, but trail mix goes stale faster than memories. The time had come to eat it.

An enormous golden butterfly fluttered across the summit and came to rest on Blue, just inches from my knee. It fluttered its wings and spread them wide, at rest. Its presence reminded me that the people I loved were with me, and always would be, even if I couldn't see or touch them.

I opened the trail mix and ate a handful of raisins, peanuts, and candy-coated chocolate pieces. The bag had gone across the Pacific and up five *hyakumeizan*, making it some of the best-traveled trail mix on the planet. It was delicious and I was hungry, so I ate the entire bag.

As I finished, footsteps approached me from behind. I turned to see another member of the women's hiking group I'd met before. Her purposeful stride and the light in her eyes made me prepare for another impromptu test of my spoken Japanese.

She got right to the point. *"You're a mystery writer?"*

"Yes," I replied in Japanese, *"I'm a novelist."*

She pulled out her phone. *"May I ask your name?"*

When I told her, she typed something on the screen and turned the phone around, revealing the Amazon sales page for my Hiro Hattori novels. *"Is this you?"*

I smiled. *"Yes, it is."*

"Thank you very much!" After a pause she added, *"Do you like Japanese mountains?"*

At that moment, every word of Japanese I knew went AWOL. I couldn't even remember the word for "yes."

After an awkward pause, I stammered, *"Hyakumeizan."*

"You're climbing the hyakumeizan!" She lit up. *"I am climbing the hyakumeizan! How many have you climbed?"*

"Six. And you? How many?"

She smiled politely. *"Ninety-nine, as of today."*

"SUGOI!" (That's amazing!)

"In August, I will climb the last one. Mount Rishiri, in Hokkaido."

My limited Japanese had returned, but I desperately wished I spoke the language better. I wanted to tell her how impressed I was with her achievement and to ask if she had any advice for me. I wanted to ask how long the challenge had taken her and which of the mountains she had found most difficult. I wanted to wish her success in Hokkaido, and to congratulate her on completing such a major feat.

I barely had the ability to return her polite goodbye.

She bowed and left to rejoin her group. I felt starstruck as I watched her go. This woman—older than me—had done the very thing I hoped to do, and even though I had barely begun to climb, she treated me like an equal and a friend.

From the summit, I hiked down the far side of Mount Kumano to see Mount Zaō's famous crater lake. The emerald pool was flanked by smoking vents that filled the air with the scent of rotten eggs.

While taking pictures of the lake, I saw a line of hikers approaching along a nearby ridge. They walked in single file, their gear a splash of brilliant color against the muted red and gray of the volcanic rocks. One of the hikers raised a hand in my direction, and a moment later the entire group broke into frenzied waving.

"*Suzan-san! Hello!*"

It was the women from the summit, now returning from a hike around the lake.

I waved back, delighted. As they disappeared from view, I took a few more pictures of the lake and then began the climb back up the ridge.

The descent began uneventfully, as horror stories often do. Aglow with joy over meeting the Japanese hikers and filled with the pride of achieving my sixth *hyakumeizan* summit, I didn't notice the dangerous rumblings in my belly until the pressure built to painful levels. I increased my pace, far less concerned with the volcano I was walking on than with the imminent, raisin-triggered eruption in my gut.

In my eagerness to share the summit moment with my mother through the trail mix she bought in Sacramento, I overlooked two very important facts:

First, chemotherapy slows digestion and bowel transit time, even after treatments finish, meaning more food stays inside your body and stays in longer than before.

Second, raisins are an excellent natural laxative.

And when raisins do their magic two kilometers from the nearest toilet, on a barren mountainside with nothing large enough to hide behind, "raisin magic" is dark sorcery indeed.

By some not-entirely-minor miracle, I reached the bathroom at the gondola station without staining either the mountain or my . . . reputation.

On the bus ride back to Yamagata, I found myself wishing I could remain in Tōhōku. I loved its snowcapped mountains and longed to see more of them immediately. However, with only two weeks remaining until our first apartment move, I needed to check in with Michael (and the visa lawyer). I planned to bounce into Tokyo for a day or two, catch up with my family, and head back off to the mountains before the summer typhoons arrived.

As it turned out, that was not to be.

10

CUCKOOS AND CHAINS

June 13–14, 2018

The morning after I returned to Tokyo from Mount Zaō, I woke to the violent hammering of rain against the window and the eerie wail of wind in the balcony railings. Already behind on my climbing schedule, I'd hoped the summer rainy season would hold off a little longer, but the rain outside suggested the typhoons had now arrived.

The rain continued for over a week, and every day my anxiety grew.

You'll never finish the climbs in time, my inner voice repeated.

On the morning of June 13, with driving rain still coming down, I jumped out of bed, switched on my computer, and panic-planned another climb. Ironically, the only *hyakumeizan* peaks far enough away to escape the typhoon, close enough to one another to justify the cost of extended travel, and with buses running to the trailheads in early June were in Tōhōku—where I'd been the week before.

Two hours later, I sat on a *shinkansen* headed north through the pouring rain with a hastily packed suitcase at my feet. The apartment buildings of Tokyo soon gave way to single-family homes and then to the deep-green rice fields of the countryside. White herons stood in the flooded paddies, gazing into the distance as if contemplating life.

My thoughts drifted back to the first few climbs. I wasn't making the clear, dramatic progress I had hoped for. One month in, anxiety still tied me in knots at every turn. If I wasn't afraid of missing a bus, I was worried about falling to my death. If I wasn't fretting about failing to reach my ultimate goal, I was frantic about immigration denying my visa a second time. And beneath it all, I was terrified my cancer might come back.

The difficulties were piling up. I felt my anxiety rise.

Cutting the anchors didn't change anything. You were foolish to think it would. Instead of letting my inner voice push me into an anxious spiral, I asked myself, *If you died tomorrow, what would you wish you had done differently today?*

I watched the rice fields speeding by outside. A jet-black crow with outstretched wings swooped down from a tree and circled over the paddies before winging off toward the distant mountains.

In that moment there was nothing I would change.

Is that true, or just what you think you're supposed to feel right now?

It was true. Right then I felt no need to grieve over the parts of my life I could not change.

Anxiety reminded me about my visa issues and the threat that my cancer might return, but neither of those was a thing that I could alter. I had wasted so much time and energy fretting about things I could not control. I hoped this year would teach me how to stop.

* * *

The Mount Nasu (那須岳) volcanic complex sits on the border between Tochigi and Fukushima Prefectures, northeast of Tokyo, in Nikkō National Park. The most popular hiking course begins at the Nasu Ropeway, crosses over the summit of Mount Chausu (茶臼岳), and curls around the side of Mount Asahi (朝日岳) en route to the high point, 1,917-meter Mount Sanbonyari (三本槍岳). Of the range's five volcanic peaks, only Mount Chausu is still active, but it's active enough to hold a permanent place on the Japanese Meteorological Agency's live volcano early-warning list—a fact I'm glad I didn't know before I made the climb.

The first gondola of the day began its climb at 8:30 a.m. with me aboard. At 8:35 I emerged from the upper station and took a "summit photo" with Mount Nasu's summit marker, which sits about a hundred yards from the gondola. Afterward, I started up the rocky trail toward Mount Sanbonyari.

The path cut switchbacks up a slope that looked more like a moonscape than a mountain. Giant jet-black daddy longlegs wandered across the rocks. I am not a spider fan, and found their size—and prolific numbers—disconcerting. I couldn't help wondering what they ate in such an isolated place.

Most likely, one another.

I followed a short detour trail to the summit of Mount Chausu (1,915 meters), where I stopped to enjoy the view and photograph the summit shrine. Nothing grew on Chausu's slopes, and the smell of sulfur lingered in the air. As I descended the opposite side of the volcano, I looked across the valley at tree-covered mountains stretching away as far as I could see, and wondered what it would be like to climb not just a hundred but a thousand Japanese mountains.

What new hubris is this? You climb six mountains, and you think you can climb a thousand?

As ridiculous as it seemed, part of me wondered if I could do it—whether I had the strength, the will, and, most importantly, the years remaining to finish such a massive task.

Beneath my boots, the rocky trail slowly changed from gray to deep brick red. Overhead the sky stretched wide and blue. The trail wound down the mountainside in front of me, across a saddle and past a mountain hut, before it disappeared from view around the side of a neighboring mountain. An hour later I reached that point. Beyond it, the trail crossed a narrow pass. The wind picked up both speed and strength as it funneled through the gap, and gusted almost hard enough to knock me down as I hurried across the opening.

On the far side of the pass, the path continued up a boulder-covered ridge to a set of enormous steel chains bolted into the mountainside.

A number of Japanese mountain trails have permanent chains installed through steep or dangerous places, both to serve as balance aids and to mark the safest route. The chains on Nasudake followed an incline steep enough to qualify as bouldering, and then crossed a ledge so narrow that my shoulder brushed the cliff face as I passed. The pebbles my boots dislodged from the path clattered down the rocky face for more than 20 meters before coming to a rest in a gully far below.

I focused on my footing and did not look down.

After almost an hour of climbing over narrow, rocky paths, the trail crossed yet another saddle and descended into an alpine wetland similar to the one on Mount Hakkōda. Raised wooden walkways offered a dryish path across the sucking, snowmelt-swollen mud field on the ground.

Birds sang in the bushes beside the trail; their unfamiliar songs made me wish I had learned more about Japanese birds before my climbs began.

As a child in California, I recognized most of the birds in my neighborhood by sight or song. I even started a short-lived bird-watching club with six other kids from school. But aside from the Asian cuckoo, whose call is easy to recognize, and the raucous cries of crows and raptors, I knew nothing about bird songs in Japan.

Beyond the wetlands, the trail ascended once again, this time through fields of *sasa* interspersed with brush just tall enough to block my view of the mountaintop. Despite my plan to worry less, the time weighed heavily on my mind. I pushed myself to move as fast as possible. Just before noon I passed through a thick stand of brush and emerged, unexpectedly, on the summit of Mount Sanbonyari. The far side of the small plateau offered expansive views of the surrounding deep-green mountains, but the peak itself had been completely hidden as I approached.

I wanted to enjoy the summit, but the unforgiving tick of the clock and the now-familiar fear of missing the final gondola off the mountain made me too uneasy to take an extended break. I shot some pictures, gobbled down an energy bar, and started my descent.

An hour later my legs began to tire, and I grew careless. On a flat patch of trail just above the steepest part of the descent, my boot slipped on a patch of scree. I tumbled backward and landed hard. Blue absorbed the worst of the fall, but I almost threw up when I thought about what might have happened if I'd fallen a couple of minutes later. Fears about visas and the future shrank to nothing by comparison.

I stood up, brushed the dirt from my pants, and forced myself to focus.

Ninety minutes later, after descending safely past the chains and across the windy gap, I began my reascent of Mount Chausu. Halfway up the slope, I heard the hissing, whistling sound of steam escaping under pressure.

Above me on the right side of the trail, a column of pale white steam surged up and out the side of Mount Chausu. It was a fumarole—a volcanic vent, where steam and gases emerge from the mountain. I hurried past it, trying not to think about news articles I'd read in which Japanese hikers were killed by pebbles flung from similar fumaroles.

I reached the gondola with time to spare, and as I rode back down the mountain, I considered the fact that the *hyakumeizan* were more dangerous than I realized. The climbs weren't technical, or even very long (by experienced hikers' standards, anyway), but they were potentially hazardous for novices like me. My knees and feet ached mercilessly from the 12-kilometer round-trip climb, and it seemed a little strange that I felt compelled to do something that scared me so much (and hurt a great deal too). Yet even in that moment, I remembered the views from the summit and along the trail, the iridescence of the stones beneath my feet, and the scent of the mountain air, and I wanted to climb again (after a rest and a desperately needed bath). The thrill of accomplishment I felt when I completed the chains, and the joy of the unexpected summit, made me feel thoroughly happy and alive.

And that, I decided, was worth a little pain.

11

THE MOUNTAIN WANTS TO BE CLIMBED

June 15, 2018

From Mount Nasu, I took a bus and then a train to the town of Inawashi-ro, in northern Fukushima Prefecture. I arrived at sunset, and felt a surge of gratitude as I left the station and saw an orderly line of jet-black taxis waiting at the stand. Neither my hotel for the next two nights, an *onsen* (volcanic hot-spring) resort at the base of Mount Bandai (磐梯山) (1,816 meters) nor the Bandai trailhead was accessible by bus. Without a taxi, I was looking at a multi-hour walk in the dark on the heels of my all-day Nasu climb.

My taxi driver recognized the hotel name and I sat back, looking forward to a relaxing ride.

As we left the station, the driver gestured out the window to his right. *"Bandai-san."*

A massive conical mountain with a flattened summit rose majestically into the orange, blue, and lavender sunset sky. In other circumstances, the view would have inspired poetry.

As it was, the only thing that came to mind was *Holy Shit, it's huge!*

When I was little, my parents told me curse words were the product of an uncreative mind: "A person who swears is telling you they can't come up with anything more descriptive."

As I stared at the unbelievably large volcano I planned to climb the following day, I was indeed unable to think of anything more creative than *HOLY SHIT*.

Originally named *Iwahashi* (rock ladder to the sky) and also known as "Aizu-Fuji" for its resemblance to Japan's most famous peak, Mount Bandai erupted violently in 1888, killing almost 500 people and collapsing on itself, dramatically changing the shape of its northern face.

From the south, it looked intact and terrifying.

By the time I reached the hotel I desperately needed a meal, a bath, and good night's sleep. The hotel restaurant—the only option for 10 kilometers in any direction—closed in 30 minutes, so I dropped my bags in my room and hauled my filthy carcass off to dinner.

In the restaurant, the wait staff walked me through the expansive all-you-can-eat buffet (which filled three rooms), explaining the options in rapid Japanese that I followed only enough to catch that the Special of the Day was horsemeat *nabe*—a hearty soup of meat (in this case, local horse) and various vegetables.

Except for fish (which I'm allergic to), I planned to sample every regional specialty I had the chance to eat during my 100 Summits journey, so I set aside my lifelong love of horses and reached for a bowl of horsemeat *nabe*.

With 27 minutes remaining before the restaurant closed, I also helped myself to tempura vegetables, roasted chicken with new potatoes, fresh-made local *soba* (buckwheat noodles), chicken and apples in creamy sauce, and a bowl of steamed white rice. I cleaned the tray with just enough time for a slice of strawberry cream-cheese cake, a tiny chocolate-orange mousse, and a bowl of honey-soba ice cream dusted with *kinako* (roasted soybean powder), along with a cup of dark, rich coffee.

When the restaurant closed, I waddled to the front desk and arranged a taxi to the Bandai trailhead in the morning. Afterward, I headed to my room, and barely stayed awake long enough to get a bath before falling into bed.

I woke on June 15 to overcast skies that threatened rain. It was my mother's 75th birthday, and due to the 16-hour difference between Japan and California, the milestone birthday would begin for her about the time I reached the summit of Mount Bandai.

At least, it would if everything went as planned.

My taxi pulled up at precisely 7:58 a.m., and as it drove me down the curving forest road to the trailhead, I tried to memorize the route. My "taxi Japanese" was more than sufficient to tell a driver where to go and handle payment when the ride was through, but I didn't feel confident in my ability to arrange a pickup at the end of a possibly-six-hour (but-maybe-longer) hike, so I planned to return to the hotel on foot.

Ten minutes later, I began to reevaluate that decision. We still hadn't reached the trailhead, and I hadn't seen another man-made structure on the way. The hike to the hotel would add at least two hours of walking to my day, and likely more.

I began to think the climb was a bad idea.

I debated asking the driver to turn around and take me back to the hotel. I stared out the window, equally frustrated by my lack of confidence and my insufficient language skills. My Japanese was improving daily, but my small vocabulary stranded me at critical moments.

Gravel crunched beneath the wheels as the taxi reached the trailhead parking lot.

As we came to a stop, the driver asked a question in Japanese.

"I'm sorry," I apologized. *"I did not understand."*

He shifted to broken English. "Come back . . . time?" He gestured to the trailhead. "After?"

I could hardly believe my luck.

I did some generous mental math, added an extra 90-minute margin, and converted the number to Japanese. *"Jyu go ji?"* (3 p.m.?)

The driver made a notation on his clipboard, accepted my fare, and wished me well on *Bandai-san*.

Delighted to have the transportation problem solved, I completed a hiking notification form—a requirement on many Japanese mountains, to provide the authorities with details about hikers' clothing, gear, and intended routes in case a person or a group goes missing—and dropped it into the wooden notification box before starting up the trail.

I walked through a misty deciduous forest so green and fragrant that I half-expected to see fairies flittering among the trees. The air felt fresh and cool, but there was no breeze. Despite the clouds, the atmosphere held neither the charge nor the scent that normally heralds rain. A carpet of last year's fallen leaves crunched softly underfoot. Birds sang in the branches overhead.

The trail meandered through the forest and up a gentle slope covered with interlacing roots that formed a natural set of stairs. Completely alone, I felt connected to the forest and the mountain in a way I never had before.

Forty-five minutes later the aromatic, earthy scent of trees gave way to a sulfurous stench I had learned to associate with live volcanoes. Around a bend in the trail, the forest ended at the entrance to the enormous shallow crater created when the 1888 eruption shattered Bandai's peak. Volcanic gases bubbled up through cracks beside the trail, smearing the gray volcanic soil with the distinctive, brilliant yellow hue of sulfur.

I crossed the crater, noting the warning signs and barriers erected to keep hikers on the trail. On the opposite side, the path led sharply upward into the forest as the climb began in earnest.

As I ascended, the pungent scent of the volcano slowly faded. The scents of the forest reemerged. A recent rain had left the trail muddy but not slippery enough to make me nervous. It slowed me down, but what I lacked in speed, I made up in persistence.

After three hours on the trail, I climbed the last few stony, treeless yards to the rocky summit of Mount Bandai.

The mist had intensified, concealing the mountain's famous views behind a curtain of impenetrable white. However, I didn't care. I laid a stone on the summit cairn in honor of Mom's birthday and felt grateful for her presence in my life. I wished she was there with me but felt glad that I would see her in exactly a month, when she came to join me for my biggest climb—an overnight ascent of Mount Fuji.

With nothing to look at on the summit, I started down—but didn't make a beeline for the trailhead. Ten minutes into the descent, I stopped at Bandai's mountain hut to investigate the delicious scent of roasting mushrooms I had noticed when I climbed past on my way to the mountaintop.

Inside the hut, a woman in her sixties stood behind a wooden counter, selling beverages, snacks, and a wide variety of what my son calls "bits and bobs," but what my father would have termed—in this case, accurately—"bells and whistles." Beside the counter, a heavy wooden table ringed with split-log benches offered hikers a place to sit and savor a bowl of soup or drink a cup of coffee.

A sign recommended mushroom soup "with Bandai-foraged mushrooms!" so I ordered myself a bowl.

Three perfectly toasted bread rounds bobbed on the surface of the dark brown soup. Beneath them, tiny flare-capped mushrooms swam in steaming broth. To call the mushrooms "special" would open the door to some inaccurate assumptions, but I doubt I'll ever taste another mushroom quite as perfect as those foraged caps, or a soup as rich and flavorful.

Afterward, I continued my descent with renewed energy. Tree roots snaked across the trail, creating such perfect natural stairs that it seemed as if Bandai wanted to be climbed. The thought was more than just a passing fancy. Everything about this mountain, from the cool, refreshing mists to the easy trail, suggested a mountain that both recognized and welcomed human visitors.

I returned to the trailhead six hours after starting what the map described as a five-hour hike—a little closer to the posted time than I had managed previously. Even better, I hadn't felt afraid. In fact, I had enjoyed myself the entire time.

I hoped that, perhaps, this was the breakthrough I'd been waiting for. Maybe overcoming fear wouldn't be that difficult after all, and maybe the remaining climbs wouldn't be as hard as I had worried they would be.

As it turned out, the last part was correct.

The coming climbs would not be nearly as difficult as I had feared.

They would be a whole lot worse.

STATION 2: FUJI, DENIED
MOUNTAIN TOTAL: 8

I fell in love with Mount Fuji in kindergarten, when I saw a picture of her perfect snowcapped cone in *National Geographic* magazine. I had longed to see her with my own eyes for more than four decades, but after dozens of unsuccessful attempts, I began to think Japan's most famous mountain veiled herself in clouds deliberately whenever I approached.

I'm not a superstitious person, but as my failures mounted, her recalcitrance began to feel personal.

Three days after my return from Mount Bandai, as the *shinkansen* carried me south toward Mount Ibuki, Fuji once again concealed herself behind a cloak of clouds.

Were this a movie-of-the-week, the protagonist would see Mount Fuji only after she proved her worth by climbing to the mountain's peak.

Were this a novel I was writing, I would never use such a sappy plot device.

However, I had no control over Mount Fuji's narrative. I simply hoped I'd get to see her—at least once—before the year was through.

12

AT LEAST THE FROG WAS HAPPY

June 20, 2018

On the morning I planned to climb Mount Ibuki (伊吹山) (1,377 meters), I woke to the heavy drum of rain against the hotel window. Uncertain whether it was safe to climb, I checked a number of online trail guides. None of them mentioned the trail becoming hazardous in rain. Since I knew that Mount Ibuki had a hiking trail up one side and a scenic highway up the other, with regular bus service connecting the visitor center on the mountaintop with Sekigahara Station on the far side of the peak, I decided to make the climb. If the rain continued, I would simply take a bus back down.

As I dressed for the hike, I discovered I had left my waterproof rain pants back in Tokyo. I remembered seeing some plastic pants at the *conbini* (convenience store) between my hotel and the station, so I hurried down the street and bought a pair. After a pit stop in the bathroom to pull the rain gear over my hiking pants, I caught the 7 a.m. bus to the trailhead.

The fact that I was the only hiker on the bus, combined with the driver's wide-eyed stare as I disembarked at the trailhead, should have been valuable clues that this was a bad idea. However, like any good B-movie victim, I ignored the warning signs.

By 7:45 a.m. I had left the trailhead far behind and the rain had become a downpour that transformed the rocky trail into a series of small waterfalls connected by puddles the size of pizzas. A fist-sized reddish frog with huge brown eyes stared up at me from the center of one such puddle. I stopped to take his picture and continued up the trail.

In the early 2000s Mount Ibuki was home to a popular ski resort with motorized lifts and a ski-in, ski-out hotel located partway up the slope. Lack of snowfall put the ski resort out of business, but the abandoned buildings and derelict lifts remain. I had read about them in the online trail guides, so when I emerged from the forested lower slopes, the decaying resort didn't take me entirely by surprise.

That said, the rain and the fact that I was the only hiker on the mountain changed what might have been merely weird into a post-apocalyptic wasteland. I half expected to see a horde of zombies shamble out of the ruined buildings, intent on devouring my brains.

Needless to say, I didn't linger long.

The rain slowed to a drizzle as I left the resort behind, still mercifully in possession of my brains. (Although if I'd been using them, I would have turned back down the mountain then.)

Just before I reached Fifth Station—the supposed halfway mark—a wild deer bounded across the trail. I caught only a momentary glimpse of light brown fur and a flash of tail, but it lifted my sodden spirit and made me feel much less alone.

Above Sixth Station, the trail grew steep and narrow. There were no trees to shelter me from the rain, which had resumed, much heavier than before. Each step became an exercise in balance as I struggled up the increasingly wet and slippery trail. I tried not to think about what I'd do if I were injured in a fall.

I pushed myself to the limits of my strength and will, but barely reached the Seventh Station by the time I'd calculated as the latest I could reach the summit and return to the trailhead in time to catch the final bus.

I had to make a critical decision.

I looked back down the trail, which had become a muddy stream.

You cannot climb back down that without falling.

A painful lump rose in my throat.

People died on the *hyakumeizan* almost every year. I knew that fact when I made my plans, and yet, somehow, I had assumed the mountains would be easier. I believed I could overcome my fear of risk without putting myself in any real danger. I had clung to those beliefs despite what I had seen on prior climbs, and now I found myself confronted with a truth that did not match my imagination.

It was stick-horse racing all over again.

As a little girl, stick horses were my passion. I had four, and I rode them in my backyard every day. I constructed jumping courses from flowerpots and overturned patio furniture, and ran through the yard, imagining myself astride a stallion, winning gold in the Olympic Games.

One afternoon when a friend came over, I suggested we have a stick-horse race. We picked our mounts and arranged the course. I shouted, "Go!" and started off at the skipping pace that (in my head) mimicked the gait of a real horse.

My friend ran straight for the finish line as fast as she could, holding the stick horse in front of her and making no attempt to "ride."

She won, of course, and my dream was shattered. I wasn't a gold-medal rider on a magnificent, prancing stallion. I was a chubby kid in Coke-bottle glasses grasping a sock attached to a stick that I desperately wished was a real horse.

As I stood alone, high on Mount Ibuki, once again my visions of victory dissolved in puddles at my feet. I cried, both for my current self and for the injured child who longed for greatness far beyond her reach.

Forty-seven years old, and I was still that little girl.

I don't want to be a failure anymore, my injured child-self cried.

Tears flowed freely down my face. I looked at the rocky trail below and at the mist that concealed the trail ahead.

Up was terrifying.

Down was worse.

Every muscle in my body ached. I had pushed myself beyond what I could handle, and yet I could not give up. Somehow, I had to get off the mountain.

I wanted the rain to stop and the rocks to dry. I wanted to feel strong and safe. I wanted to succeed. Most of all, *I wanted a bus.*

I had passed the Seventh Station. As between the bus at the trailhead and the one at the top of the mountain, the top was closer.

Decision made.

In the hour that followed I lost the trail three times and had to double back along the rocks to find my way. With every step, my aching thighs and pounding feet hurt worse. My fingers scraped against the stones as I grasped for balance. More than once, I accidentally grabbed one of the giant earthworms that emerged from the ground to escape the watery mud.

I was hungry, exhausted, and terrified that I would fall or that my dwindling strength would fail before I reached the top.

My inner voice chimed in.

For once it didn't work against me.

Take one step. Just one step more. You don't have to climb the entire mountain right this minute. You just have to take one step.

I took that step. And another. And another, until I finally dragged my muddy, rain-soaked body over the final rise and past the marker for Station Ten, where the trail evened out for the final hundred yards to the summit. I splashed along it, only to stop in disbelief at the sight of a 10-foot chain link fence across the trail, just yards from the summit marker.

And the gate was padlocked shut.

In the fictional, stick-horse version of this story, I emerged atop the summit as the sun burst through the clouds and a rainbow arched across the peak.

In the real world, a padlocked gate denied me the final yards.

I could see the marker, but I couldn't get there.

Slowly, I turned away from the gate and followed the path around the summit plateau to the visitor center where I could catch the bus. The rain, which had faded to a drizzle, once again became a downpour—one last kick to a fighter already down.

Inside the visitor center, the staff sat around a table, warm and dry, enjoying cups of tea. They sprang to their feet in shock as I crossed the parking lot, and by the time I walked through sliding doors the tea had disappeared and the staff stood waiting at their stations.

One of them approached me, wearing a look of confused concern.

"Hello," he said in English. "Where did you come from?"

I answered in Japanese. *"Amerikajin desu."* (I'm an American.)

"No, yes, okay. But . . . did you climb?" His voice rose dramatically on the final word, implying that, despite appearances, this could not be true.

I nodded and switched to English. "From the trailhead."

"In the rain?"

I switched to Japanese again. *"What time is the bus to Sekigahara?"*

An older man behind the counter answered. *"Bus?"* He shook his head. *"There is no bus today."*

I desperately hoped I had misunderstood. *"No bus?"* I repeated in Japanese.

He gestured to the window. *"It is raining."*

THAT'S PRECISELY WHY I NEED THE BUS.

Unable to comprehend the brilliant stroke of planning that cancels buses when it rains (in retrospect, it's true few people visit mountains on a rainy day), I grasped at my last remaining straw. *"Takushii desu ka?"*

In my desperation, it didn't occur to me (and wouldn't, until much later) that I hadn't asked "Is there a taxi?" but, instead, inquired *"Are you a taxi?"*

To his credit, the elderly gentleman didn't bat an eye. *"It is expensive."*

" That's okay ."

My inner voice was screaming, *Whatever it costs! Just get me off this mountain!*

He exchanged a glance with the younger man, who spoke to me in English.

"He worries because the taxi is expensive." The young man wrote a number on a piece of paper: ¥10,000. The equivalent of a hundred US dollars.

I had worried it would cost much more.

"That's fine," I said in Japanese. *"Please call a taxi."*

With a nod, the older man picked up a phone and dialed. When the call connected, he spoke for a moment, listened as the other party answered, and then slowly turned his face away before he whispered, *"Gaikokujin."*

A foreigner.

No doubt, a response to the dispatcher asking who on earth would climb Ibuki on a day like this.

When the taxi arrived, I stripped off my filthy plastic pants to avoid destroying the spotless white lace covers on the seats. To his credit, the driver did a remarkable job of pretending this was all routine. We chatted on the drive, and when he heard that I wrote novels set in 16th-century Japan, he turned the meter off and gave me a drive-by tour of the site where the famous Battle of Sekigahara took place in 1600.

Later, as he dropped me at the station, I said, *"Thank you for rescuing me from Mount Ibuki."*

Only then did he crack a smile. *"It was no problem."*

That night, I tried to decide if I could credit myself with a climb of Mount Ibuki. The summit marker was only meters past the gate. I had not reached it, but I'd climbed as far as anyone could go that day.

My friends and family said, "You climbed. It counts. Especially after everything you went through."

Still, I felt conflicted. I had climbed the mountain, but I hadn't touched the summit marker. I wished I had the time to return to Mount Ibuki—this time, by bus—to hike those final meters, but I had nonrefundable reservations, and other scheduled climbs, in the days that followed.

Someday, I would return for those final meters—by the end of the year if possible and, if not, then when I could. Until then, I would count the climb as done, if not entirely complete.

13

WALKING ON THE ROAD
June 21, 2018

The morning after my miserable adventure on Mount Ibuki, I caught the earliest possible train to Shimoichiguchi, a tiny station in southern Nara Prefecture. The tiny, open platform was a far cry from the tourist crowds in deer-filled Nara City. I arrived an hour before the first bus left for Dorogawa Onsen, a hot-spring town not far from Mount Ōmine (大峰山) (1,719 meters)—a *hyakumeizan* I was not allowed to climb.

Since the early eighth century, Mount Ōmine has been the headquarters of *Shugendō*, a monastic faith that focuses on the realization of spiritual power through challenging ritual tests designed to refine a worshipper's courage and devotion. Historically, all practitioners were male, and women were prohibited on the sacred peaks where *Shugendō* was practiced. In modern times both men and women are allowed to practice *Shugendō*, and most of the sacred mountains welcome visitors of any gender. Ōmine alone maintains its ban (and that, on the honor system only).

The mountain's ban on female climbers is a controversial topic, both politically and in trekking circles, but I had not come to Japan for political reasons. I loathe being told that my gender prevents me from doing anything I want to do, but also have profound respect for other people's earnest faith and private practices.

My feelings about Mount Ōmine were complex, to say the least.

After long and careful thought, I decided not to violate the sacred prohibition. I had come to the mountains on a spiritual quest and it seemed hypocritical to disrespect the mountain's sacred status. Ultimately, I decided to treat Mount Ōmine as I would a temple: by showing respect for the beliefs of those who worshipped there. In this case, that meant I could not climb.

I had read that a sign near the trailhead declared "No women allowed beyond this point" and decided to use the sign as an ersatz summit marker. Afterward, I hoped to find something else to hike in the area, ideally about the length of the trail up Mount Ōmine.

While I waited for the bus, an elderly man approached and handed me a tourist map to the nearby open-air flower museum. Not wanting to be rude, I accepted the map and set it on my lap. As I did, I noticed another map on the opposite side, labeled ŌMINE AND TENKAWA GORGE. To my delight, it showed not only the hiking trail from Dorogawa Onsen to the base of Mount Ōmine—a map I needed and did not have—but also a second nearby trail that followed the Tenkawa ("River of Heaven") through Mitarai Gorge.

My plans for the day were set.

The road to Dorogawa Onsen paralleled the lower portion of the swiftly flowing Tenkawa. The rushing river mirrored the steel blue of the clouds that hung low overhead, threatening yet another storm.

Once again, I was heading out alone to hike on a rainy day. I felt a chill. Memories of Mount Ibuki rose like hungry ghosts to suck my confidence away. I took meditative breaths to slow my pounding heart and reminded myself that neither the trail to the base of Mount Ōmine nor the one through Mitarai Gorge would be steep or dangerous.

My fear abated slightly, but not much.

Dorogawa Onsen swarms with visitors during the autumn foliage season, but it was a ghost town on an overcast Thursday morning in late June. I was the only person on the bus and the narrow streets were deserted. All the shops were closed.

The last bus back to Shimoichiguchi Station left the far end of the gorge just after 6 p.m., which meant I had almost eight hours to complete a pair of hikes that, together, should take no more than five.

Surely not even I could screw that up.

A set of steep stone stairs led into the forest on the left side of the road, just past the bus stop. Life-sized statues of foxes and lions lined the steps, their stony faces guarding the approach to a wooden torii. I climbed the stairs and found myself in a forest shrine. Just past the worship hall, an abandoned-looking monorail station huddled at the base of a massive pine. Its metal track curled up the mountainside, the upper terminus hidden in the trees.

I had to investigate.

As I approached the station, wondering what a monorail was doing in the forest, I saw a camera-style doorbell by the entrance. Above the button, but below the camera, a sign read "Ring for train."

Never one to argue with a sign, I pushed the button.

A speaker squawked and a female voice said, *"Good morning"* in Japanese.

I responded in kind. *"One person, please."*

I hoped that was enough to call the train.

"One moment, please," the woman said, and the box went silent.

Three minutes later, a four-car train designed to look like a chain of logs came gliding silently down the track. The woman at the helm wore overalls and a happy smile. She waved me in, and when I took a seat in the narrow car, the monorail began a slow trip up the mountain through the trees.

At the upper station, the smiling conductor led me toward a sign that explained the 300-yen fare for the monorail also included entry to a nearby limestone cavern. The price seemed like a bargain, so I paid the fare and went inside the cave.

Dripping water from the recent rain, combined with the spiked stalactites and stalagmites, made me feel as if I walked through the drooling jaws of a stony beast. Colored lights illuminated many strange and beautiful formations. Deep in the cave, I found a Shintō shrine dedicated to the deities of the mountain, along with a display of oblong fox skulls that apparently belonged to former residents of the cave.

Later, I followed an earthen path across the mountainside to Dorogawa Onsen's famous suspension bridge, which spans the Tenkawa at a height of 120 meters above the river's rushing flow. The bridge wobbled beneath me as I crossed, but not enough to scare me, and I stopped at the center to enjoy the view. I felt a thrill as I watched the river flowing far beneath me. It was difficult to believe how exciting—how absolutely *cool* —my once dull life had now become.

On the far side of the bridge, a path descended to the bank of the Tenkawa and joined the trail that led to Mount Ōmine. Wooden signs at intervals along the path reminded me, in Japanese and English, that women were not permitted beyond the trailhead at the base of the sacred mountain. Every time I passed one, I thought (in the voice of the ancient crusader knight from *Indiana Jones and the Last Crusade*), *The woman cannot pass beyond the Great Seal.*

The Tenkawa flowed so high from recent storms that it spilled across the bank and flooded sections of the trail. I picked my way through the puddles, hopping from stone to stone. Between the extra time it took to navigate the flooded trail and my earlier detour to the monorail, cave, and suspension bridge, I didn't even reach the temple at the base of Mount Ōmine until past the time when I had planned to start my hike through Mitarai Gorge—and I was still several kilometers from that trailhead.

I took selfies with the sign at the Ōmine trailhead, which did in fact proclaim "No Woman Admitted," and then hurried down an asphalt road away from the sacred mountain. I arrived at the starting point of the 7.5-kilometer hike through Mitarai Gorge more than an hour later than I planned.

Despite my need to catch the final bus, the scenery refused to let me rush. The gently undulating earthen trail followed the mighty Tenkawa's turbulent course through the steep-sided gorge. Dense forest overhung the path, filling the air with the rich scent of earth and the freshness of recent rain. Dozens of waterfalls cascaded down the sides of the gorge to join the roaring river. Smaller rivulets trickled down the massive, overhanging stones, sprinkling my head in a way that felt like a baptism from the mountain. The feathery ferns that clung to the rocks unfurled their fronds like questing fingers reaching for the path.

A butterfly fluttered across the trail, and then another. Moments later, dozens of them surrounded me, their wings a living blizzard in the air. They swirled and fluttered around me for more than a minute before slowly disappearing into the forest from whence they came.

I stood transfixed until the raucous cry of a crow reminded me that I was on a timeline.

A short while later I stopped to watch the Tenkawa gather strength as it flowed between enormous stones at the entrance to the first of several cataracts. The river's voice increased, its constant rumble rising to a thunderous roar of water over rocks.

The sound made my heart sing, and I thought of how much my father would have loved this place. An Eagle Scout, he adored the mountains and the majesty of waterfalls. I wished he could have lived to share the wild freedom of this place with me. But even as I had the thought, I knew he never would have come. His fear of airplane flights and unknown places would have kept him home.

My dad instilled a love of nature in my heart, but it was Mom whose sense of adventure gave me the strength to go and see it.

I dallied at each of the suspension bridges that crossed the river, taking photographs and enjoying the elevated views of the river's flow.

Eventually I emerged from the forest at one end of a concrete bridge that crossed the river to an asphalt road. I crossed, but found neither a bus stop nor a trail marker on the other side.

Clearly, I had made a wrong turn somewhere. The trail hadn't branched, so it seemed impossible that I was lost, but the lack of a bus stop (or a sign) indicated that something had gone badly wrong.

I consulted the trail map to no avail.

If only you had an interactive map that could show you exactly where you are . . .

Wanting to slap myself in the forehead for my density, I pulled out my mobile phone and checked the GPS, which—as expected—knew exactly where I was.

Better yet, it knew exactly where the *bus stop* was and how to get there.

I plotted a course and set off down the asphalt road, amused to find myself smack in the middle of just the kind of obnoxious math problem I'd hated back in high school.

"If a hiker who has already walked 13.5 kilometers leaves a bridge located 1.77 kilometers from the nearest bus stop, hoping to catch a bus that departs in exactly thirty minutes, how fast must the hiker walk to reach the bus stop in the allotted time?"

With no disrespect to my former algebra teachers, the answer is *as fast as humanly possible.*

I made the bus with six minutes to spare and climbed aboard, wobbly-legged from the effort but proud of myself for finishing my second-longest hike to date (on a mountain that I didn't even climb).

Better yet, I was learning to ride through life like a leaf in a river instead of trying to dam the river's flow or change its course. I had begun to understand that, sometimes, the unexpected path was more rewarding (and more fun) than the boring sameness I'd mistaken for stability.

14

TOO MANY BEES

June 22, 2018

The morning after my adventure in the gorge, I checked out of my hotel and left my suitcase in a locker at the station, planning to retrieve it on my way back through to Tokyo that night. (The presence of coin-operated lockers in most Japanese bus and rail stations made traveling easy and saved me from having to carry more than I needed for a single hike.)

With the suitcase stowed, I caught a train and then a bus to the border of Nara and Mie Prefectures, home to Mount Odaigahara (大台ヶ原) (1,695 meters), the highest mountain in Mie and, according to an ancient Japanese chronicle, the place where the first emperor, Jimmu, assumed the throne of Japan.

As I waited for the bus, a little garbage truck drove by, its speakers playing jingling music to warn pedestrians of its approach. Strangely, it played the exact same tune as the ice cream trucks that sent me screaming homeward as a child to raid my piggy bank or beg my mom for money for a Bomb Pop.

The garbage truck awakened a compulsive need for ice cream, further dampening my already lukewarm feelings toward my preclimb breakfast of Calorie Mate and canned café au lait.

"Calorie Mate" is a Japanese meal-replacement bar in shortbread cookie form. Its distinctive rectangular boxes occupy significant real estate on the shelves of every Japanese supermarket and *conbini*, and although the plain, no-nonsense yellow packaging did not inspire confidence, Christopher had said it wasn't bad, and he was right. It's no eggs Benedict or cherry Danish, but the lightweight cookies were an easy and nutritious way to fill my stomach when I needed something fast, light-weight, and portable.

A bus pulled up 10 minutes before the one to Odaigahara was due to leave. For the first time since my climbs began, I was able to read the sign and knew it wasn't the one I wanted even without asking the driver to confirm its destination. As it drove away, I realized the breakthrough had come, appropriately, on Christopher's birthday.

For the past two years, my son—who majored in Japanese language and spoke it fluently—had refused to translate anything for me if he believed I could read it on my own.

"READ, Mom," he would tell me. "You can do it, and you need the practice. Read."

The proper bus arrived nine minutes later—right on time—and I climbed aboard for the two-hour journey to Mount Odaigahara. As the bus rolled through the countryside, my thoughts returned to the problem of my visa. Weeks had passed and I'd heard nothing from the immigra-tion lawyer. At this point, another rejection would leave me with precious little time to find an alternative solution. I fretted about the situation for almost an hour—until the bus turned up a sphincter-clenchingly narrow mountain road with such steep drop-offs on the downhill side that I couldn't even see the ground below. In most places, the road was barely wide enough for two small cars to pass, and the bus was too wide to pass anything at all.

I clutched the armrest and hoped we wouldn't encounter any opposing traffic.

Half an hour into the nerve-wracking ride, I saw a bicycle tire hanging from a tree branch high above the road. I couldn't imagine the most dedicated cyclist trying to ride up (or down) this punishingly steep and narrow route, and didn't want to imagine how that tire ended up in a tree 10 meters off the road.

Periodically, I caught tantalizing glimpses of misty mountains through the trees. The closest ones were vibrant green, the ones in the distance, gray.

At 11 a.m. the bus pulled into the enormous parking lot at the Odaiga-hara Visitor Center. I checked the posted bus times carefully. Only two buses made the long run to and from Odaigahara daily. I'd arrived on the first one. Missing the next—and only—return trip was not an option.

After filing a hiking plan and picking up a map at the visitor center, I started along the forested trail toward the true high point atop Mount Hidegatake (1,695 meters), where a viewing platform offered 365-degree views of the mountains that surrounded the Odaigahara Plateau.

I reached the summit in precisely the amount of time described on the trail map and celebrated my victory with cookies and a break to enjoy the view. A sign claimed that on clear days you could see Mount Fuji from the viewing platform but, although the day seemed clear to me, Fuji did not appear.

Instead of heading back to the visitor center, I continued along a loop trail that circumnavigated the huge plateau. Near its center, I found a statue commemorating the first emperor of Japan and the famous crow that led him to the throne.

According to ancient Japanese chronicles, a divine crow named Yatagarasu (八咫烏) led Jimmu across Japan, from the region known as Kumano to Odaigahara (in a region then known as Yamato, now called Nara). When they arrived, Jimmu was granted the right to become the emperor of Japan. Yatagarasu, whose name means "eight-span crow," is a powerful symbol of the sun goddess Amaterasu—the highest deity in the Shintō pantheon. This sacred crow is honored at hundreds of Kumano shrines across Japan, and crows have historically been considered important messengers of the divine.

I loved these confident, raucous crows, and saw them everywhere in Japan. During my initial visit in 2015, and on every visit since, they had appeared at important junctures and interacted with me in ways that often made me wonder whether they were leading me to a special destination too.

Beyond the statue, the trail continued toward a fang-shaped rocky outcrop known as Daijagura, whose narrow, tapering point extends over a chasm at vertigo-inducing heights. Hikers who climb out to the end are rewarded with dizzying, unimpeded views of forested mountains and dazzling waterfalls.

I clambered up and over a set of boulders and along the winding trail to Daijagura. The air smelled of vanilla mixed with pine. When I reached the outcrop, I climbed up and inched along it sitting down, because it felt too high and exposed to stand. I only went about halfway to the end before I lost my nerve, but counted it as a victory.

Six months before, I would not have dared to climb onto the narrow rock at all.

The visit to Daijagura put me slightly behind the estimated trail times, but I still returned to the visitor center more than half an hour before the bus was due to leave. For once, I wasn't even sore—though, admittedly, the climb had been less challenging than usual.

A trip to the gift shop yielded a commemorative pin and an unusual ice cream sandwich featuring *matcha* (powdered green tea) flavored ice cream, whole adzuki beans, and mochi (pounded glutinous rice) all stuffed inside a crispy wafer shell. It was delicious!

After eating it, I walked across the parking lot. As I approached the wooden bench beside the bus stop sign, a distinctive buzzing filled the air. A dozen bees crawled on the bench, while others hovered in the air nearby.

I'm allergic to bee stings, so I left the bench to the bees and retreated toward another bench on the opposite side of the parking lot.

But there were bees all over that one too.

The parking lot had benches at all four of the cardinal compass points, and every one was occupied by bees. In fact, no matter where I tried to stop and rest, the bees were there—if not when I arrived, then moments later. I didn't know what drew them, but they only left me alone if I kept moving. By the time the bus arrived, I was tired of walking and truly tired of bees. In fact, I was so worn out that I fell asleep in my seat before the bus had even left the parking lot.

15

MAGIC IN THE MUNDANE

June 23–24, 2018

I returned to Tokyo with only four days remaining until our first short-term apartment lease expired on June 28. Even so, I hoped to sneak in one more climb before Michael and I made the crosstown move from Shinjuku to Sumida Ward. The only *hyakumeizan* I could reach, climb, and return from within that window was Kurumayama (車山) (1,925 meters), the highest point on the Kirigamine (霧ヶ峰) Highlands in Nagano.

Kurumayama, which means "car mountain," sounds decisively unromantic, but Kirigamine ("misty mountains") derives its name from the fog that rises up to the plateau from the valley surrounding nearby Suwa Lake.

According to my hiking guides, Nagano's Alps—in winter, home to some of the best skiing and snowboarding in Japan—were among the world's most beautiful hiking trails in the summer months. I couldn't wait to see them.

The night before I left for Nagano, I sat up in bed at 3:30 a.m., awakened by a panicked thought: *What if the bus to Kirigamine doesn't run in June?*

In Japan, the mountain buses run only at certain times of year; in some cases, they run only on weekends and holidays, and they have extended service gaps during the rainy season. When I planned the Kirigamine climb, I'd checked the scheduled times, but not the dates of operation.

I climbed out of bed and checked the bus company website. Sure enough, there was no service to Kirigamine from June 15 to July 14, presumably due to the summer rains, and the distance to the trailhead was far too long for taxis.

I lay down, now wide awake. My hotel in the historical town of Suwa was nonrefundable, because I'd made the reservation within 24 hours of the check-in date. I had chosen to stay in Suwa, half an hour by train from Chino (where I had to catch the trailhead bus), because the town was home to one of Japan's most important Shintō shrines.

Although frustrated with my foolish oversight, I decided I would go to Suwa anyway. If possible, I would find a way to the mountain; if not, I would see the historical sights and enjoy whatever experience awaited.

On the train to Chino City in central Nagano, I thought about the way rebooting my life had plunged me into the very kind of half-plotted chaos I created when writing fiction. I wondered how I could have believed that leaving my old life behind for a year in the mountains would transform me into a different person overnight. Had I truly thought I could absorb the Big Existential Lessons without running into any serious problems?

To my amazement, I really had been that naive.

Most of the lessons I had learned so far were obvious-in-retrospect things like "insects are jerks," "don't climb mile-high mountains in the rain," and "remember to take food . . . but don't take raisins."

Valuable truths, but not the epic victories I hoped for.

At Chino Station, I made a beeline for the bus depot across the street. I knew from experience that Japanese websites didn't always post bus schedules accurately (see: Mount Ibuki) and hoped there might be an alternate bus I hadn't seen online. As it turned out, there *was* a bus, and although it had just departed for its last run of the day, it ran the next day too.

While I waited on the platform for the local train to Suwa, an enormous crow swooped in and landed on a rafter overhead. He cocked his head and watched me without fear.

"Are you Yatagarasu?" I asked in Japanese.

He cocked his head to the other side.

As the train pulled in, he spread his wings and flew off in the direction of Suwa Shrine.

Historians believe Suwa Grand Shrine was already well established by the seventh century, based on references in the eighth-century chronicle

Kojiki. Today, Suwa Shrine consists of four holy complexes arranged at different points around Lake Suwa.

I visited two of the Suwa shrines and walked a stretch of the Nakasendo, a 17th-century mountain road that once connected Kyoto with the city of Edo (now Tokyo). As I strolled past narrow wooden homes and inns that had stood for centuries, I came upon a spring-fed fountain shaped like a snarling dragon carved from stone. A narrow stream of water emerged from the dragon's mouth and splashed into a stone-rimmed pool. Small porcelain teacups sat on the fountain's rim, inviting passersby to take a drink.

Before I left the United States, I would never have used a random cup to drink an unknown trickle of water drooling from a statue's mouth. The risk of germs, contamination, and litigious fountain owners would have made me hurry past. But in Japan, I filled a cup and drank.

The day was warm but the water felt icy cold on my lips and teeth. It tasted pure and clean, like melted snow. When I finished, I set the cup in a basket beside the fountain and said a silent thank you to whoever left (and hopefully washed) the cups so visitors like me could taste the water from this mountain spring.

As sunset approached, I wandered along the promenade at Suwa Lakeside Park and sat on the seawall near the shore. A gentle breeze blew off the lake as the setting sun transformed the water's surface into shimmering gold.

Small waves lapped softly against the grassy shore. A family strolled across the lawn nearby, the parents holding hands as their toddler flirted happily with the ducks that waddled on the green belt near the lake.

Not far away, a trio of skateboarders practiced tricks on a concrete slab in front of an outdoor amphitheater. An elderly man sat on the uppermost tier of seats, watching the teenaged skateboarders with contentment on his wrinkled face.

An enormous jet-black crow circled overhead and landed beside me on the wall, so close that I could have touched him. He watched me through intelligent eyes.

"I get it," I told him. "I'm on a quest to the place I'm supposed to be."

That night, I woke from a nightmare in which my cancer had returned. Burning pain in my sternum prevented me from going back to sleep, so I lay awake and worried. I ran my hands across my chest, feeling my ribs beneath the scars as I searched for lumps or unexpected growths. I didn't find anything unusual, but each time I worried that I might. Until (and unless) my visa came through, my health insurance let me see a doctor only in emergencies—and cancer checkups, though important, didn't qualify.

In the morning, I rode the bus to the sightseeing lift at the base of Mount Kirigamine and bought a ticket to the top. The slope was steep, but the lift hung low. In places, my dangling feet almost brushed the ground.

Unlike the other lifts and gondolas I'd ridden, which ended at least an hour's hike below the summit, the Kurumayama Lift carried riders to within two minutes of the summit marker. Had I known the lift went *all* the way to the summit I would have climbed, despite my rule about taking lifts.

The mountaintop was lovely, with 360-degree views of the snow-capped alps and the Yatsugatake Mountains. The Shintō shrine on the summit featured one of the loveliest white torii I had ever seen.

And yet, it didn't feel special.

Asphalt roads curled through the nearby mountains, cutting dark black lines across the mountainsides. Hotels and lodges dotted the slopes, marring the view—at least, by comparison with my other recent climbs.

I wished I had skipped the mountain and stayed in Tokyo . . . but the moment I had the thought, I felt guilty about my attitude. I decided to walk along the rocky trail that wound through the highland area near the summit park and find a way to appreciate the day.

Fifteen minutes past the summit, movement drew my eye to the side of the trail. A brilliant orange butterfly the size of a silver dollar fluttered up from the grass and landed on my hand.

I gasped in surprise and it flew away.

Moments later another one, nearly identical to the first, rose up from the other side of the trail and landed briefly on my arm. A third one settled on my pants and stayed for several minutes. When it left, another butterfly flew across the trail and landed on my hiking poles. Its twin alighted on my hand, unfurled its wiry tongue and dabbed my skin to taste the salty sweat.

I stood dumbstruck, and remembered hunting for tiny, golden fiery skippers in my neighbor's marigold bed when I was six years old. I stalked the little butterflies with care, waiting to pounce until they folded their wings together (I had learned that, in that pose, they were less likely to escape).

When I caught one, I cupped it carefully in my hands and waited for its frightened fluttering to cease before I opened my fingers to see it resting on my palm. I always let the butterflies go free, but loved the feeling of holding them in my hands.

Two years later, I read an article in *National Geographic* that explained how touching the delicate scales on a butterfly's wings could interfere with its ability to fly. My heart hurt as I read it; I had seen the dust-like scales on my hands after catching butterflies, and hated that my love for them had made me cause them harm.

I never captured butterflies again.

On Kirigamine, the butterflies caught me.

I spent the better part of half an hour watching the butterflies fly around. I felt a thrill each time one stopped to rest on my pants or walk on my waiting palm. Dozens of other hikers passed, but none of them seemed to care about the butterflies at all.

Eventually, the last of the butterflies disappeared into the grass. I returned to the summit, filled with happiness and peace.

The experience transformed my attitude and my opinion of Kuruma-yama. A day that began as an anticlimactic flop ended up a treasured memory, the mundane transformed to magic in a flash of butterfly wings.

STATION 3: STILL WAITING
MOUNTAIN TOTAL: 12

At the end of June, Michael and I began our second short-term lease, in a small apartment near the Tokyo Skytree. I hoped by the time the six-week lease term ended in mid-August, I would have my visa and we could finally find a place to call our own.

That said, I hadn't heard a peep from my lawyer or the Immigration Bureau.

My immigration status was the last thing I thought about each night and the first thing on my mind when I woke each morning. (The second thing was how badly my muscles hurt from all the climbs.)

I worried about what would happen if the Japanese government rejected my second long-term visa application. Generally, a citizen of the United States can receive only two tourist visas—and stay a total of 180 days in Japan—each year. I had already come to Japan in March to apply for my first, failed, visa, and might not qualify to return again after my tourist visa ran its course.

As if that wasn't bad enough, the typhoon season had arrived in earnest.

16

DAISEN'S GIANT CHIPMUNK

June 30–July 1, 2018

At the end of June, a huge typhoon bore down on Tokyo from the east. With the forecast promising a week of thunderstorms and heavy rain across north and central Honshu, I went west—880 kilometers west—to Daisen-Oki National Park in Tottori Prefecture.

Mount Daisen (大山) (1,710 meters) is the highest peak in Japan's Chugoku Region, an area that encompasses most of western Honshu, including Hiroshima, Okayama, Shimane, Tottori, and Yamaguchi Prefectures. Due to its sacred status, Mount Daisen was closed to visitors until the Meiji Era (1868–1912), and Daisenji—the Buddhist temple at the base of the mountain's northwest slope—remains a draw for many Buddhist pilgrims. *Shukubo*, or temple lodgings, near the mountain offer overnight stays for religious and secular travelers alike.

During the five-hour *shinkansen* ride from Tokyo to Tottori (where I'd transfer to a local train), I considered the massive amount of time it took to travel between the *hyakumeizan* peaks. The mountains were spread across the length and breadth of Japan's four major islands; in many cases, they were more than a day apart by train. Buses to some *hyakumeizan* trailheads ran only in the summer; other *hyakumeizan* had no buses to their trailheads at all.

Transportation challenges aside, I questioned my original decision to climb the *hyakumeizan* in a year. When I made that plan, I hadn't known how many beautiful, historic mountains existed in Japan, or that confining myself to *hyakumeizan* would leave so little time to experience the places I would visit. More importantly, the goal of becoming the first non-Japanese woman over 45 to climb Fukada's mountains in a year had begun to feel at odds with my deeper purposes: to face—and overcome— my fears, reset my life, and learn important truths about the mountains and myself. Achieving the *hyakumeizan* goal required a heavy focus on logistics: when I wasn't actively planning climbs or watching weather forecasts, I was traveling, and although I took a necessary break from logistics to make the climbs, I was always hurrying. I found myself with precious little time to absorb and reflect on my experiences, let alone enjoy them.

I was so busy *doing*, I had no time to think or feel.

I felt trapped between irreconcilable objectives. And yet, I had set a goal to climb the *hyakumeizan* in a year, and I had never failed to reach any major goal I set.

But what if, to reach the goal, you must fail yourself?

* * *

In Tottori, I boarded a local train that trundled through the mountains underneath a leaden sky. Storm clouds perched like angry gargoyles on the mountaintops. A steady rain began to fall as the train rolled on past villages too small to warrant a streetlight—some, too small to warrant an asphalt road.

Once or twice an hour, the train chugged into a station and disgorged a passenger or two. Most of the stations consisted of little more than a 50-meter concrete platform, some of which didn't even have a roof to block the rain.

I disembarked at Yonago Station. Due to its proximity to Daisen-Oki National Park, the station had not only a roof but a *conbini* and a tiny visitor center. The silver-haired volunteer behind the counter spoke perfect English—in which, he explained that the only bus to Daisen didn't leave for three more hours.

"But," he added, "the taxis have a flat fee rate of 2,800 yen to the Daisen Visitor Center, if you're interested."

Twice the bus fare, but a quarter of the standard rate for an hour-long taxi ride.

Five minutes later, I was in a cab and on my way.

By the time we reached the visitor center, the rain was coming down so hard I suspected I would need an ark by morning. I went inside for a hiking map and waited for a break in the pouring rain before I hurried up the narrow, cobblestoned street to my temple lodging at Sanraku-sō.

I had stayed in *shukubo* before and I loved everything about them, from the simple, traditional guest rooms to the scent of incense in the air. Most of all, I loved the temple meals, cooked in the ancient, vegetarian *shojin ryori* (temple cuisine) style, which was my favorite food—not only in Japan, but in the world.

My guest room at Sanraku-sō had tatami-covered floors and a low wooden table flanked by cushioned backrests. Rain drummed on the temple roof as I sipped a cup of hot green tea and nibbled on the crispy pear gaufrette the temple gave me as a welcome treat. The comforting scents of tatami and sandalwood perfumed the air.

Later, I sat in a private dining room and savored a delicious nine-course meal of local vegetables and tofu, with each dish designed to inspire the eye as well as the palate. Tiny vegetables carved to resemble flying herons sat beside a plate of konjac and tofu sliced to look exactly like sashimi. I watched a flaming hot pot cook my delicate tofu soup as I sampled a plate of crispy mountain vegetables foraged on Mount Daisen and pickled at Sanraku-sō.

I hoped the rain would clear so I could climb, but I could think of far worse fates than having to return.

* * *

In the morning, I woke to the welcome glow of sunshine, dressed, and shouldered Blue for the five-hour round-trip hike.

Mount Daisen's lower slopes are home to the largest beech forest in Japan, nicknamed the "Green Dam" for the way it retains water. Hundreds of species of birds and animals call the forest home, and as I started up the earthen trail I hoped to see some wildlife.

Daisen didn't disappoint—at least, not if you count a Japanese hiker wearing a full-body, hooded chipmunk suit (complete with ears and tail) as "wildlife."

Chipmunk Man also wore an enormous grin and a pair of high-top hiking boots, and greeted me with a gleeful *"Good morning!"* in both English and Japanese before he turned and bounded up the slope. His unfazed wife and mortified tween son (both dressed in normal clothes) echoed his greeting and followed gamely in his wake.

I ran into Chipmunk Man and his family several times along the trail, and despite the sweltering temperature—more than 30 degrees Celsius

(86 Fahrenheit)—and sweat-inducing humidity, Chipmunk Man never lost his happy grin. By the time we reached the halfway point, his son's humiliated stare had even softened to resigned acceptance.

On Japanese mountains, it's customary to say hello to everyone you pass, and on crowded days the trails ring with *ohayoo gozaimasu* (good morning) and *konnichiwa* (hello/good afternoon). The rain's retreat brought hundreds of hikers to Mount Daisen on the day I climbed, so my morning consisted largely of greetings with little snatches of nature in between.

Above the forest, the shrubs grew short and the trail grew steep and rocky. Dense foliage grew close to the path on either side. In places, there was barely enough room for a single hiker to ascend or descend along the rocky slope. Lines of hikers formed above and below these bottlenecks, as people waited to take their turns through the narrow sections.

I felt nervous when these waits took place at the edges of steep cliffs (as they often did), but they also offered a welcome chance to rest my aching legs and enjoy the expansive views. Beyond the forested slopes of Daisen and the surrounding peaks, the Sea of Japan glittered like a sapphire.

At one such stop, I looked more closely at the mountains surrounding Daisen, many of which were listed on my trail map. I wished I had time to stay and climb them all, or even one or two. The desire to climb a hundred mountains resonated in my mind and heart, but once again I wondered if they had to be Fukada's hundred peaks.

The trail grew increasingly steep and jagged. Clouds closed in and the temperature dropped. I climbed through shifting mist that made me feel as if the world beyond the mountain had disappeared, leaving only a never-ending, rocky climb.

Abruptly, the rocks disappeared, replaced by a set of wooden steps that led up to a wooden boardwalk measuring only a meter wide. Waist-high climbing ropes were strung through thin metal posts on either side of the wooden walkway. The boardwalk was designed to protect the delicate grasses covering Mount Daisen's summit area, and offered no protection against the winds that howled across the mountaintop. As I crossed the narrow walkway, shivering in the unexpected cold, I clutched the climbing ropes to keep the wind from blowing me off the edge.

The boardwalk ended at a concrete platform and a two-story block-shaped hut. I hurried across the final meters and climbed the last few stairs to the summit marker, the freezing wind forgotten in my rush to reach another mountain goal. I was shivering, but I felt triumphant. I had reached the top of my thirteenth *hyakumeizan*—and my hair was long enough to take a summit picture with no hat. Best of all, I had enjoyed the climb.

That night, after my descent, I lay on my futon at Sanraku-sō and listened to the rhythmic patter of rain that once again fell on the temple roof. I remembered reading that, in his later life, Kyūya Fukada said he would have changed a few of the mountains on the *hyakumeizan* list if he had known his hundred peaks would become such an important part of the Japanese climbing lexicon.

As I drifted off to sleep, it occurred to me that if Fukada could change his mind about the *hyakumeizan*, I could too.

17

ALL ROADS LEAD TO KYOTO
July 2–3, 2018

In addition to being the former capital of Japan and one of the world's great cities, Kyoto was a convenient place to break up my journey from Mount Daisen to Kōyasan, a sacred mountain on the Kii Peninsula in Wakayama Prefecture. An overnight stay in Kyoto also gave me the chance to climb, and spend the night on, sacred Mount Hiei (比叡山) (848 meters), the headquarters of the Tendai sect of esoteric Buddhism.

Hiei is not a *hyakumeizan* peak, but I had to sleep somewhere, and a *shukubo* on another sacred mountain sounded like an excellent choice to me.

Mount Hiei sits slightly north of Kyoto City, on the border between Kyoto and Shiga Prefectures. In the early ninth century, a Japanese priest named Saichō returned from studying Buddhism in China and established the Tendai sect of esoteric Buddhism in Japan. Shortly thereafter, he founded Hieizan Enryakuji, a temple high on the slopes of Mount Hiei, to serve as a center for Tendai training and religious practice. In 1994 the temple became a UNESCO World Heritage Site, in recognition of its deep religious and historical significance.

I planned to climb to the summit of Mount Hiei the afternoon I arrived, before spending the night at Hieizan Enryakuji Kaikan, a *shukubo* that was as different from Sanraku-sō as possible while still retaining all the essential elements of a temple stay. Enryakuji's enormous, seven-story "guest house" had a marble lobby, gift and coffee shops, and a restaurant, all of which reminded me more of a four-star hotel than a thousand-year-old Buddhist temple. And yet, my guest room had a tatami floor, traditional futon bedding, and a view of the forested mountain I'd come to climb.

A less-pleasant similarity to Sanraku-sō appeared when I looked out the guest room window. Angry clouds—the darkest and heaviest I had seen since my arrival in Japan—hung low in the sky, obscuring the mountaintop.

Hoping I could beat the rain to the summit and back, I laced up my boots, grabbed Blue, and headed out.

As I crossed the lobby, the desk clerk's forehead furrowed with concern.

"Pardon me," he asked hesitantly, in Japanese, *". . . are you going out?"*

"Hieizan—" I forgot the verb for "climb," so I raised my hiking poles and smiled.

His worry deepened. *"But . . . it's going to rain."*

"That's okay," I lied. *"I like the rain."*

"It's going to rain," he repeated, clearly torn between concern for my well-being and the social obligation not to contradict a guest.

I felt a flash of guilt. A Japanese guest has a similar obligation not to put the host in an awkward position. However, the clerk wasn't technically my host, and I had come to climb this mountain. With my shuttle leaving for the train the following morning at 9 a.m., if I wanted to climb, it had to be that day.

I hurried out the lobby doors as an enormous boom of thunder cracked the sky.

The downpour that followed was so sudden and intense that I was drenched in the seconds it took me to turn around and get inside.

A second, louder roll of thunder rattled the lobby doors as they closed behind me.

The clerk looked just as startled as I felt.

"It's raining," I said (unnecessarily). *"I think I'll go to the coffee shop instead."*

I sat by the shop's enormous plate glass windows and drank cappuccino as the storm raged on outside. Forked lightning stabbed across the sky, and peals of thunder shook the glass.

Later, in my room, I watched as curtains of mist floated through the pouring rain like gauzy veils. Unexpectedly, I did not feel disappointed that I missed my chance to climb the mountain. The sudden storm felt too much like a judgment of my plans. Either God or Mount Hiei, or both, said *not today*, and I accepted that decision.

As I watched the rain, an unaccustomed sense of peace fell over me.

I had spent my life so focused on my goals that I hadn't ever learned what it truly meant to *rest*. I celebrated victories, but always with my eyes on the next big target. I perpetually told myself that I would relax as soon I reached *this* goal, but every time, another goal was waiting just beyond it.

In Tōhoku, I had decided to treat each day like a treasure box, but one month later I was still too busy hurrying from mountain to mountain to open the treasure boxes and enjoy the wealth of memories they contained.

I spent the rest of that rainy afternoon and evening in deliberate relax-ation. I watched the rain. I soaked in the *onsen*, and I lingered over another delicious, seasonal *shojin ryori* meal. I thought about the moun-tains I had climbed and how much I loved my new life in Japan.

As I went to bed I realized—with no real surprise—that I had no intention of leaving Japan when the year was through. The thought wasn't new. I had dreamed about living in Japan for years, and mentioned that desire to friends and family. But this time, the thought was more than just *I'd like to stay*; it was, *I will.*

I would need a job to qualify for a long-term visa and didn't know what kind of job (aside from teaching English, which did not appeal) a middle-aged lawyer/novelist could do. However, depending on the immi-gration bureau, I had somewhere between eight weeks and eight months to figure out the answer.

* * *

I passed a fitful night, beset by nightmares that grew more intense as the hours passed. Shortly before 5 a.m., I abandoned the pretense of sleep. Outside the window, thick gray mist obscured the world; it even hid the trees across the road from the *shukubo*.

But it wasn't raining.

With two hours until breakfast—four until my shuttle left for the station—I had time to give the climb another try.

When I slipped out the lobby doors at 5:05 a.m., the clerks had not yet come on duty. Swirling mist surrounded me as I climbed the stone steps through the temple grounds. The crunching of my boots on the gravel path was the only sound I heard. The air felt chilly but refreshing, and my legs felt strong, already recovered from the Daisen climb.

One by one, Enryakuji's sacred buildings appeared through the mist and vanished behind me, swallowed by the heavy clouds that covered the mountaintop. The gravel path came to an end behind a vermilion pagoda. From there, an earthen trail led upward through the forest, cutting switchbacks up the slopes of Mount Hiei.

The air was rich with moisture and the scents of earth and pine. Fat drops of water plummeted from the trees at random intervals, the residue from last night's rain. One of them landed on my neck, splashing my ears and trickling down my back.

At a crossroads where two trails met, I saw fresh deer prints in the mud. I scanned the forest, hoping for a glimpse of tawny fur, but saw only the massive, misty trees. Still, as I walked where the deer had walked, I felt connected to the sacred forest and the wild things that lived there.

I reached the mountaintop just as the rising sun peeked through the clouds. To my surprise, the trail ended at an asphalt parking lot. An access road—for visitors who wanted to visit the summit shrine and museum without the climb—ran up the far side of the mountain, which explained why I hadn't seen it from the trail.

I crossed the parking lot to the summit marker, took a photo, and began my descent immediately. The rising sun transformed the mist to gold. I felt the strongest I had ever been, both physically and emotionally, and though I regretted having spent so many years in the pursuit of never-ending goals, I also felt I had taken an important step toward real change.

Back at the temple, I paused in front of the worship hall, which enshrines a statue of Amida Nyorai, the Buddha of Infinite Light. I felt grateful for the storm. Without it, I would have missed this misty dawn.

For centuries, Japanese poets have written haiku to commemorate profound experiences. Inspired by overwhelming joy and the beauty of the rising sun, I composed my own:

> Hiei summit, dawn
> breaks above the misty trees.
> I must journey on.

As I finished my poem, I walked face first into an enormous, sticky spider web, which triggered an impromptu performance of the *ARGHSpider!* flail-dance and completely shattered my contemplative mood.

Later, after breakfast and a shower hot enough to expunge the memory of the giant web, I took a shuttle bus, three trains, a cable car, and a local bus to the summit of yet another sacred mountain, where I planned to celebrate the release of my sixth mystery novel with a climb of a historic peak.

18

GODDESS OF ALL THAT FLOWS
July 3, 2018

The tsunami that followed the Great Tōhōku Earthquake of 2011 damaged the Fukushima Daiichi Nuclear Power Plant, north of Tokyo. In the wake of the disaster, scientists measured increased radiation levels on Mount Adatara, one of the *hyakumeizan* peaks. The levels had returned almost to normal by 2018, but my oncologist advised me to avoid any unnecessary radiation, so from an overabundance of caution I omitted Adatara from my climbing list. As a *"hyakumeizan* stand-in," I chose Bentendake (弁天岳) (984 meters), also known as Mount Benten, one of the eight peaks that rise in a circle around the sacred mountaintop plateau of Kōyasan like the petals of a lotus flower.

Kōyasan has been the headquarters of Shingon Buddhism since shortly after Kōbō Daishi (774–835)—also known as Kūkai—founded the esoteric Buddhist sect in the early ninth century, when he returned from studying in China. Since that time, Kōyasan has remained an active center of Buddhist study and worship. Like Mount Hiei, it became a UNESCO World Heritage Site in 2004. Kōyasan is also home to Japan's largest cemetery, Ōkunoin, which contains more than 250,000 graves and monuments for the dead.

I fell in love with Kōyasan during a research trip in 2016, when the sacred mountain inspired the setting of my sixth mystery, *Trial on Mount Kōya*. The novel was scheduled to release on July 3, 2018, so I decided to kill two birds with a single stone and climb Mount Benten on the book's release day.

The fact that this meant back-to-back climbs on Mount Hiei and Kōyasan was a historically interesting bonus. Kōbō Daishi studied esoteric Buddhism in China at the same time as Saichō, who founded both the Tendai sect and Hieizan Enryakuji. The priests were friends at the time they established their respective esoteric Buddhist sects, but later had a falling out over theological differences and were still rivals when they died.

When I arrived on Kōyasan, I left my suitcase at the 1,100-year-old temple where I planned to spend the night and caught a bus to the Bentendake trailhead. The trail began at the *nyonindo* (women's hall), a historical building at the edge of the Kōyasan plateau. Until the Meiji Era (1868–1912), women were prohibited from entering the sacred precincts of Kōyasan. Instead, female pilgrims stayed at one of several *nyonindo* located along a trail—now known as the *Nyonin-michi* (women's route)—that circles the perimeter of the sacred valley and climbs across its holy peaks.

The forested trail to the summit of Mount Benten started with a sharp incline but quickly evened out along the side of a steep mountainside. Tall *koyamaki*, prehistoric pines native to Wakayama Prefecture, grew all around the path. The mountain dropped precipitously away from the left side of the trail, which in places was less than half a meter wide. The ground felt stable beneath my boots, but the women who hiked this trail in centuries past wore woven sandals and would have needed nerves of steel—especially in winter, when the snow disguised the true edge of the trail.

Bright green ferns sprang from the earth. Tiny butterflies and moths danced in the air. Overhead, the forest canopy rang with the songs of birds I wished I recognized, along with the staccato calls of crows.

I had spent so much time studying the history of this holy place that I felt a deep connection to the mountain. I was neither a Buddhist nor Japanese, and yet I felt a physical aching in my chest as I thought of all the pilgrims—men and women—who had walked this path in the centuries before me. I imagined how the women, in particular, would have peered through the trees, hoping for a glimpse of the temples in the sacred valley.

Near the summit of Mount Benten, the trail climbed sharply upward through a gully with sides higher than my head. Halfway up the narrow defile, I heard a rumble of thunder in the distance.

A flash of panic followed.

You don't want to be here when it rains.

I tried to hurry, but the slippery, rocky ground demanded caution. Overhead, the sky grew dark. My shadow on the ground, already faint, disappeared completely.

The wind began to gust. The birds fell silent, except for the crows, whose urgent calls now felt like warnings meant specifically for me.

The trail, though narrow, was not dangerously steep. The forecast hadn't called for rain, so downpours and landslides were both unlikely. Still, I began to shake—and not from cold.

I was angry with myself for being scared, and yet the memories of Mount Ibuki flooded back as my fear increased.

At the top of the gully, the trail changed back to dense-packed earth. Thick tree roots created natural steps, enough like the ones on Mount Bandai to inspire a positive memory. I increased my pace and prayed the rain would wait until I reached the *shukubo*. I revised the thought almost at once: I only *needed* the rain to wait until I reached the summit of Mount Benten and descended to the *Daimon* (Great Gate) on the other side.

The wind blew hard and the clouds were dark, but it hadn't started raining when I reached the beautiful Shintō shrine on the small summit plateau. Guardian lions carved from stone watched over the peak-roofed structure that enshrined the *kami* (deity) of the mountain. A trio of vermilion torii gates stood at the entrance to the sacred space. Like the mountain, the shrine is dedicated to the goddess Benzaiten, patron of water, music, words, and everything that flows (including money). A syncretic deity, Benzaiten (or Benten) is the Japanese form of the Hindu goddess Sarasvati. According to Shingon belief, she has protected Kōyasan since Kōbō Daishi consecrated the summit of Bentendake, and enshrined her there, many centuries ago.

The air now held the scent of approaching rain, so I took my summit photo and continued down the far side of the mountain. Shortly past the summit, the *koyamaki* gave way to a forest of other pines intermingled with maples and tall bamboo. Insects swarmed from the undergrowth as I passed, surrounding my head and shoulders in visible swarms. I flailed my arms and jumped around in a futile attempt to avoid becoming dinner for every insect on the mountain.

On the positive side, the bugs made me forget about the rain.

Mercifully, the swarms remained behind in the forest when I reached the end of the trail and emerged into the open area where the massive *Daimon* stands.

The red, two-story wooden gate rises 25 meters into the air. Elaborate, colorful carvings of waves decorate the upper level, representing a prayer that this incarnation of the gate (which dates to the 18th century) would not burn to the ground as previous versions had. The *Daimon* marks the official entrance to Danjo Garan, the oldest temple complex on the mountain, which also serves as the headquarters of the Kōyasan Shingon Buddhist faith.

I felt as if 12 centuries' worth of female pilgrims stood there with me, straining their eyes for a glimpse of the holy ground on the far side of that massive gate. I invited them into my mind and heart, bowed deeply, and prayed—for those women, and for every other woman who was ever told she could not live the life she wanted. When I finished, I straightened and stepped through the gate, symbolically carrying all of them with me into Kōyasan.

In a moment I could not have timed any better if I'd written it as fiction, the rain arrived. Enormous raindrops pelted my head and spattered Blue as I hurried toward the *shukubo*, anticipating a steaming bath, a delicious evening meal, and a good night's sleep.

I got all three.

STATION 4: VISA AT LAST
MOUNTAIN TOTAL: 15

Three days after I returned to Tokyo from Kōyasan, I received an email from my immigration lawyer.

"Congratulations! I received your certificate of eligibility today!"

The Japanese government had granted my visa application.

My residence card would be issued in the next few weeks. When I received it, we could sign a long-term lease. More importantly, Michael would finally qualify for a visa, as my spouse.

Since his existing tourist visa and the lease on our short-term apartment would expire before my residence card arrived, we would still have to make one more short-term apartment move, and Michael would have to make a two-week "tourist visa reset" visit to the United States at the end of August.

But before that, I had plans to climb the tallest mountain in Japan.

And when I did, I would not climb alone.

19

EVEN ANTS LIKE KAKIGORI

July 13, 2018

The day after I received the life-changing news about my visa, I went to the airport to meet my friend Laurie and her daughter Kaitlyn, who were flying in from California. My mother was scheduled to arrive a few days later, and at the end of July the four of us would attempt an overnight ascent of Mount Fuji (富士山) (3,776 meters), the tallest mountain in Japan.

I barely slept the night before my friends arrived. I had met Laurie, her husband David, and their children Chris and Kaitlyn several years before, at Epiclesis church in Sacramento, California. Laurie mentioned that Kaitlyn—then a ninth-grade homeschool student—had an interest in writing fiction. A newly published debut novelist myself, I offered to take a look at Kaitlyn's stories.

I had never known a person her age to write so fluidly, especially without any special training. When Laurie asked me for advice about writing programs, I offered to teach Kaitlyn's English class—and thus began a three-year, much-beloved weekly ritual. Laurie, Kaitlyn, and Chris came to my house each Tuesday morning, and our writing classes soon included not just lesson time but home-cooked breakfasts and long talks about every aspect of our lives. When Kaitlyn graduated from high school the summer before my departure to Japan, she and her family had become much more than friends. They were my family too.

I didn't miss much about the United States, but I missed Laurie, Chris, and Kaitlyn every time another Tuesday rolled around. When Laurie and Kaitlyn bought their tickets for Japan, I almost cried for joy.

As I hugged them at the airport, I felt like a desert receiving a shower of refreshing rain.

Three days after Laurie and Kaitlyn arrived in Japan, we traveled an hour west of Tokyo to climb Mount Takao (高尾山) (599 meters), see the sights, and get some exercise before our upcoming trip to Fuji.

In addition to its many hiking trails, Mount Takao is home to flower gardens, thousands of maple and cherry trees, a monkey park, and Yakuoin, a Shingon Buddhist temple famous for its statues of bird-headed *tengu* (mountain spirits). Established in 744 as a base for Buddhist worship in eastern Japan, the temple was restored in the 14th century by a Shingon priest; thereafter both the temple and Mount Takao flourished as a center of *Shugendō*, the syncretic faith practiced throughout the sacred mountains of Japan.

Laurie, Kaitlyn, and I arrived at the base of Mount Takao at midmorning, with the temperature and humidity rising quickly. As we walked to the funicular that would carry us halfway up the mountain, I cast a glance at the overcast sky and hoped it wouldn't rain.

Near the upper funicular station, we visited the Mount Takao Monkey Park and Wild Plant Garden. The monkey park is home to approximately 40 Japanese macaques, many more of which roam free on the forested slopes of Mount Takao. A glass wall on the ground floor separates the visitors from the monkeys—though who benefits most from this arrangement is unclear. A spiral staircase leads to an open-air viewing platform on the second floor, and my friends and I trooped up for a topside view.

The day we visited, four tiny baby monkeys were monopolizing the bucket-swings and stealing food from the other macaques, to our vast amusement and the great chagrin of their simian peers. Laurie, Kaitlyn, and I bought monkey treats from the keeper and tossed them to the macaques, who caught the kibbles with reflexes that put Major League outfielders to shame.

The monkeys all looked up and screeched as rain began to patter on the rocks.

"They get excited when it rains," the laughing keeper said in Japanese.

"So do I," I deadpanned.

Laurie, Kaitlyn, and I waited out the rain in the forested flower garden adjacent to the monkey park, where the broad-limbed trees kept us mostly dry. The smells of earth, wet growth, and the occasional scent of a flower perfumed the air. I visited with Laurie as we strolled along the gravel path. Nearby, Kaitlyn—a talented naturalist—photographed the plants.

When the rain passed, we continued up the mountain, taking a longer, earthen trail that crossed a suspension bridge en route to the peak. As we hiked, I confessed that I was thinking about changing my *hyakumeizan*-only goal and instead attempting to climb a hundred famous, sacred, and historically important Japanese mountains within the year.

I felt relief when Laurie and Kaitlyn expressed complete support. They reminded me that this was a journey of self-discovery, not a mountaineering challenge. I hadn't expected them to disapprove, but I trusted them to be honest, too, and their support moved me one step closer to accepting the decision (which, in retrospect, I had already made, though at the time I lacked the courage to admit it).

As we reached the summit, a white butterfly the size of a 500-yen coin (or a US quarter) flew out of a tree and landed on my hand. It unfurled its springlike tongue and tapped my skin. When it finished, I expected it to fly away.

Instead, it stayed.

I raised my hand to Laurie's, and the butterfly walked over. To our mutual delight, it relaxed on her hand as it had on mine.

Eventually the butterfly fluttered off. We took summit photos and crossed the summit park to a shop selling *kakigori*: fluffy Japanese shaved ice flavored with syrups and other toppings. Laurie and I chose Blue Hawaii flavoring, while Kaitlyn opted for the more traditional Japanese toppings of adzuki beans and sweetened condensed milk. We found seats at a nearby picnic table that, on a clear day, supposedly offered lovely views of Fuji (though even after three visits to Mount Takao, I knew this only secondhand).

Three huge black ants wandered around the tabletop. Eventually, they found the drips of melted *kakigori* that fell from our bowls, and stuck their heads in the tiny puddles, drinking them up so quickly we could see the pools shrink. Afterward the ants ran around the table like a trio of toddlers on a sugar high.

We took an alternate trail down the mountain in order to visit Yakuoin and see the bird-faced *tengu* statues. Just past the temple we stopped again, at a vendor selling one of my favorite treats: grilled *kurogoma dango*. The traditional Japanese snack is made from balls of mochi mixed with black sesame, stuck on skewers, and brushed with a sweet soy or miso glaze before being grilled above an open charcoal flame. The result is crispy on the outside, chewy inside, and has a delicate flavor that combines the sweetness of the glaze with savory sesame.

Laurie and Kaitlyn loved the *dango* as much as I did, and the entire day made me feel as if the smile would never leave my face. I enjoyed the way hiking on my own gave me space to think and time to move at my own pace, but after so many months alone in the mountains, Laurie and Kaitlyn filled a void I hadn't even realized was there.

As we rode the funicular down the mountain, I received an anxious text from my mom in California. With barely 12 hours until their flight departed for Tokyo, Mom and my stepfather, Spencer, had lost the key to their fireproof safe—which had Mom's passport locked inside.

The allegedly-but-not-actually-24-hour locksmith Mom had called could not get anyone to their house until eight o'clock the following morning (California time), three hours before their flight to Japan was due to depart from LAX. Not only would Mom and Spencer be unable to reach the airport three hours early, as the airlines recommended, but they would be lucky to make the flight at all.

Mom and Spencer could take a later flight, but that would delay their arrival in Japan by at least an entire day. With only three full days remaining before we were scheduled to climb Mount Fuji, and no way to change our reservations at the mountain hut, any delay would jeopardize Mom's ability to make the 16-hour time adjustment and prepare for the Fuji climb.

Mom was 75 years old and had no recent experience in the mountains.

"Jeopardy" was the last word I wanted to associate with our upcoming climb.

20

ON MOUNT INARI
July 16, 2018

Mom and Spencer made their plane with minutes to spare. Their safe was ruined—the locksmith said that drilling it open was the only way for them to make the flight—but as between a fireproof safe and a timely flight to Tokyo, the fireproof safe was easier to replace.

The evening after Mom and Spencer arrived in Tokyo, all five of us (sans Michael, who had opted to remain behind with Oobie) took the *shinkansen* to Kyoto.

Once again, Mount Fuji hid herself behind the clouds as we sped past.

After spending the night in Kyoto, all four members of "Team Fuji" headed twenty minutes farther south to Fushimi Inari Shrine for a climb of 230-meter Mount Inari (稲荷山). (Spencer was recovering from recent spinal surgery; like Michael, he had opted out of all the mountain climbs.)

Fushimi Inari *Taisha* (Shrine) was established during the eighth century and moved to its current location a century later. The shrine is dedicated to Inari Ōkami (one of Japan's most popular Shintō deities) and is the largest of Japan's Inari shrines. Fushimi Inari is famous for the thousands of vermilion torii that line the mountain's slopes. Hundreds of statues, most of them shaped like Inari's messenger foxes, stand guard beside the brightly colored gates. More than a dozen sub-shrines at numbered locations along the trail serve as prayer points for the many pilgrims who climb Mount Inari as a devotional exercise; they also offer climbers a place to rest.

By the time Team Fuji started up the stone and concrete steps that pave the trail to Mount Inari's summit, the temperature was already almost 40 degrees Celsius (104 degrees Fahrenheit), and the humidity was rising too. Cicadas screeched and rattled in the trees like choruses of tiny banshees.

We tried to climb together, but our paces soon diverged, and we shifted to hiking alone or in pairs. We waited for one another at every sub-shrine, but that meant the slowest climbers had the least opportunity to rest before we resumed the climb. The pace was not a real concern on little Mount Inari, but I worried about what would happen when we reached Mount Fuji. Each of the stations on Fuji's trail was farther from the others than the entire length of the trail up Mount Inari.

A small, traditional restaurant clings to the side of the mountain halfway up Inari. Despite the hordes of visitors that throng the paths, the restaurant almost never has a wait because the tables are reserved for people willing to order entire meals (and ice cream doesn't count).

By the time Team Fuji reached the restaurant, the sun was blazing overhead and the four of us were drenched in sweat. It took no effort to persuade the team to stop for an early lunch.

A refreshing breeze washed over us as we stepped inside; oscillating ceiling fans and open windows kept the restaurant cool. We removed our shoes and stepped onto the elevated, tatami-covered floor. The hostess offered us a table by the window with a breathtaking, bird's-eye view of Kyoto in the valley far below. We knelt on cushions around the table and enjoyed a leisurely meal of soba (buckwheat noodles) and *inari-zushi* (rice and sesame seeds wrapped in paper-thin fried tofu skin), along with a selection of traditional iced summer beverages popular in the Kyoto region.

Laurie and Kaitlyn both chose deep green, sweetened *matcha*. The opaque green liquid struck the perfect balance between sweetness and rich, grassy tea. Mom selected a "lemon squash," which looked and tasted like sparkling lemonade. I picked a drink I had never tasted: an ancient specialty made from barley sugar, ginger, and spring water, served over large cubes of ice. It was delicious, not too sweet, and left me feeling cool, refreshed, and energized.

Sharing the food I loved with the people I loved filled me with overwhelming joy. I'd found this little restaurant on my first solo research trip to Japan. The trip itself was a watershed: my first time traveling overseas alone, and also when I finally learned to enjoy eating in restaurants by myself. When I returned from that research trip, I had told my mom, and also Laurie and Kaitlyn, about the restaurant on Mount Inari. At the time, I never thought I would have the chance to experience it with them. Watching them eat the food I had described to them so long before, and desperately wished that they could taste, left me deliriously happy.

After lunch, we continued to climb—and the thermometer did too. The air became so hot that it hurt to inhale. We dripped with sweat. The trail itself was far from challenging—just endless stairs—but the unyielding heat and humidity took a toll.

When we passed a team of workers replacing a damaged torii with a new one, I could hardly imagine the effort it must have taken to carry the heavy wooden beams up a mountain in the oppressive heat. Their labor made me even more aware of the thousands of torii that lined the slopes, each one inscribed with the name of the person or company whose donation paid to build the sacred gate. Each gate had been carried up the mountain, piece by piece, a labor of love as well as a sacred offering.

Team Fuji reached the summit of Mount Inari as the clock struck noon. We arrived as a group and celebrated with summit photos and bottles of water that we dumped on one another's heads instead of drinking. The lack of shade on the summit made it a less than ideal place to rest, so we stayed just long enough to catch our collective breath before we started down.

Just above the halfway point, I saw a familiar blue-and-white cloth flag outside a sub-shrine shop. I pointed. "They have *kakigori*—"

I didn't need to finish the sentence. The others were already making a beeline for the shaved ice vendor.

As we settled on benches outside the shop with heaping cups of soft, pink, strawberry-flavored ice, a Japanese couple asked where we were from and where we were traveling in Japan. The answers led to an extended conversation about our upcoming attempt to climb Mount Fuji. We communicated well even though the couple knew only rudimentary English and I spoke equally basic Japanese. Impromptu conversations still outstripped my vocabulary, but my anxiety level no longer shot through the roof when a stranger asked a question.

Team Fuji descended Mount Inari in less than half the time it took us to ascend, motivated primarily by a collective desire to escape the crushing heat. When we finished, I felt confident that Laurie, Kaitlyn, Mom, and I were as prepared to climb Mount Fuji as four women of disparate ages with little collective climbing experience were ever likely to be.

Whether any of us was actually capable of reaching the top of the highest mountain in Japan remained to be seen—but the next few days would tell the tale.

21

MOUNT FUJI
July 19, 2018

Just before dinnertime on July 18, Team Fuji (and Spencer) arrived in the city of Fujinomiya, southwest of Mount Fuji, where Spencer would wait during our ascent. The overcast sky hid the mountain so completely that we weren't even sure which way to look. The lack of visibility made me sad; the next day's forecast called for rain, with thunderstorm warnings.

If the rain materialized as more than showers, I would have to call off the climb.

We dropped our bags at our hotel and crossed the street for a celebratory pre-climb dinner at a local restaurant. The elderly Japanese owner took an instant shine to Spencer, even though she spoke no English and he no Japanese. Their back-and-forth teasing made me feel better about leaving him alone for the next two days. If nothing else, he would have company when he came to eat.

After dinner Team Fuji walked to a nearby *conbini* for final mission-critical supplies: bottled water, packaged nuts, half-sized wooden pilgrim staves to carry up the mountain, and Blue Hawaii–flavored dessert parfaits.

Back in my room on a sugar high, I sorted my gear and packed Blue for the two-day climb. Last of all, I carefully added a circular wooden amulet I'd bought at a Shintō shrine three days before. The Tao-shaped amulet was designed to be split into two halves, and each half kept by one of two people who shared a personal tie. The pieces would keep their bearers connected, no matter how great the distances between them. I planned that Mom and I would split the amulet on Fuji's summit and keep the pieces as mementos of our climb.

I ran a bath and used the final envelope from a box of "Fuji bath salts" I had bought in Japan in 2016. Exhausted from the mental and physical preparations, I fell asleep in the tub and woke up with my fingers and toes so wrinkled they could have passed for pale prunes. I moved to the bed and slept like a rock—assuming rocks have nightmares about thunderstorms.

At 5 a.m. the rising sun interrupted my fitful rest. I rolled over, hoping to sleep until the alarm went off at eight.

Get up and check the view.

I dragged myself out of bed and to the window, not expecting to see anything but clouds.

But this time, at long last, Fuji was there.

The massive, flat-topped mountain rose above the surrounding plain, veiled lightly in mist, with the sun about to rise above her shoulder. She was one of the most beautiful things I had ever seen.

She was also enormous.

I had known she was big. At 3,776 meters, her summit was more than two miles high. But those numbers had not prepared me for her staggering size.

I thought about calling Mom and Spencer, or Kaitlyn and Laurie, but didn't want to deprive them of the sleep they would need in the hours to come. Besides, the mountain would still be there at breakfast.

Except . . . she wasn't.

By eight o'clock, Mount Fuji had cloaked herself in clouds, and my climbing companions had to be content with the pictures I took at dawn.

At breakfast, we reviewed our climbing plan. We would catch the 10:30 bus to the Fujinomiya Fifth Station trailhead (elevation 2,400 meters) and begin the ascent from there. We would climb independently as far as Goraiko Sansou, the Seventh Station mountain hut where we had reservations for the night. Over dinner at the hut, we would finalize our plan for the summit push. Personally, I hoped to leave the hut at midnight, climb through the night, and reach the top in time to see the sunrise from the highest elevation in Japan.

The Fujinomiya route was supposed to be the easiest of Mount Fuji's four main hiking trails—but "easy" is a relative term, as my relatives and I would soon discover.

We took an official "Team Fuji" photo at the trailhead and started up. Within minutes, we strung out along the broad dirt trail that curled around the wide base of the mountain. To my left, dramatically high above, a small white building perched on a ridge at the base of what looked like the final summit push. (I would later learn that this was just Ninth Station, and that it was still two hours' climb below the summit.) To my right, Mount Fuji's shoulder sloped down toward the city of Fujinomiya, which was already half concealed by clouds.

The overcast sky trapped heat, and the temperature soared to 33 degrees Celsius (91 degrees Fahrenheit). Trails of sweat ran down my face and back. I debated slowing down to wait for Mom and the others but worried that if I did, they would feel rushed and try to hurry on my account.

Before I decided what to do, I reached Sixth Station, making the issue moot.

Kaitlyn arrived a couple of minutes later, and we paid the station attendant to burn the first of the official station brands onto our pilgrim staves. He returned the sticks to us still warm and smelling of charred pine. The brand included an image of Mount Fuji, the year, and the station number, along with the kanji (Chinese characters adopted for use in written Japanese) for "sea of clouds." With mounting excitement, I imagined what the staff would look like, covered in brands, when the climb was through.

Mom and Laurie arrived, and once they got their brands we all pressed on toward Seventh Station.

Soon the earthen path gave way to rocks and unstable scree. The group strung out again, and our progress slowed. I lowered my head and tried to focus, but I worried about Mom and Laurie—specifically, about the duty I owed them, as the leader of the group. Each of my climbing companions had said, repeatedly, that getting me to the summit was the goal, whether or not they made the summit too. Still, I debated what to do if I had to choose between reaching the summit and leaving them behind.

With so much going through my head, I barely established a climbing rhythm before I reached the Seventh Station hut. Kaitlyn arrived about 30 minutes later, and we celebrated with hugs and photos, stowed our packs in our sleeping cubbies, and waited on the overlook, watching the sea of clouds until the rest of the team arrived.

At sunset, after a simple but tasty meal of Japanese curry, rice, and *tsukemono* (pickled vegetables), we crawled into our cubbies—plywood cubes with foam pads on the floor—to get some rest before the summit climb.

A mountain hut on Fuji in the height of climbing season is the antithesis of restful. The stifling, sweaty heat, close air, and constant whispers, thumps, and laughter from the other hiking groups made it impossible to do anything more than drift uneasily in and out of consciousness.

At one point, I heard crying. I sat upright, thinking it was Mom. Just that morning, she received the news that her lifelong friend, Geraldine, had died after a long and difficult illness. Mom still wanted to climb Mount Fuji—and had dedicated her efforts to Geraldine—but I worried about the added stress impacting her ability to climb. As it turned out, it was a stranger crying, but worry wound me up so tightly I was on the verge of tears myself.

When my alarm went off at 11:45, I was more than ready to escape the stifling hut. I planned to hold a brief team meeting to establish critical turn-around times and a communication plan, but Mom and Laurie were already gone. Kaitlyn reported that they had left for the summit half an hour before.

I shouldered Blue and stepped outside into darkness so deep and complete—and air so unexpectedly cold—it took my breath away. The Milky Way ran like a silver river across the sky. Beside it, Mars glowed brilliant red, looking down like the eye of God.

Kaitlyn and I switched on our headlamps and began to climb. Our breath plumed out in front of us, clearly visible in the chilly air. Insulation, many bodies, and the heat given off by the compost toilets kept the hut uncomfortably warm, but outside the temperature had dropped to just above freezing.

I hiked as fast as possible to generate warmth, and wished for a heavier sweater.

Kaitlyn and I caught up with Mom and Laurie half an hour after we left the hut. I felt a surge of relief when I saw them together. I was worried about Mom alone in the dark on this massive mountain. She was active and worked full time, but she was over 75 and had no mountain training. In fact, none of Team Fuji, aside from me, had trained extensively for the climb.

Although struggling with the scree and altitude, Mom and Laurie told us not to wait for them. Kaitlyn and I continued up the trail, but I didn't feel comfortable leaving them behind. Halfway up the next switchback, where I knew the darkness would disguise my presence, I told Kaitlyn to go ahead, turned off my headlamp, and watched Mom and Laurie's lights bobbing up the trail. They were climbing well, but they didn't seem to be moving fast enough to reach the top by dawn, despite the many hours that remained.

I hesitated, torn between the desire to reach the summit and the urge to stay with Mom and Laurie. If we did not reach the top by dawn, we would not make it there at all. We had to descend all the way to the Fifth Station trailhead that day, and an ascent that took more than five or six hours would not leave us with sufficient time to reach the trailhead by dark. Failing to make Mount Fuji's summit would put an absolute end to my *hyakumeizan* goal as well, because the mountain huts were fully booked for the rest of Fuji's two-month climbing season.

I felt guilty. Good leaders don't leave the team behind, and if one of them got hurt I'd be too far away to help.

On the other hand, Mount Fuji was the jewel in the *hyakumeizan* crown, and an important personal climb for me as well. After so many years of trying and failing to see Mount Fuji, I had started to believe that if I wanted to see her at a distance, I would have to prove my worth by standing on her summit.

I shivered in the darkness as I struggled with the choice.

Mom and Laurie's headlamps stopped to rest and then continued.

Cold air seeped into my muscles. My knees grew stiff. I looked at the stars and prayed for an answer, but heard only the distant crunch of gravel under hikers' boots.

All my life, my mom had supported my dreams and helped me reach them. When I was little she sewed me a perfect replica of Snow White's dress, so I could pretend I was Snow White. When I was in high school, she persuaded my dad to let me ride the horses I loved so much, despite his concerns about the safety of equestrian sports. When my son was a toddler, and money tight, Mom paid for me to attend the writers' conferences that helped me to become a published author. And when cancer threatened to derail my plan to climb the *hyakumeizan*, Mom had never stopped believing I would beat the cancer and make the climbs.

She had not come 5,000 miles to see me fail.

Tears flooded my eyes and transformed the beam of her headlamp into a liquid blur. I wiped the tears away and set my jaw as I turned and continued up the slope.

22

SUMMIT DAWN

July 20, 2018

When I reached Eighth Station shortly before 2 a.m., Kaitlyn was already there and resting on a bench near the station marker. We texted Mom and Laurie, who replied that they could see Eighth Station, but their description suggested they were more than an hour behind us. My concern that they might not reach the summit by dawn solidified into certainty. The question now was whether they were climbing fast enough (and had the strength) to reach the top at all.

The freezing cold made waiting for them impossible. The station huts were closed for the night, except to people sleeping there, and sitting on a bench in the cold for hours was not a viable alternative.

Kaitlyn and I continued up the mountain, hiking silently in tandem.

Anxiety about Mom and Laurie hampered my pace. I stumbled over stones. My fingers grew painfully cold, even after I pulled them into the sleeves of my thin sweater. I had brought a hat and earmuffs, insulated boots, and warm wool socks—but I'd have traded every bag of trail mix in Blue for a pair of mittens to warm my freezing hands.

By 3 a.m., Kaitlyn and I had passed Station Nine and begun the final leg of the summit climb. Above us, hundreds of headlamps bobbed across the upper slopes like fireflies dancing in the summer sky. I stopped, mesmerized by the beauty of the scene and by the staggering number of other hikers climbing the mountain through the night.

Kaitlyn and I joined the line of hikers, which stretched all the way to the summit, and spent the next hour walking virtually head-to-tail with dozens of other climbers. At some point, we got separated in the crowd. With no way to descend and no space to even step out of line, I continued on my own, my headlamp one more pearl in the endless moving string. Despite the countless hikers all around me and the beauty of the starry sky, I felt lonelier than I had at any point on my climbs to date.

The trail grew steep and narrow. The line moved upward in single file. My stomach growled from hunger and my legs burned from the constant climb, but there was no place to stop and rest. I couldn't even pause for breath without holding up a line of hikers that stretched behind me for more than half a kilometer.

I hoped my mom was safe. I hoped I hadn't made the wrong decision leaving her behind. I remembered the wooden amulet in my pack, and a spark of hope ignited in my heart. Mom would not reach the summit with me, and maybe not at all, but I could stand on the mountaintop and bathe the amulet in the light of the rising sun. It would link us to each other, and the summit, even if I reached the top alone.

It would not be the same, of course, but if I couldn't have the dream I wanted, I would have to change my dream to fit the reality I had.

Thoughts of the amulet renewed the strength in my tired legs. My stomach snarled, but I had no way to retrieve a snack so I pushed through the hunger pangs.

At 4 a.m., the eastern sky grew pale, and the world began to take on definition. The line of hikers continued to move at a snail's pace. I wondered if I would reach the summit before dawn. My feet and legs grew leaden. The strength I drew from my plans for the amulet faded as my hopes began to fray.

A streak of pale pink appeared on the eastern horizon. I craned my neck, but the slope was too steep, and the hikers ahead too numerous, to see the summit.

You won't make it by dawn. You're going to fail.

It surprised me just how much I needed to hold that little amulet in the rising sun and, through it, give my mom the summit too. Exhausted and at the end of my emotional rope, I didn't know if I could even be happy about reaching Fuji's summit if I missed the dawn.

At that moment, the trail widened. The hikers in front of me dispersed, and I stood before a white wooden torii that rose up against the lavender sky.

I had reached the summit, minutes before dawn.

My phone buzzed with a text from Kaitlyn: "Where are you?"

I stepped through the sacred gate. "On the summit."

"I am too!"

Two minutes later we found each other and shared a photo and a hug. A yellow glow appeared in the pale sky as we walked to the crater's edge. I pulled the wooden amulet from my pack and held it high as the first rays of the rising sun passed over the mountaintop.

Tears flowed freely down my face. I sobbed from exhaustion, joy, grief, accomplishment, pride, pain, and so many other feelings that I couldn't start to quantify them all. I placed a stone on the summit cairn for each member of Team Fuji, and one more for Geraldine. My sobbing ceased, but I remained entirely overwhelmed by what I had achieved, not only that night but since beginning the 100 Summits journey.

Shouts rang out behind me. I turned, and my heart dropped into my hiking boots.

Kaitlyn and I were on the summit, but not at the highest point.

A rise on the far side of the summit crater held a weather station and the coveted summit marker that I had to touch to call the climb complete. I almost started to cry again—this time from exhaustion—but seized control of my emotions just in time. I had a job to do. I returned the amulet to Blue, now baptized by the sun but still intact. I wanted Mom to have the honor of splitting the wooden disc in two.

Kaitlyn and I sent texts to Mom and Laurie. As I expected, they were nowhere near the summit. While waiting to hear what they planned to do, we made the long, slow walk around the crater rim and up the final rocky slope to the summit marker. On the way, I composed an emotional haiku:

> Pilgrims climbing high;
> sunrise, fire across the sky.
> Thank you, Fujisan.

Kaitlyn and I remained on the summit long enough to drink a cup of coffee, brand our staves at the summit shrine, and snag a few minutes' rest. Kaitlyn napped, but my emotions were snarled worse than a dozen kittens in a bathtub full of yarn. I had no strength to sort them out. It would take months, if not years, to unpack the experience. In that moment, I was content to sit and *be*.

Half an hour later, Kaitlyn woke up and we started our descent. By then I knew, via texts, that Mom and Laurie had stopped their ascent at dawn. Laurie's knees, which had given her trouble in the past, refused to let her reach the summit. Mom continued up when Laurie stopped, and thought she might have made the summit, given time, but she, too, stopped at sunrise, just above a deep red torii that marked the halfway point between Stations Eight and Nine.

Since the stations were closed during our ascent, Kaitlyn and I stopped at each one to brand our staves as we descended—a pilgrimage in reverse. At 10:30 a.m., almost 11 hours after leaving Seventh Station the night before, we reached my mom. I stayed to descend with her while Kaitlyn hurried on to meet up with Laurie farther down the trail.

Four hours later, Team Fuji reunited at the Fujinomiya Fifth Station trailhead, sweaty and exhausted after almost 15 hours on the trail. We dragged our jellied legs and tired bodies onto a bus for Fujinomiya, where we retrieved our bags (and Spencer), and caught an evening train to Tokyo.

Laurie and Kaitlyn returned to California two days later. I was sorry to see them go. I didn't know when I would see them again, though I knew it would be far too long.

Mom, Spencer, and I headed south to a golf resort on the coast of the Izu Peninsula, where Mom and I originally planned to climb Mount Amagi (天城山). However, I suspected Mom had seen enough of mountains for a while, so I opted for a few days' rest instead.

The morning after we arrived in Izu, I showed Mom the amulet I'd bathed in the dawn on Fuji's summit. She split the wooden Tao, and we each kept half as a memento of our shared adventure on the highest mountain in Japan.

I cried when Mom and Spencer boarded the plane for California a few days later, but although the child inside me sobbed, *I want my mommy back*, she could not stay. Mom had clients waiting in Los Angeles, and I had more than 80 mountains left to climb.

23

TIDAL SHIFT
August 7, 2018

I spent the last week of July and the first week of August completing the final paperwork for my residence card, helping Michael prepare for his 10-day visit to the United States, and packing up our rental apartment for yet another crosstown move.

The typhoons had ended, replaced by pavement-scorching summer heat.

During those busy weeks in the wake of the Fuji climb, I also thought about my goals. I could feel myself growing stronger and more confident with every ascent, but the kind of personal growth I hoped to realize was not compatible with the single-minded, destination-focused drive required to climb Fukada's mountains in a year. I hated hurrying through the climbs to "check the boxes" instead of giving each mountain the time and attention it deserved.

As the first week of August drew to a close, the time had come to make a choice.

My inner voice said, *Set the record. You can focus on yourself when the climbs are through.*

But the mountains had taught me an important lesson about my inner voice.

Sometimes it helped me, but it also lied.

With three days left until Michael's flight to the United States, I went to the mountains to make my choice. I couldn't reach a *hyakumeizan* and return before he left Japan, so instead I opted for Shiroyama (城山) (562 meters), a historic mountain in the coastal city of Yugawara, 90 minutes south of Tokyo.

Outside of Japan, few people even know the mountain's name, but Shiroyama changed the course of Japanese history. In the late 12th century, Yugawara—then called Doi-go—was ruled by Sanehira Doi, a nobleman whose castle sat on Shiroyama's summit. During the early days of the Genpei War (1180–1185), a civil war between the rival Minamoto and Taira clans, a young Minamoto general named Yoritomo lost a critical battle and fled to Doi-go with the Taira on his heels. Sanehira Doi concealed Yoritomo and his followers in a cave on Shiroyama for 10 days while the furious Taira searched the area. When his enemies left, Yoritomo emerged from the cave, gathered a new army, and returned to war.

Five years later, Yoritomo led the Minamoto clan to victory. The government he established in Kamakura, just north of Doi-go, was staffed with warrior-administrators who became known as samurai. In the spring of 1192, Emperor Go-Toba made Minamoto Yoritomo the first shōgun of Japan, and the age of samurai officially began. If not for that cave on Shiroyama, Minamoto Yoritomo would not have lived to become the shōgun or to create the first samurai government.

I didn't have 10 days to hide, but I hoped the mountain would change my future too.

Mountain guides call August the "least ideal time" for hiking in Japan, and they are not wrong. Even on the coast, the air felt like an oven. The five-minute walk from Yugawara Station to the former Doi clan temple at the base of Shiroyama left me gasping like a koi on a riverbank.

According to my map, the trailhead sat atop a hill behind the temple at the end of an asphalt road. I emerged on the far side of the temple grounds to find a road so steep I could hardly believe cars used it. Waves of heat rose off the asphalt, and I panted as I climbed.

Half a kilometer above the temple, the road dead-ended at a wall. I saw no sign of a trailhead and couldn't figure out where I'd gone wrong. When I opened the GPS on my mobile phone, I discovered that the trailhead road, which was parallel to the one I'd taken, began at a different exit from the temple grounds. I had used the wrong gate.

I retraced my steps down the blazing road, around the temple, and up the proper road to the trailhead. Once on the mountain, I hiked upward through a forest of giant pines, alone except for a handful of birds and the constant screeching of cicadas. The temperature and humidity were almost unbearable, even in the shade. The birds were panting, beaks spread wide against the oppressive heat. Only the cicadas seemed unfazed; they shrieked and rattled like a thousand blaring car alarms.

Even in the heat, the forest was beautiful. Dust motes glittered in the sun that filtered through the pines. Swallowtail butterflies swooped through the air between the trees, and blue-gray moths rose from the grasses as I passed.

Sweat beaded on my skin, rolled down my back, and formed a pool of dampness on my chest. My sternum ached. I worried, because I didn't know whether or not the ache was normal. When my residence card arrived, I could register for Japanese National Health Insurance. After that, I needed to find a doctor and arrange my first post-cancer checkup as soon as possible.

A recurrence was unlikely, and the five-year survival rate for the cancer I had was very high, but my subconscious didn't care about statistics. Even thinking about cancer made me tired, so I stopped beside the trail for a drink of water and a rest. The air was completely still—without a breath of wind—which made the heat seem even more intense.

When I resumed the climb, I shifted my thoughts to the decision I had come to make, but found myself distracted by the vanilla-pine scent of the forest, the screaming cicadas, and the outrageous number of tiny butterflies and moths that flew among the trees.

On the summit, I discovered that a layer of clouds had rolled in off the ocean, blocking out the sun and obscuring the coastal views for which the peak was famous. My original plan had called for lunch at the castle ruins near the summit, but the heat had killed my appetite. Instead I took some pictures, checked my map, and began the five-kilometer descent.

As I hiked, the songs of tree frogs joined the cicadas' roar. The temperature dropped, and the air took on the distinctive scent of rain. I increased my pace, though not from fear; even soaking wet, the wide, flat trail would not be slippery.

The threatened rain did not arrive, and by the time I reached the station I felt coated in a crust of dust and sweat. In a fit of longing for physical comfort, I bought a reserved-seat ticket in the first-class car (the "green car" in Japan) for the 90-minute ride to Tokyo.

The enormous, plushy seat and air conditioning felt like heaven after the scorching mountain trail. As the train pulled out of Yugawara, I marveled at how thoroughly the circumstances of my life had changed. I had traded driving a private car for the rumble of wheels on steel tracks, and a sprawling home with a private swimming pool for tiny apartments (that, thus far, were even filled with someone else's furniture).

Instead of stars outside my window, I looked out on the brilliant lights of Tokyo.

For 47 years, I had thought of myself as a "country mouse," and yet I adored my city life completely. It seemed strange to have lived so many years and still be learning things about myself.

I considered the tidal shift in my *hyakumeizan* plans. In the beginning, I had loved the goal as much as I loved the mountains. My achievement-oriented brain had trouble conceiving of the mountains as a goal unto themselves.

Since beginning the climbs, I had learned otherwise. The mountains had become my mentors, my cathedrals, and my friends. They deserved to be treated as more than merely numbers on a list.

My pride resisted, but if I was honest with myself—and the mountains accepted nothing less—I didn't care about the mountaineering record anymore. I had climbed enough mountains to prove I could physically climb the *hyakumeizan* in a year. The challenge that remained was just logistical.

The week before, my son had asked, "Mom, when will you realize it's not about the mountains?"

As my train rolled north toward Tokyo—toward *home*, I understood that he was right.

The 100 Summits project was, and had always been, a vision quest: a chance to look inside myself and find the strength to claim the life I wanted.

That was the story I longed to live.

That was the story I wanted this year to tell.

24

TO PLAY WITH CROWS
August 14, 2018

On August 12, I received my long-awaited residence card, and with it, permission to remain in Japan for another calendar year. The visa dated from the issuance of my residence card, as opposed to the application date, which meant I would have time to look for a job in Japan when the climbing year was through. I celebrated with dinner at a fry-it-yourself tempura restaurant and another set of climbs.

My love for Kōyasan derived in part from my long-standing fascination with Kōbō Daishi's influence on Japanese culture. In addition to his religious and philosophical accomplishments, the eighth-century priest is credited with creating the phonetic kana syllabary used (in conjunction with modified Chinese characters known as kanji) to write Japanese. While that particular claim may be apocryphal, Kōbō Daishi left his mark—and name—on many aspects of Japan.

Mount Kobo (弘法山) (235 meters) sits two hours southwest of Tokyo, in the city of Hadano, which was once home to the Hatano clan (a branch of the noble Fujiwara family) from whom the city's name derives. Local history says that Kōbō Daishi spent 100 days (which could mean a literal 100 days, or simply "a long time") in meditation on the mountain that now bears his name.

I planned to climb Mount Kobo as part of a 10-kilometer "station to station" hike from Hadano Station to Tsurumaki Onsen Station. The trail led up and over not only Mount Kobo but three other small mountains, though the last one—125-meter Mount Azuma (吾妻山)—was so small that I decided not to count it toward my goal.

Technically, all four of the mountains (including Kobo) fell below the international mountaineering standard, which requires a "mountain" to measure at least 1,000 meters high. However, the Japanese geological survey (and numerous mountain guides) classified all of them as mountains, and I decided to adopt the Japanese government's definition. ("When in Rome, do as the Japanese would do.")

On the train to Hadano, I wondered yet again if other people would think me a failure for changing my mountain goal, or disregard my climbs because the mountains were not *hyakumeizan*. But as soon as I started fretting, I heard my son's voice in my head:

The only rules are the ones you make.

By the time I reached Hadano, my worries had vanished. I felt an added spark of excitement about the climb because—unlike the ones that went before—I didn't have a detailed trail guide, or even a map, to tell me what these mountains had in store. I would have liked a map, but found the unknown element exciting.

Assuming I could find the trailhead.

As I left the station, I passed a table with a sign extolling the beautiful hiking routes through Koboyama Park . . . and a stack of printed hiking maps. The maps were all in Japanese, but I read well enough to understand them. *Score!*

Without the map, I would not have found the trail. I could see the mountains from the station, but the entrance to the hiking trail lay two kilometers from the train, hidden beneath a stand of trees on the far side of two bridges and a garden that filled the summer air with the pungent scents of fertilizer and vegetable plants baking in the sun.

Despite the mountains' smaller stature, the start of the trail looked properly steep, with a narrow earthen path that curled upward through a forest of maple and cherry trees. It amused me that in the last three months I'd had gone from *holy shit, that's far too steep* to feeling reassured that a mountain trail was *steep enough* to climb.

Sunlight dappled the forest floor. In the treetops, countless cicadas shrieked like metal singers practicing for Battle of the Bands. Even in the shade, the heat made sweat roll down my neck and back. I gulped down water and sucked on candies to stave off dehydration.

The trail climbed steadily to the top of Mount Asama (浅間山) (196 meters), my first summit of the day. I stopped just long enough for pictures of the summit marker and the lovely view of Hadano through the trees before continuing over a sunny ridge and down a forested slope on the far side. Near the bottom of the slope, a set of public toilets stood beneath the trees. Each toilet stood in a separate, cylindrical structure designed to look like the trunk of a cartoon tree. I had never seen anything quite like them (not outside a theme park, anyway) and laughed at the unexpected "Privy Grove."

Beyond the toilet-trees, the trail began another steep ascent. Grasshoppers startled up from the brush beside the trail, clattering like tiny helicopters. Large black butterflies, and smaller orange ones, flew back and forth among the trees. The cries of crows rang overhead, more numerous than usual, and the calls themselves were less aggressive than I was used to.

A few minutes later, I reached the clearing at the summit of Mount Gongen (権現山) (245 meters), where an octagonal, two-story overlook offered an unimpeded view across the treetops toward Hadano. I also discovered the reason for the crows' unusually happy cries. Strong updrafts near the mountaintop plateau provided an aerial playground for a dozen of the large, black birds. The crows were riding the currents with their wings outstretched and their talons dangling down as if enjoying the feel of the wind across their feet.

Periodically, one of the birds would tuck its wings to its sides and dive toward the treetops. Just before it reached the upper branches, it would snap its wings open, catch the wind, and ride the updraft back into the sky. The corvids called to one another like a group of children on a playground.

I sat on a bench for half an hour to watch them swoop and glide. The entire time, I wished that I could join them in the air.

I'd brought a sandwich, but felt nauseous when I tried to eat, so I put my lunch back into Blue and continued down the trail. At the time, I didn't think about the fact that nausea is an early sign of heat exhaustion. (Lack of awareness is another.) I drank plenty of water on the trail, but had overlooked the need to replace the sodium my body sweated out in the summer heat.

Another descent, a hike across a ridge, and a short ascent brought me to the forested summit of Mount Kōbō, where, according to legend, Kōbō

Daishi spent 100 days in meditation. The mountaintop was smaller than Mount Gongen's open clearing and fairly crowded—but not with people. Rows of Buddha statues, a large wooden tower with a cast-bronze bell, a famous well, and several signs explaining the mountain's history and connection to Kōbō Daishi filled the summit almost to capacity.

By that time, I had a pounding headache and finally realized I was suffering from the heat. I had already passed the midway point of the 10-kilometer hike, so I drank more water and continued on toward Tsuruma-ki Onsen (at that point, the fastest way to escape the heat).

After another hour's descent along a gentle, root-strewn ridge and yet another short ascent, I arrived atop of Mount Azuma (125 meters). My head felt like a swarm of angry bees had taken up residence behind my eyes, but I still stopped long enough to take a selfie with the summit marker.

I chose the hike in part because I wanted to experience a "station to station" mountain climb. I liked the thought of hiking in one direction the entire way and seeing new terrain on the descent. However, the logistics of the hike prevented me from knowing just how far I was from my destination. My legs began to wobble, and I felt a weakness that did not bode well unless I reached the station, and some air-conditioning, soon.

A few minutes later, I reached a fork in the trail that wasn't on the map.

Two trails led down the mountain, but they went in opposite directions. Each trail had a sign, but they were written only in Japanese, and an incorrect choice would lengthen my hike significantly. My nausea had returned, my knees felt weak, and my need to escape the heat was becoming urgent.

I searched for the kanji that meant "station" (駅, or *eki*, in Japanese) but it wasn't there.

(*Read, Mom. You have to read.*)

I studied the sign and tried to ignore the pounding in my head. I searched my memory, willing myself to recognize the characters.

And I did.

The right arm of the sign pointed to 鶴巻温泉. The first kanji was a mystery, but I recognized 巻 (*maki*, "roll") due to my love of deep-fried spring rolls, and knew that 温泉 meant *onsen* ("hot spring bath"). Together, they read _____ *maki onsen* . . . and I had to get to *Tsuru-maki Onsen* Station.

I chose that path, and an hour later I was on the train to Tokyo, with my station-to-station climb complete—and a mild case of heat exhaustion caused by sodium depletion. I stayed at home to rest for the next few days, and although I recovered quickly, the incident served as a wake-up call to the dangers of hiking in the heat.

Fortunately, the summer was almost over, and in just three weeks I would be heading somewhere extremely cool—in every sense of the word.

STATION 5: HOME SWEET HOME
MOUNTAIN TOTAL: 22

With Michael off to the United States for a visa-renewing visit with his parents, I took a break from the mountains and dedicated myself to finding an apartment we could rent for at least a year.

Since we hoped to live near Christopher, I visited the realtor who helped my son find his apartment in Tokyo's Meguro Ward. To her credit, she didn't bat an eye when I told her Michael and I had a cat, no gainful employment in Japan, and needed to move in the next three weeks. (In Tokyo, any one of those requests would have made things difficult. All three? I basically asked her to find me a unicorn.)

The realtor disappeared into her office for almost an hour. When she returned, she said, "I found one place, available now, where the owner will accept self-employed foreigners with a cat."

One place.

The words fell like a hammer.

"But," she added, "it's not far from your son. Would you like to see it?"

She drove me to a tree-lined residential street in Meguro. As we turned a corner, the realtor gestured out the window. "There's even a *conbini* on the block."

I did a double take. "I know that 7-11!"

The only apartment in Tokyo that met our needs was less than 200 yards (100 yards, if you're a crow) from my son's apartment. It was also newly renovated, sparkling clean, and even had a fancy, high-tech Japanese toilet seat.

I loved it instantly . . . and we got the keys three days after Michael returned from the United States—less than a week before I left for Hokkaido.

25

HOKKAIDO NATURE TOURS
September 6–9, 2018

I'd wanted to visit Hokkaido since I memorized the names of Japan's four major islands (Hokkaido, Honshu, Shikoku, and Kyushu) in first-grade geography class. Hokkaido is the second largest island (after Honshu) and the farthest north. Its shape resembles a widespread paw—appropriate, given the island's many bears. It was originally home to the indigenous Ainu people, and although Hokkaido contains almost 25 percent of Japan's total arable land, much of the island's mountainous landscape remains in a natural, wild state.

Hokkaido is also home to nine of the *hyakumeizan*, most of which are live volcanoes and all of which are difficult to reach by public transportation. For those reasons, I decided not to climb alone in Japan's far north. Instead, I arranged a private, 12-day custom tour through Sapporo-based Hokkaido Nature Tours. My itinerary included not only transportation but also lodgings, rest day activities, and a trio of experienced, professional mountain guides. All I had to do was show up, enjoy myself, and climb.

I had been looking forward to the trip since chemo, counting down the days for almost a year.

And then, with my planned departure only 48 hours away, disaster struck.

On September 6, 2018, a magnitude 6.6 earthquake rocked Hokkaido. More than 40 people lost their lives, and every one of the island's 2.95

million households lost electricity when the power failed. The airports closed. All public transportation ceased.

In the wake of the temblor, I felt conflicted about my trip. People had died, and parts of Hokkaido were disaster zones. According to the map, the affected areas were not near the mountains that I hoped to climb, but it still seemed inappropriate—if not unsafe—to go. On the other hand, anticipation of this trip got me through chemotherapy. I'd thought about it every single day for months on end.

On September 7, I emailed Ido Gabay, the owner and founder of Hokkaido Nature Tours, to find out whether the trip was even possible. He replied almost instantly and reassured me that my climbs were not in the damaged areas. He left the decision up to me, but said that he and my other guides were prepared for, and still planning on, my trip. In fact, he had sent his guides to check the mountains and confirm the hiking trails were safe.

Ido's confidence reignited my excitement. I was going to Hokkaido after all!

That is, I was if I could get there.

After the quake, the rail companies canceled every train in Hokkaido, the airports closed, and the buses ceased to run. The *shinkansen* was scheduled to resume its service to Hokkaido on September 8—the day I had a ticket to depart—but the bullet train went only as far as Hokuto, on Hokkaido's southern tip. My original itinerary called for me to take a local train from Hokuto to Lake Tōya, several hours to the north, where I would meet the first of my guides from Hokaido Nature Tours. With local trains not running, I couldn't reach the lake, but I found a highway bus that was resuming runs from Hokuto to Sapporo on the morning of September 9. I bought a ticket and emailed Ido. Within an hour he confirmed that my first Hokkaido Nature Tours guide would meet me in Sapporo instead.

* * *

On the five hour, 800-kilometer ride from Tokyo to Shin-Hakodate-Hokuto Station, I tried to figure out a way to stay in Japan when my climbing year concluded. The obstacles seemed insurmountable. My license to practice law was valid only in California, but I didn't want to return to law practice anyway. I needed a job to get a long-term visa, but any job I accepted would need to give me time to write and travel.

I fell asleep as the train streaked north through Tōhōku and woke as it glided into the station at Shin-Hakodate-Hokuto. I roused myself just long enough to disembark, check into my hotel, and crawl into bed.

The following morning, I bounded out of bed like a kid on Christmas and hurried across the parking lot to the bus stop with my gear in tow. Heavy clouds hung over the mountains near the station, and the air held the scents of rain and rich, dark earth.

Signs at the bus stop indicated local service would resume that morning, but I didn't see anyone on the street, either on foot or in a car.

When the highway bus arrived, I presented my ticket and stowed my suitcase in the cargo hold. As I took my preassigned place in window seat 1D I thought about the fact that, but for Hokkaido Nature Tours, my climbs in Hokkaido would have been a bust. I would have ended up with tickets on trains that did not run and reservations at hotels I couldn't reach. The fact that I wasn't relying on public transportation for the next two weeks meant no delays and no missed opportunities.

In Sapporo, I met my first guide, an American expat with a brilliant smile and a bushy beard. He reminded me so much of a mountain ascetic that I called him "the Yamabushi"—a name he liked so much, it stuck. We loaded my gear in a van emblazoned with the distinctive logo of Hokkaido Nature Tours and began the two-hour drive to Niseko, where we planned to spend the night before our scheduled climb of Mount Yōtei (羊蹄山) (1,898 meters), a conical volcano whose distinctive shape had earned it the nickname "Ezo Fuji." ("Ezo" being the former name of Hokkaido.) En route, we stopped for lunch at one of the Yamabushi's favorite noodle shops, where a bowl of delicious udon almost made me forget the sky was threatening rain.

As we left the restaurant, the Yamabushi asked, "Do you like ice cream?"

Minutes later, we were eating fresh gelato at Niseko's Takahashi Dairy Farm. I chose a two-scoop cone, with a scoop of rich espresso and a scoop of the lightest, creamiest cookies-and-cream I had ever tasted.

Outside, beyond the bright red barns, Mount Yōtei's perfect cone rose impossibly high above the broad, flat plain. The garland of clouds around the massive peak made me second-guess the next day's climb.

Three weeks before, I'd wondered if Mount Kobo was too small. That afternoon, I had no doubt that Mount Yōtei was far too big.

By the time I finished my gelato, my sense of adventure had returned. I had climbed Mount Fuji. I could climb her smaller cousin too.

We still had more than an hour until our check-in time, so the Yamabushi suggested a visit to Niseko Yumoto Onsen, a sulfurous hot spring bath at the base of nearby Mount Chisenupuri.

Like most *onsen*, Niseko Yumoto had separate bathing areas for men and women. After the Yamabushi and I made plans to meet at the lobby in an hour, I headed through the curtain on the women's side. To my delight, the bathing area had not only indoor pools but four *rotenburo* (open-air baths) as well. Opaque white water bubbled up from the ground into steaming pools of varying size and temperature. I moved from one to the next, relaxing in the heated water and shivering as I pattered through the freezing air to the next pool down the line. The allotted hour flew by.

En route to the guesthouse, the Yamabushi pulled the van to the side of the road so I could photograph Mount Yōtei bathed in alpenglow from the setting sun. The volcano's upper slopes glowed pink; a wreath of blue and salmon clouds made a halo around the peak. I shivered with anticipation. In twelve hours, I'd be climbing toward the top.

That night at 10:58 p.m., I heard rumbling and my bed began to shake. Growing up in California, I had experienced enough earthquakes to recognize that this one—which I estimated at a 3.5 on the Richter scale—was not immediately dangerous.

Not where I was, anyway.

The earthquake lasted more than 15 seconds, but eventually the rumbling faded and the room grew still. I checked online and learned the quake—an aftershock from the larger one three days before—had measured 5.0 at the epicenter (though near me, it was in fact a 3.5). No damage was reported in Niseko, and the quake would not affect my climb.

That said, I hoped we wouldn't have more aftershocks while we were on the mountain.

26

PEEPING TOM

September 10, 2018

Before arriving in Hokkaido, I wondered how I'd react to climbing with a guide after so many months alone in the mountains. The Yamabushi made it easy. By the time we reached the Yōtei trailhead, we were laughing like old friends.

As we hiked along the trail, he taught me about the plants and trees that grew on the mountain and about the natural history of Hokkaido. He walked behind me, letting me set the pace (and, I noted, gauging my strength and stamina), though he offered to take the lead anytime I asked.

The lower portion of the hike went quickly; we passed Station Four in less than an hour. Tall trees overhung the trail, and groves of *sasa* (bamboo grass) rose higher than my chest on either side. Above Fourth Station, the trail grew noticeably steeper. The trees began to thin, and I caught glimpses of the patchwork quilt of dairy farms and lakes that surrounded the base of Yōtei, far below. In the distance, misty mountains disappeared into the clouds.

The overcast sky kept temperatures cool, but I drank a lot of water to replace the fluids I was sweating out. Eventually, some of that water needed to come out a different way, and around Seventh Station I mentioned that I had to make a pit stop.

The Yamabushi said he would wait around the next bend in the trail and hiked away. When he disappeared, I stepped off the trail (we hadn't seen any other hikers on the mountain, so I didn't bother going very far) and undid the drawstring of my hiking pants. No sooner had I squatted on the ground than I heard rustling in the underbrush. Something—from the sound of it, something large—was headed through the trees in my direction.

I immediately thought of the bears for which Hokkaido is famous, and of a headline reading *American Mystery Author Caught with Pants Down—Killed by Bear.*

The rustling grew louder. I tried to hurry, but there's only so much you can do when a liter and a half of water catches up with you.

The rustling stopped on the far side of a nearby log, and my anxiety dropped by several notches. A 12-inch log would not conceal even the smallest bear. Still, bear or not, I could think of several things I didn't want to encounter with my pants around my ankles. In fact, pretty much the entire world fell into that column, one way or another.

The rounded top of a gray-green head appeared above the log, followed by a greenish-yellow eye and a pointed beak.

"Susan?" The Yamabushi's voice was distant but concerned. "Are you okay?"

"I'm fine," I called back. "There's a wood pigeon here. Be there in a minute."

The pigeon watched as I pulled up my pants and prepared to leave.

The Yamabushi laughed when I told him about my avian Peeping Tom, and agreed the pigeons do sound larger when they're walking on the ground. I suspected he only said it so I wouldn't feel embarrassed about mistaking a one-pound bird for a full-grown bear (it didn't work, but I appreciated that he tried).

Five hours into the climb, we passed Eighth Station. By that time, the Yamabushi was in the lead. When he stopped short, I froze behind him, once more thinking *bear.*

He pointed to a scrubby tree at the side of the path. "*Ezo shimarisu—*chipmunk."

The small, striped creature watched us for a moment, turned, and scampered off along a branch. Although brief, the sighting made me forget my aching legs and the soreness in my chest. Before I came to Hokkaido, I made a list of animals I hoped to see, and with the chipmunk I had now seen two on my first hike. (Although the first—a green wood pigeon—had admittedly seen far more of me.)

A few minutes later the Yamabushi and I arrived at the rim of Yōtei's yawning summit crater, which measures 700 meters in diameter and 200 meters deep. The brush that covered its steep, sloping sides already showed the deep burnt orange and vibrant gold of autumn. A small pond at the bottom reflected the cloudy sky.

The Yamabushi pointed to the far side of the crater's edge. "That's where I dropped in two years ago."

Earlier, he had mentioned climbing Yōtei every winter with a snowboard on his back to carve fresh trails through the virgin snow—but snowboarding *into the crater* was an entirely different level of extreme.

"You've got to be kidding," I said, though I knew he wasn't.

I was mightily impressed.

Two trails led around the crater to the summit marker at the true high point. The longer one required us to hike three-quarters of the way around the crater rim. Gray clouds were rolling in, and given the consistent pace we had maintained so far, the Yamabushi suggested we take the shorter path, across a ridge of jumbled rocks that rose above the edge of the crater like dragon's teeth.

Minutes later we were clambering up and over the massive stones. I had done a little bouldering and indoor rock wall climbing years before, and recognized the ridge was not technically difficult. Still, the gusting wind and terrifying drops on either side changed the equation in my mind.

The stones were damp with fog and quickly soaked my lightweight gloves. The slippery gloves made it hard to get a firm grip on the rock, but the stone was far too cold to climb without them. I felt off balance, and my pack seemed to pull me backward.

I clung to the rock as if paralyzed.

If I moved, I would fall. If I fell, I would die.

The clouds closed in, obscuring my view of the crater. My world collapsed to a few meters of mist-slick stone. The wind blew harder. I could not go forward and could not go back the way I came.

I had never been so terrified.

I clutched the boulder and began to cry.

"Susan."

I couldn't even look in the direction of the Yamabushi's voice.

"You can do this." His reassuring tone pierced through my terror. "It's not far. You're almost there."

And you can't stay here.

I forced myself to evaluate the available options and told myself that although I could choose any one I wished, I had to choose—and once I had, I had to execute that choice.

Option 1: let go of the rock and fall, to my death or otherwise.

Not a *good* option, but I made myself consider, visualize, and reject it consciously.

Option 2: surrender the summit and go back the way I came.

If the summit was close, this struck me as only slightly less foolish than option 1.

Option 3: keep going to the summit (and ask the Yamabushi if we could descend by the longer route around the crater rim).

I selected option 3.

Ten minutes later, with the Yamabushi encouraging me every careful step of the way, I finally reached the summit of Mount Yōtei.

As we celebrated with a box of chocolate-covered almonds, I asked, "Can we go back the long way, even if we're short on time?"

He nodded. "I was already planning on it."

He told me later that my confident strength on the trail had made him think the ridge would present no problem. What he couldn't have known—because I hadn't either—was how much exposed high places terrified me. He warned me, gently, that some of the other mountains I planned to climb were also steep, but added that he believed I had the skills to reach the summits if I focused on the trail and not my thoughts.

We descended as quickly as my aching knees could handle, but sunset caught us on the trail. We finished the descent in the dark, as bright green moths fluttered in and out of my headlamp beam. My feet throbbed and my left knee hurt so badly that I struggled not to limp. I tried to hide my pain from the Yamabushi, afraid that if he knew, he would cancel the next day's climb.

At the trailhead, we tossed our packs in the van and drove to Sapporo. The Yamabushi dropped me off at my hotel, and I soaked my aching joints in a steaming bath. I felt humiliated by my lock-up on the summit ridge, and mortified that I had cried, but also deeply satisfied with the fact that I had pushed beyond my boundaries to complete the climb. I was also glad I'd booked a tour. I would not have reached the summit on my own.

My next *hyakumeizan*, Tokachidake (十勝岳) (2,077 meters), was higher than Mount Yōtei, but the trail started at a higher elevation, so the hike would take less time. After the bath, my knee felt fine, and the muscles in my legs and back no longer ached. I felt confident that a good night's sleep would leave me ready for whatever Mount Tokachi had in store.

Had I known what actually awaited me, I guarantee I would not have slept at all.

27

TOKACHIDAKE

September 11, 2018

On the morning of September 11, 2018, the Yamabushi and I drove from Sapporo to Daisetsuzan National Park in central Hokkaido, a distance of almost 200 kilometers. An hour from the trailhead, the Yamabushi pointed out the windshield toward a line of mountains on the horizon. "See the smoke?"

A pale white plume rose into the air from the top of a huge volcanic peak.

That can't possibly be . . . "Tokachidake?"

He nodded. "That's a fumarole. The summit is behind it."

Even the fumarole looked too high for the five-hour climb my online hiking guide described. I wondered—not for the first time—what I'd gotten myself into in Hokkaido.

At the trailhead, the Yamabushi ducked into the visitor center to check the volcano's status and ensure it was (relatively) safe to climb. (There is no "safe" when hiking on a live volcano. Hikers die in the Japanese mountains every year, and volcanoes present additional challenges, even for experienced climbers. I was smart to have a guide.) When he returned with the all-clear (more accurately, the "statistically improbable this mountain will choose to murder us today"), we started across the gentle, rocky slope toward the emergency hut at the base of the mountain, where the real climb began.

The sun shone in a bright blue sky. Light breezes kept the temperature cool and floated fluffy clouds across the heavens. I could not have imagined a more perfect day.

Above the hut, the trail grew steep and slick. We climbed across a hardened lava flow, along a narrow path worn smooth by years of hikers' boots. I bent forward, fighting gravity with every tiny step. I had no idea how—or if—I could descend it without tumbling into the sharp volcanic rocks that lined the trail. My anxiety rose with every step, though I tried to remind myself that coming down was a problem to deal with later.

At the top of the slope, we stopped for snacks on a ridge that ran between two of Tokachidake's massive smoking craters. Hunger transformed my simple salted *onigiri* into the tastiest rice ball on the planet. To this day, the taste of salty, tender rice balls, slightly chilled, takes me back to that happy time on Mount Tokachi.

When we finished eating, the Yamabushi led the way across the level ridge between the craters. To the right, the giant fumarole we'd seen from more than an hour away sent clouds of sulfurous smoke into the air.

That's mountain farts, my inner 10-year-old chortled as I passed the steaming plume.

Clouds rolled in to block the sun, and the land became a moonscape. Nothing grew on the gritty volcanic tuff that crunched like gravel underneath our boots. The summit towered high above us, stark and gray, like the skull of the mountain.

The final slope to the summit ridge looked steeper and more difficult the closer we approached. The route ascended a ridge of sharp, compressed volcanic tuff across the remains of a lava flow. I could not see a trail up the slope.

The Yamabushi said the trail had probably washed away in the summer storms, leaving only the jagged face of the lava flow, which was covered with pebbles and chunks of broken rock. The face was steep enough that in places I could reach straight out and touch the route ahead without bending over.

As I climbed, I felt off-balance and about to fall, but the Yamabushi bounded up the slope like a mountain goat. He made it look so easy that I thought it must be easier than it seemed. I tried to follow, and told myself that I could do this.

No, you can't. It's too exposed. You're going to fall.

I bit my lip. The Yamabushi would let me turn around if I asked. In fact, if he knew how I felt, he would probably make me turn around. I fought back tears, equally upset by the likelihood of a dangerous fall and by my need to admit that I couldn't reach the summit.

Halfway up the 100-meter face, I couldn't take another step. "I don't think I can do this."

The Yamabushi pointed to a wooden stake protruding from the top of the rise. "Do you see that marker?"

From where I stood, it looked more like a toothpick.

"That's the top," he said. "You're almost there."

I suppressed the urge to tell him we had wildly different definitions of "almost."

He let the comment hang, allowing me to make the call.

I had not come all this way to learn I was too weak to climb this mountain.

Hoping I'd feel safer without Blue, I cached my pack behind a boulder (completely forgetting that my jacket and my wallet were inside). Without it, I felt stable enough to follow the Yamabushi up the slope. With each steep step, I reminded myself that my guide had climbed this mountain more than once. If he believed I could reach the top, then I could reach it.

Every step was a conscious exercise in pushing myself beyond my personal boundaries. I focused on the rocks, and on my boots, and pushed all other thoughts aside.

One step at a time, I climbed that slope.

As it turned out, the wooden marker was not the top of the mountain— only the top of the lava slope. Then again, the Yamabushi hadn't *said* it was the summit. He had said "the top" and let me draw my own conclusions.

Well played, Yamabushi.

The final ridge to the summit was broader, flatter, and far less terrifying than the lava slope. It also had a clear, if narrow, trail. The Yamabushi let me lead, and a few minutes later I climbed across a pile of rocks and reached the summit of Mount Tokachi (2,077 meters).

The clouds broke up the moment I reached the mountaintop, and golden rays of sun illuminated the nearby peaks and the plains beyond. This was the view, and the achievement, I'd imagined during the miserable days when chemotherapy ravaged every system in my body.

Imagining this moment had sustained me through that pain.

I'd expected to break down when I reached the summit of Mount Yōtei, but I hadn't. As a result, I was completely unprepared for the tidal wave of uncontrolled emotion that washed over me on the summit of Mount Tokachi. I burst into giant, shuddering sobs, even worse than the ones I'd cried atop Mount Fuji.

Which (understandably) freaked out the Yamabushi.

To his credit, he did an excellent job of concealing his concern. I tried to explain my tears but found it impossible to convey how hard I'd fought to reach this golden summit and how much it meant to me.

After I regained control, we took summit photos and enjoyed the view. Long before I tired of the mountaintop, the Yamabushi mentioned we should probably think about starting down.

I had been trying *not* to think about it.

On the descent, I followed both the Yamabushi and his advice to focus on the trail (and not my thoughts). Periodically, I glanced at Blue, a brilliant spot of color near the bottom of the dark gray slope. Before long, I realized that we were moving fast and that the slope, while steep, was neither as dangerous nor as frightening as I remembered. I still didn't like the feeling of exposure. I could hike even the narrowest of routes without concern if there were trees, or even knee-high foliage, between the trail and a drop-off. But without barriers, terror reigned.

Understanding the source of the problem did not cure it, but it gave me an important tool that I hoped would help me on the climbs to come.

Since I'd learned the real meaning of "terrifying slope" on the upper mountain, the steep descent to the mountain hut proved no significant obstacle. I descended carefully, but the slope inspired no fear.

As we approached the mountain hut, the sinking sun transformed the western sky into a blaze of scarlet fire. The mountain blazed with pink and orange alpenglow. When I looked down, I, too, was bathed in rosy, glowing light that matched the glow inside my heart—because, despite its challenges (and partially because of them), my day on Tokachidake ranked among the best experiences of my life.

The stabbing knee pain I experienced on the descent from Mount Yōtei returned an hour above the mountain hut. Each time I bent the joint, it felt as if my knee might lock and not unbend. The injury slowed me down, and we barely reached the hut by dark.

With no lights close to the mountain, the Milky Way was clearly visible overhead. I would have liked to stop and stare but had to keep my focus—and my headlamp—on the trail. The last kilometer to the trailhead, though flat, was dangerously rocky, and my knee hurt more with every step.

I hiked on through the inky darkness, struggling with a difficult decision.

My itinerary said I would begin a two-day, overnight ascent of Mount Poroshiri in the morning.

My knee said I was unfit to make that climb.

On the long, dark hike back to the van, I told the Yamabushi about my knee and asked him to contact Ido about canceling the Poroshiri climb.

"Are you sure?" he asked.

I desperately wanted to climb Mount Poroshiri, but climbing on an injured knee could derail my remaining climbs, not just in Hokkaido but for the rest of the 100 Summits project. This wasn't chickening out or not being tough enough. This was triage.

"Yes, I'm sure."

Once again, Ido revised my itinerary with blinding speed. I would spend two nights in Furano, with a rest day in between, after which my next guide, Takuto, would pick me up to resume my climbs (assuming that my knee recovered properly). With the plans complete, the Yamabushi drove me to nearby Tokachidake Onsen for a therapeutic hot spring bath. To my delight, the *onsen* had four large *rotenburo* (open-air baths) with tiny shielded lights along the paths. I relaxed in the steaming water, feeling the pain fade from my tired muscles and injured knee as I watched the stars shine overhead.

Later that night, I said a last goodbye to the Yamabushi in the lobby of my hotel in Furano. He left as he arrived, with a brilliant grin, and as I watched the van pull out of the parking lot with him behind the wheel, I hoped he knew how much I enjoyed our climbs (despite my tears).

The next evening, after a day of rest, I took a walk to test my knee, which seemed as good as new. On the way, I stopped for dinner at a local restaurant that had a panoramic view of a massive nearby peak that I assumed was Poroshiri. I stared at the beautiful mountain all through dinner, wishing I had climbed it.

As I paid my bill, I asked the restaurant owner if the lovely mountain was Poroshiri.

"No," she replied, "that's Mount Tokachi."

"*That's* Mount Tokachi?" I could hardly believe it.

"*Do you know Tokachidake?*" The woman's husband asked in Japanese.

I nodded. "*I climbed it yesterday.*"

His eyes went wide. "*To the top?*"

When I confirmed this, he and his wife offered sincere congratulations—and their surprise did not offend me in the least.

I was more than a little amazed myself.

28

TAKUTO AND TOMURAUSHI

September 13–14, 2018

On the morning of September 13, I waited in the hotel lobby for my next Hokkaido Nature Tours guide. I knew his name was Takuto, and I had read the short biography Ido sent me by way of introduction (along with the ones for the Yamabushi and for Ido himself, who would act as my final guide), but I still felt a little nervous when the Hokkaido Nature Tours van pulled into the parking lot. The Yamabushi had been a fantastic, knowledgeable guide and teacher, with a dry sense of humor that matched my own. I didn't know what to expect from someone new.

I needn't have worried. I liked Takuto instantly and felt at ease before we even left the parking lot. During the two and a half hour drive to Tomuraushi Onsen, where we planned to spend the night before the long ascent of Mount Tomuraushi, I learned that Takuto shared my love of natural and human history, and he told me about the history of Hokkaido and the indigenous Ainu people.

The troubled history between Japan and the Ainu bears some striking, and not entirely coincidental, similarities to the history of indigenous tribal peoples in the United States. Today, the Ainu and their culture have begun to receive more recognition and respect, but the situation remains highly complex and sensitive.

Mount Tomuraushi (トムラウシ) (2,141 meters) derives its name from an Ainu expression meaning "place with many flowers," a reference to the colorful wild blooms that cover the mountain during the spring and summer months. Because we were not hiking until the following day, I had plenty of time to enjoy the hot spring baths and delicious food at Tomuraushi Onsen before calling it an early night.

I needed the rest. In the morning, I would start the most arduous one-day climb of my 100 Summits quest.

September 14 dawned cloudy, but at 6:45 a.m. Takuto and I arrived at the forested trailhead, raring to go. The trailhead sign reported a distance of 9.2 km to the peak, and as I hiked along the muddy trail, I hoped my knee could handle 18.5 kilometers over rough terrain.

At the start of the hike, Takuto explained that another group of hikers had seen a bear near Tomuraushi Onsen around five o'clock that morning, before dawn. The hikers had scared the bear away, but it might still be in the area, so we had to stay alert.

Hokkaido's native mammals are more closely related to those in Russia's Sakhalin and Kuril Islands than to animals found elsewhere in Japan. In particular, Hokkaido is home to the Ussuri Brown Bear (*Ursus arctos lasiotus*), one of the largest brown bear species, whose dark coat can also look completely black. Generally, the bears avoid contact with human beings, but like all wild animals, they can be aggressive if surprised or cornered.

I was glad Takuto and I had bear bells on our packs to warn the bear of our approach.

After the first kilometer, the trail grew steep and rocky. I felt unexpectedly strong, given the two other mountains I had climbed that week, and the heavily forested slope had lots of underbrush, so I relaxed and enjoyed the climb.

Takuto seemed content to hike in silence, striking his poles together on occasion to warn off unseen bears. I had enjoyed my trail talks with the Yamabushi, but didn't mind having time to think. My thoughts soon drifted into all-too-familiar territory. I worried that I was hiking too slowly to reach the summit before our turn-around time and that I would run out of strength before I got there. I worried about what I would do, and where we would live, when the climbs were over. I worried about my cancer coming back.

My breathing grew ragged. My legs began to ache. We hadn't hiked that far, but I was too much in my head to find my pace.

After an hour on the trail we emerged from the forest and entered a marshy section where wooden boards created a path through the sticky mud. The trees on either side of the trail had begun to display their autumn foliage, and the brilliant gold and orange leaves transformed my attitude as well. I found my hiking rhythm, and my worries disappeared. Instead of thinking about all the things that might go wrong, I listened to the birds and stared in delight at the colorful foliage that transformed the path into a tunnel of vibrant colors.

At 9:30, we stopped for "lunch" on the bank of a rocky riverbed. Takuto taught me about the local plants, and said the river ran so high in spring and summer that hikers needed water shoes to ford it. That cloudy morning, we hiked across the stones without even wetting the soles of our boots.

Beyond the river, the trail ascended a steep gully full of late-blooming wildflowers. Enormous, fuzzy bees crawled in and out of the purple and orange blossoms. Takuto had already told me that Hokkaido's bumble-bees were not aggressive, so I didn't worry about getting stung. I watched their fuzzy rumps wiggle into the flowers and thought about my child-hood love of peanut butter and honey sandwiches on sourdough toast.

The trail was one of the steepest I had climbed so far, but the flowers, and the fact that we climbed through a gully rather than on a ridge, meant that it didn't feel exposed. Logically, I knew the delicate wildflowers would not block a fall, and yet, their presence at the side of the trail made me feel secure.

You know how ridiculous that is, my inner critic commented.

I did, but I was having too much fun to care.

At the top of the gully the trail crossed a fall of enormous boulders that looked like a river of stones flowing down the mountainside. As we crossed from stone to stone, I heard a series of chirps and trills from higher up the slope.

"Do you hear them?" Takuto grinned. "Pikas!"

Of all the animals I hoped to see in Hokkaido, the northern (or Japanese) pika was number two on my list. The fuzzy, guinea pig–like rodents inspired the Pokémon character Pikachu. Highly reclusive, the little herbivores live in rocky mountain crevices, and Tomuraushi was one of the few places I would have a chance to spot one.

The pikas' chirps increased as we approached the area where they were hiding.

"They're warning each other about us," Takuto said.

At that moment, a pika appeared on a nearby rock, chirped an alarm, and darted for cover. I only saw its fuzzy body for a moment, but even a glimpse was thrilling—for Takuto as well as me. He said he heard them fairly often, but rarely saw them.

He had barely made the comment when we noticed another pika sitting on a rock about 10 yards ahead. We crept toward it for a better view until it dashed beneath a stone.

We continued climbing, only to see another pika higher up the slope.

Eventually we left the pikas and their slope behind, and I followed Takuto along a ridge, down a rocky descent, and up another fall of boulders. At that point, it was almost eleven o'clock, and we hadn't even seen the summit. I wasn't tired (though I could certainly tell I had been hiking for almost four hours), but I had concerns because, when we began the climb, Takuto explained the importance of returning to the trailhead by dark, due to the possibility of bears. Night came early in September, and every hour we hiked increased the time required to return.

I didn't ask what time Takuto set for our turn-around barrier, mainly because I didn't want to hear him say we wouldn't have time to reach the summit. I had not failed to reach the top of any mountain I had tried to climb, and I didn't want Tomuraushi to be the first.

At last the peak came into view. The sight punctured my hopes like a dart in a balloon. The rocky summit rose high above us on the far side of another rocky valley.

It's still more than an hour away.

As if reading my thoughts, Takuto said we had only thirty minutes left to climb if we wanted to reach the trailhead by dark. After delivering this news, he started down the trail toward the summit.

Why bother going on? We can't possibly reach the summit in half an hour.

I felt angry and disheartened but kept hiking, because a germ of hope still glimmered in my thoughts. Takuto was too skilled a guide to push me if we wouldn't make the summit. If he *knew* it was hopeless, he would have asked me if I wanted to turn back.

The twelve o'clock deadline came and went, and still we climbed. We crossed the valley and started up another set of boulders. Takuto didn't mention the time, and I didn't remind him. Instead, I pushed my body as hard and fast as possible, calling on reservoirs of strength I didn't know I had.

The summit loomed above us, hidden in the shifting mist.

Takuto stopped to check the time at the base of the final push—a steep rise of enormous boulders that looked like the mountainous love child of the final ridge on Yōtei and the terrifying slope on Tokachidake, covered in a carpet of spongy moss. My chest felt squeezed by a giant hand. My pulse increased.

It was 12:40. If I wanted this, I had no time for fear.

I followed Takuto up the mossy rocks. The route was steep, and the wind was blowing hard. The terror came, but I forced it down. I could not afford to lock up as I had before.

Once again, Takuto stopped. He pointed to a stone five meters above us and waved me past him, giving me the honor of reaching the summit first.

As I climbed the final meter, he called, "Welcome to Tomuraushi!"

Two other climbers were already on the summit—a married couple who had just completed their 100th *hyakumeizan* climb. I blinked back tears of joy, both for myself and because I felt so proud and humbled to witness the end of their *hyakumeizan* journey.

Takuto and I spent barely five minutes on the summit before starting our descent, but they were worth every physically and emotionally taxing moment of the hours I spent to get there, plus the six additional hours it took us to descend. We almost—but not quite—managed to reach the trailhead by dark.

More importantly, we did not meet a bear.

29

LAKE AKAN AND MEAKAN

September 15, 2018

Due to the size and number of the peaks on my itinerary, Ido had also built in several rest days, each of which included an adventure of its own. On September 15, Takuto took me to see traditional "stop and go" horse racing in the city of Obihiro and then to a famous moorland *onsen* on the way to Lake Akan. While driving to the lake, we saw five families of red-crowned cranes, including several babies, and Takuto mentioned (yet again) how fortunate I was with seeing wildlife. I had come to Hokkaido for the mountains but was seeing animals that other people planned entire trips to see—and didn't always get to.

He also told me more about the Ainu, including the fact that they worshipped owls as powerful guardian deities. I, too, had a lifelong affinity for owls (in fact, "owl" was one of my first spoken words). I had hoped to see an owl in Hokkaido but, given their nocturnal nature, my hopes weren't high.

Takuto dropped me off that evening near a traditional Ainu village on the shore of Lake Akan. As the sun went down, I wandered through the shops of local artisans and carvers, looking for a wooden owl to buy as a souvenir.

My father had both a passion and a talent for woodworking, and I thought of him as I watched the artisans carving at benches and tables near the entrance to their open-fronted shops. I didn't know what Dad would have thought about my decision to climb 100 Japanese mountains, but my breast cancer diagnosis would have devastated him. As much as I missed him, I was glad, at least, that he had been spared my suffering.

I walked from shop to shop and searched the storefronts, confident that I would know "my owl" when I saw it.

Thousands of wooden owls stared back at me from shelves and counters. Some were hand-carved, others mass-produced, in every possible shape and size. I looked at every owl in every shop, but my owl was not there. I felt disappointed, but also suspected I wanted too much from a souvenir owl. No object could capture the treasured essence of my time in Hokkaido.

At the final shop, I stopped to watch the artisan—a man about the age Dad would have been—carving an owl from a piece of ash.

He looked up. "Please come in."

"Thank you." I gestured to his work in progress. "I like the owls. Which ones did you make?"

Clearly honored by the question, he gestured to three short shelves beside his carving table, which held a parliament of wooden owls. Most were large, with outstretched wings. I looked at each one carefully, but once more my hopes began to fade—this time, with the added awkwardness of their creator looking on.

Then I noticed the littlest owl on the lowest shelf. It was much smaller than the others, about the size of a bookend. The artisan had carved it perched on a branch, with folded wings. It stared at me through round black eyes, their pupils burned into the wood.

I felt it instantly: *This was my owl.*

As I reached for it, a smile burst onto the artisan's face.

"That is a good owl." He laid his hand on his chest. "The owl is my god. When I carve, I ask the owl's spirit to come inside."

He wrapped my owl carefully in bubble wrap and paper to protect it on the journey. I carried it close, in both hands, as I left the shop and started down the darkened street.

When I passed the Shintō shrine around the corner from my *ryokan*, I heard a deep, low hooting through the trees. I stopped and listened. Once again, the owl called from the trees inside the shrine. I hugged my wooden owl, overcome with joy.

The next morning, on the drive to the trailhead, I told Takuto about the wooden owl and how I heard a real one at the shrine. He said it was a rare and special sign.

Last day of chemotherapy. With Jaime (L) and Vickie (R), my chemotherapy nurses, on the day I "graduated" from chemotherapy. Their cheerful smiles and positive attitudes helped me climb the first—and most difficult—"mountain" of them all.

The summit bell on the peak of **Mt. Iwaki (岩木山) (1,625 m)** with the "sea of clouds" spreading out beneath—a sight I never thought I would see except in photographs or out an airplane window.

Atop Mt. Akakura, in the Hakkoda range. My hair had started growing back—but little did I suspect that after more than four decades with absolutely straight hair, my head would soon be covered in corkscrew curls.

Japan's world-famous *shinkansen* (新幹線)—also known as the "bullet train"—a high-speed rail system that carries passengers across the country at speeds up to 320 kph. During my mountain year, I rode all seven *shinkansen* lines, and logged well over a hundred hours of travel on these high-speed trains (along with several hundred more hours on the local and express trains that travel to places the *shinkansen* does not go).

Okama (御釜) Crater, on Mt. Zao. A volcanic crater lake named for its resemblance to a traditional cooking pot. The lake, which is also known as the "Five-Color Pond" because it changes colors based on the weather, measures 360 meters (1,200 feet) in diameter and 60 meters deep.

My first clear sight of Mt. Fuji (3,776 m), at dawn on the morning we began our ascent of Japan's highest and most famous peak. For years, she had veiled herself in clouds every time I approached, but that morning she finally deemed me worthy of an unobstructed view.

Team Fuji 2019. (L–R) Laurie Bolland, Kaitlyn Bolland, me, and my mom (Paula Ross-Jones), on the afternoon we began our ascent of Mt. Fuji's Fujinomiya Trail. Less than 24 hours later, Kaitlyn and I would watch the sun rise from the top of the highest mountain in Japan.

In Shinto belief, torii (lit.: "bird residence") mark the entrance to a sacred space. Although all of Mt. Fuji is considered sacred, this white torii gate stands at the top of the Fujinomiya trail, marking the entrance to Fuji's summit plateau. On a clear day, it's also an excellent place to view the "sea of clouds" spreading out beneath the holy mountain.

Mt. Yōtei (羊蹄山) (1,898 m) also known as "Ezo Fuji" for its location ("Ezo" is an alternate name for Hokkaido) and its resemblance to Japan's most famous peak. This was my first climb with the Yamabushi, my guide from Hokkaido Nature Tours, and the site of my encounter with an avian peeping Tom.

A misty morning in Takahara, near the start of the ancient Kumano Kodo Nakahe-chi—the "Imperial Route" through the mountains of Wakayama Prefecture that Japanese nobles and royalty have used since the tenth century to make pilgrimages to the three Kumano Grand Shrines (Kumano Hongu, Kumano Hatayama, and Kumano Nachi).

The Otorii (great torii) at Kumano Hongu Shrine, as seen from the mountain pass where pilgrims have first laid sight on Kumano Hongu Shrine for over a thousand years. This torii, the largest in the world, stands 33.9 meters high and weighs 172 tons. It was constructed in 2000 on the original site of Kumano Hongu Shrine (the shrine itself was moved to adjacent, slightly higher ground in 1891, after a disastrous flood).

For more than 1,700 years, pilgrims have journeyed through the mountains of Wakayama Prefecture to Kumano Nachi Shrine. Nachi Falls has the longest uninterrupted drop of any waterfall in Japan (133 meters), and is rated among the most beautiful waterfalls in the country.

This brilliant red torii stands near the top of Mt. Tsuruma, just outside the *onsen* (hot spring) resort of Beppu on the island of Kyushu. I traveled to Japan's southernmost major island in midwinter to escape the snow—but clearly, that plan didn't work out as intended.

With Annamaria Alfieri on Koyasan. Annamaria and I traveled to Koyasan, one of Japan's most beautiful and sacred mountains, shortly after her husband's death. "If there was ever a place for a woman to contemplate a loss like mine," she later told me, "Koyasan was it."

"The owl put his spirit in the statue, to protect you from now on."

* * *

Mount Meakan (雌阿寒岳) (1,499 meters) is the tallest of the nine overlapping cones of the Akan volcanic complex. Her triple summit crater features two small ponds and many smoking fumaroles. She has erupted 43 times in the last century, and although each one was small in geological terms, her temper makes her worthy of respect.

Takuto and I arrived at the trailhead at 8 a.m. A short time later, we passed a sign that showed a topographical map of Mount Meakan overlaid with concentric rings spreading out from the mountain's crater. A bright red arrow labeled "you are here" sat on the outermost ring, next to a warning printed in Japanese. I couldn't read it but understood it nonetheless.

"If you cannot make it back across this line before Mount Meakan gets angry, you won't make it back across this line at all."

The little girl who wouldn't enter a bounce house walked right past that sign, not worried in the least.

As we climbed, Takuto shared the legend of Mount Meakan. According to local belief, the volcano (which is female), is the wife of nearby Mount Oakan. Many centuries ago, Oakan was seduced by the perfect conical shape of neighboring Mount Akan-Fuji, and had an affair (precisely how mountains accomplish this wasn't mentioned in the story). When Mount Meakan learned of her husband's betrayal, she lost her temper and erupted. Her furious jealousy continues to this day, as revealed by her ongoing eruptive fits.

Past Third Station, the forest gave way to stands of stunted pines barely taller than my head. Periodic openings between the trees revealed expansive views of Lake Akan and the surrounding mountains, including unfaithful Oakan and cone-shaped Akan-Fuji (which was indeed a lovely little mountain).

I expected to feel sore, but my muscles had finally adjusted to the aggressive pace. The barrier of tiny pines made the rocky trail seem safe, and my confidence did not fade even after we climbed above the tree line. The final push to the summit followed a rocky trail that carved steep switchbacks up the mountain. Three weeks earlier it would have terrified me, but compared with the other mountains I experienced in Hokkaido, Mount Meakan was an easy climb. The change in my attitude and skills made me enjoy the trail even more.

As I hiked the final 100 meters to the summit, I looked down into the crater's steaming pools of volcanic mud. Multiple hissing fumaroles sent columns of steam into the air along the crater walls. I felt a rush of exhilaration when I reached the summit, adding yet another active volcano to my list of successful climbs. The physical achievement was not a major one—most of the other mountains I had climbed were taller and more difficult—but after a lifetime of reading about other people climbing mountains, *I* was climbing them, and it felt profoundly empowering.

After a stop for summit photos and an early lunch, Takuto and I started down the trail. I felt increasingly sad as we descended. When we finished the climb, we would return to Lake Akan, and my time with Takuto would end. On the positive side, I would also finally meet Ido Gabay, with whom I had corresponded for many months. Anticipation of that meeting blunted my sorrow, though I wished I could have spent more time with Takuto too.

Shortly before we reached the forest, we saw a pair of hikers trying to climb Mount Meakan via a rocky gully far from the posted route. From the look of things, it wasn't going well.

"That looks dangerous," I said.

Takuto nodded. "But they want adventure."

"It doesn't seem like a very nice adventure. They're not getting anywhere."

"You have to get somewhere," Takuto agreed. "Otherwise it's not an adventure, it's just getting lost."

A final piece of wisdom that applied to more than merely climbing mountains.

30

WATER OVER ROCK
September 16–17, 2018

As I expected, Ido Gabay and I hit it off immediately—and not only because Ido has a positive, easygoing attitude and a wicked sense of humor (although both of these are also true). Before settling in Hokkaido, Ido spent more than a decade living and traveling in more countries than many people can even name. He understood what it meant to break away from "safe" and undertake a personal odyssey to find out who you truly are and what you want your life to be.

Hokkaido Nature Tours was among the fruits of his odyssey.

I looked forward to seeing the results of mine.

After leaving Takuto at Lake Akan, Ido drove me to the base of Mount Shari (斜里岳), a 1,547-meter stratovolcano in northeastern Hokkaido, not far from the Shiretoko Peninsula. Due to the mountain's remote location, we planned to spend the night at a mountain hut beside the trailhead to allow for an early start the following day.

That evening, Ido offered to carry my gear and water on Mount Shari so that I could climb without a pack. I refused, because I felt I didn't deserve to climb if I couldn't carry gear.

Ido replied that we hadn't come here to prove anything. "We came to climb the mountain and have fun."

He wouldn't offer to carry your gear unless he thought you were too weak to do it.

I suspected my inner voice was wrong. Even so, I struggled with the choice. Eventually, I put the final decision off until morning and went to sleep.

For more than 20 years, I had suffered from chronic, recurring nightmares about a former boyfriend with whom I had a turbulent, unhealthy relationship. I fought with him in my dreams at least twice a month, and every time I woke up in a sweat, unable to understand why a relationship that ended more than 20 years before still caused me anguish.

That night, in the hut at the base of Mount Shari, I dreamed of him again.

We were standing in a fast-food restaurant, waiting for our food. Strangely, I had the feeling that we weren't in a relationship anymore, and I didn't know why we were in a restaurant together. When our number was called, we learned that the clerk had gotten the order wrong. I winced in anticipation of my former boyfriend's customary furious explosion. To my surprise, he pointed out the error calmly and waited for the clerk to correct it.

As we left the restaurant with our food, I mentioned that it looked like he had dyed his hair to remove the gray. He said he didn't want to, but had to, "because at my job, people care about my age."

"You shouldn't care so much about what other people think," I said.

He stopped walking and looked at me. "Thank you. That's really good advice. I'm going to take it."

He got into his car and, for the first time ever, we parted friends.

I woke up with tears in my eyes, instantly aware that for all these years, I had not been dreaming about my ex-boyfriend at all. His face was merely the one my own subconscious chose to wear.

For more than two decades, I had been fighting with myself.

That night in the mountains of Hokkaido, my conscious mind extended an olive branch, and my subconscious mind accepted it.

To this day, I have not had another nightmare.

My epiphany inspired something else as well: when Ido and I set off just after dawn, Blue stayed behind in the mountain hut, and Ido carried all the gear.

We took the "old trail" up the mountain, following a forested route that paralleled a twisting river. As we climbed, we crossed the river more than a dozen times, hopping from stone to stone as crystalline water flowed around us. Without a pack, I felt both light and in control. The air smelled fresh and damp. I reveled in the splashing, trickling sound of water over rock—two elements that, when combined, create a song that makes my heart sing too.

A little over an hour into the climb, we reached a place where the trail ran up the side of a flowing waterfall. The route alternated between steep hiking and bouldering—simple climbing but "real" rock climbing nonetheless. The rocks had plenty of natural hand- and footholds, and although the stones were slippery in places, climbing up the side of a waterfall felt so magical that I enjoyed every minute of the experience.

I was so focused on enjoying the waterfall that I didn't pay enough attention to the trees that overhung the trail. After I banged my head on a branch for the second time, Ido warned me every time I passed a low-hanging tree.

As we climbed, Ido shared his encyclopedic knowledge of the plants and animals, geology, and history of Hokkaido. He asked what I'd seen on my other climbs, and we talked about my adventures with Takuto and the Yamabushi. When I mentioned the pikas were number two on the list of animals I hoped to see, he asked about number one.

"A tanuki," I said, "but I know they're really rare."

Revered in Japan since ancient times, first as a forest god and then a trickster, tanuki (also known as "raccoon dogs," even though they're neither raccoons nor dogs) are associated with good luck and wealth (in part because the words for "testicles" and "gold nuggets" are Japanese homophones, and the male tanuki has disproportionately large . . . nuggets . . . a characteristic exaggerated even further in statues and artists' renderings). Ido said he had seen fewer than 10 of the elusive creatures in all his years of living in Hokkaido . . . "and one of them was roadkill."

After several hours of climbing, the deciduous trees and rhododendrons that lined the trail gave way to the low scrub pine and ash that grow profusely on the wind-scoured upper slopes of Hokkaido's mountains. We started up a slippery, graveled stretch of trail that felt just steep and exposed enough to trigger my concern about descending. Aware of the speed at which "concern" could spiral into fear, I channeled my inner Gollum (from *Lord of the Rings*) and told myself the slope was just "a tricksy bit we'll navigate carefully later on—we'll watch for it, like we do for tricksy Hobbitses." (Weird, I know, but it actually helped.)

I noted where the slippery patch began, how many steps it took to cross, and a memorable landmark where it ended (so I'd know where it began on the way back down). My tension eased as I filed the knowledge away for later use.

A few minutes later I reached a second stretch of slippery trail, which I mentally marked as "tricksy number two." Once again, my anxiety responded to the fact that I had a plan. On the way back down, I would count these sections in reverse, secure in the knowledge that when I passed them, only an easy hike to the trailhead would remain. (Ido had mentioned that, on the lower part of the descent, we would take the easier "new trail," which did not require a descent of the waterfall.)

At 11:50 a.m., after four spectacular, sunny hours on the trail, we reached the summit. We stopped for lunch and watched the clouds move lazily across the sky. Forested mountains rolled away in all directions, green up close and fading to blue-gray in the hazy distance.

On the descent, I navigated the "tricksy bits" more slowly than I would have liked, but since I knew where to expect them and how long they were, I felt no real fear. Later, we saw a tiny mole, about the size of a field mouse, running up the rocky trail. I had never seen a mole, except in photographs, and watched in fascination as he scurried past my boots. Ido said they rarely leave their burrows, because if they do, the small blind creatures are easy prey for birds and foxes.

We had barely reached the halfway point on our descent when the clouds closed in and thunder rumbled overhead. We stopped for our raincoats, and Ido put a cover on his pack as rain began to fall.

Thunder cracked, closer and louder than before. Ido was not concerned, but my memories of the rain on Mount Ibuki flooded back— along with everything I'd read about the danger of lightning in the mountains. The trees that lined the trail were slightly taller than Ido (and well above my head), but not tall enough to reassure me.

As usual when terrified and in the company of others, I talked too much. I don't remember how many times I mentioned how dangerous it was to be on a mountain in a thunderstorm (more than enough to embarrass me, in hindsight), but Ido remained both calm and patient, reassuring me while keeping us moving at a pace that would have been impressive even on flat ground.

A few minutes into the thunderstorm, we overtook a Japanese couple hiking toward the trailhead, and the four of us continued as a group. Ido talked with the couple in Japanese, while I focused on keeping my mouth shut and not flinching every time the thunder rolled. I expected one of us to get fried by a lightning bolt at any moment.

Ido pointed out mountain ash and rhododendrons near the trail, and I appreciated his efforts to distract me. They even would have worked, had the cracks of thunder not been growing steadily louder as the storm approached and passed above us.

Eventually the thunder faded and the rain stopped falling. The sun broke through the clouds just as we reached the trailhead hut, where Ido and I said goodbye to the Japanese couple and went inside for a post-climb cup of coffee.

Hundreds of red and black ladybugs were swarming over the porch and clinging to the screens of the mountain hut. The hut keeper tried to sweep them off the porch and picnic table, but they merely flew in circles and returned. Eventually, she gave up, and we drank our coffee with the ladybugs. They crawled over every surface, forcing Ido and me to shield the tops of our mugs with our hands to keep them from falling to their coffee-flavored deaths.

When we finished, we loaded our gear into the van and left the parking lot, with Ido at the wheel and me riding shotgun. Just around the first turn, my mouth fell open at the sight of a dog-sized, black-masked animal in the center of the road.

Ido hit the brakes as the two of us pointed out the windshield and yelled in unison, "TANUKI!!"

The tanuki stared at us for a moment before it ran into the bushes beside the road.

A final, magical encounter to conclude another perfect mountain day.

31

RAUSU RAINBOW

September 18–19, 2018

After leaving Mount Shari, Ido and I drove to Utoro, a town on the coast of the Shiretoko Peninsula in northern Hokkaido. Our *ryokan* sat a block from the ocean, directly beside a river where the wild salmon spawn. The salmon weren't running yet, so Ido and I made plans to spend the next day nature-spotting in other parts of the peninsula.

In the morning, I planned to wash some laundry before I left for my hike with Ido, but the *ryokan* owner said the salmon run had started, so I decided my dirty clothes would have to wait.

I hurried across the road to find the river teeming with enormous fish that ranged in color from iridescent silver to charcoal gray. They struggled up the stream against the current, the water barely deep enough to cover their gleaming bodies. Their glistening backs broke the surface as they leaped and wiggled along the riverbed. Some took refuge in deeper pockets of water near the banks, but most of them splashed and strained, drawn by the powerful impulse to return to the place of their birth to spawn and die.

That afternoon, Ido and I took a hike at *Shiretoko Goko* (Shiretoko Five Lakes). Just before sunset, as we reached an elevated portion of the wooden boardwalk overlooking the Sea of Okhotsk, the clouds broke up and the sun appeared, a handbreadth above the horizon. I stopped at the rail to watch it send its final golden rays across the sea.

Without a word, Ido continued up the boardwalk, leaving me alone with the sunset and my thoughts.

Mostly, I thought the wind was really cold.

Between the gusts, I thought about how much I'd learned in Hokkaido. My guides had shared their knowledge of history, nature, and practical hiking skills. I could feel myself overcoming the worrying habit that had wasted so much of my time and energy for so many years. Most importantly, I had learned to accept myself in a way I never had before.

As the Sea of Okhotsk reflected the golden light of the setting sun, I felt deep gratitude to Ido and my guides, and to Hokkaido too. My time in Japan's far north was almost over, but I knew that, like the salmon, I would return.

On the morning of September 19, I woke to the sound of rain against the window. I prepared myself to hear that Ido had canceled my final guided climb, but he said the storm would pass. Sure enough, the rain stopped and the sun emerged at precisely the time we planned to leave.

Mount Rausu (羅臼岳) is a conical volcano that rises 1,660 meters above the center of the Shiretoko Peninsula. It last erupted about 500 years ago, and although it lacked both fumaroles and smoking craters, I had heard that on a clear day it was possible to see the Kuril Islands from the mountain's upper slopes. Russia currently controls the southern Kurils, making Rausu one of the few places where it's possible to see "Russia" from Japan.

As we drove along the winding mountain road to the trailhead, I stared at the enormous, saucer-shaped lenticular cloud that perched like a hat atop not only Mount Rausu but the entire mountain range that ran along the spine of the peninsula. The cloud's dark underbelly gave me pause, but the sky was otherwise clear in all directions, and I hoped the weather would cooperate.

The lower portions of the trail cut switchbacks through the forest, gaining altitude with every turn. Ido pointed out puffballs and other fungi growing along the trail, and we alternated between conversation and companionable silence. After an hour on the trail, we reached an overlook with a view of the sparkling Sea of Okhotsk, which stretched deep blue beneath a pale blue sky.

A sign at the overlook said we still had 5.9 kilometers to climb to reach the summit. I wasn't physically tired but felt emotionally drained. I wasn't sure I had the distance in me. Still, I didn't want to bail out on my final climb with Ido, so when he asked if I was ready to continue, I said yes and doggedly followed him up the trail.

We hiked along a narrow path between the trees. Refreshing mist hung in the air. My mental fatigue lifted as I climbed, and by the time we reached a marker that declared us only two kilometers from the top, I felt as if I'd barely hiked at all. Beyond the marker, the trail switchbacked up a rocky gully with no trees. The wind began to howl. The temperature dropped, and it looked like there might be rain on the summit ridge.

At the top of the gully the trail crossed a saddle covered in scrubby brush before turning right and ascending toward the summit. A break in the clouds revealed the ocean far below. The Kuril Islands rose from the sea, their spiny ridges looking like the back of a giant dragon. They looked almost close enough to swim to. I would have been tempted, were the water not so cold.

Scrubby brush lined the lower portion of the final rocky climb, and I felt secure despite the wind and mist. However, the trail soon grew steep, the brush disappeared, and I found myself following Ido up a wall of boulders. Yellow arrows were painted on the rocks to mark the route, which wove upward through the massive stones. I focused on the climb, and mentally marked the tricksy bits—until the rain began.

The rocks grew cold and slippery. My gloves and hiking pants got soaked. The combination of falling rain, large boulders, and an exposed, high trail proved too much for even my inner Gollum to ignore.

I clung to the stones, unable to advance, and hated myself for feeling so afraid.

I began to cry, as much from anger as from fear.

Above me, Ido stopped and asked if I wanted to turn back.

I didn't, but when I said so, he replied that he could see me locking up.

"I'm scared," I said.

In a neutral tone, he explained that the rest of the climb wasn't technically difficult but that our time was running out.

I don't remember how—or if—I answered.

"It's not dangerous," Ido said, "but I also can't ensure your safety."

His words unlocked something I already knew: in the mountains, every person is responsible for himself.

They also prompted me to make a conscious choice.

I had gotten myself up this mountain, and I would get myself back down—but before that, I was going to the summit.

My world collapsed to the rain-spattered boulders on which I stood. I found my next handhold, and a place to set my foot, and I moved upward.

As I climbed, the rain grew lighter and then ceased.

The wind picked up—not a gentle breeze, but the kind of wind that blows away a storm. It whipped past as if trying to tear me off the mountainside.

Still I climbed, entirely focused on the rocks and on the yellow lines that marked the trail.

Until, at last, there was no more trail to follow.

The wooden summit marker sat atop an enormous stone a little higher than the rocks around it. I felt no need to climb that final unprotected meter into the howling wind and asked Ido—who was waiting to take my picture when I reached the top—to take the summit photo of me standing just behind the rock instead.

He ignored me. "Throw your leg over, like riding a horse."

For 12 days the Yamabushi, Takuto, and Ido had pushed me—not beyond my actual limits, but beyond the ones that I perceived. Not one of them let me settle for anything less than the absolute best I could deliver. I trusted them and, in the process, I had learned to trust myself.

I threw my leg over the rock and rolled—ungracefully but safely—onto the summit of Mount Rausu. Ido took a picture of me sitting with the sign.

As we retreated off the ledge, a rainbow arced across the mountainside beneath us, touching down on the far side near the sea.

The clouds closed in again as we descended, but the rain held off, and we reached the trailhead four and a half hours—almost to the minute—after we left the summit. I felt physically and emotionally drained, but the climb remains among the best, and most vivid, memories of my life.

32

FROM SNOW TO SNOW
September 20–21, 2018

On the morning of September 20, Ido drove me back to Daisetsuzan National Park in central Hokkaido, where I planned to continue my climbs alone—but not before one last adventure with Hokkaido Nature Tours.

Sōunkyō Gorge cuts a 24-kilometer gash through Daisetsuzan National Park along the upper reaches of the Ishikari River. Its towering vertical sides are among the best sites in the world to view columnar jointing, a geological phenomenon that occurs when igneous rock (volcanic magma) cools and contracts. Intersecting fractures in the rock form natural prismatic columns oriented in the same direction, like clumps of enormous matchsticks fused together.

In addition, Sōunkyō Gorge is known for its waterfalls.

Ido hadn't known how intense an affinity I had for the flow of water over stone when he planned that final day, but he could not have chosen a better parting gift. We hiked a secret trail past numerous waterfalls that cut elaborate trails down cliffs of columnar joint. A raptor circled overhead, silhouetted against the cerulean sky. At the end of the hike, we drove to Hagoromo Falls, a 270-meter, seven-tiered waterfall that ranks among the most beautiful locations in Japan.

Late that afternoon, Ido dropped me off at Shirakaba-so, a mountain lodge near the base of Mount Asahi (旭岳) (2,291 meters), where I had one last surprise: Takuto was behind the reception desk. He worked at the lodge before joining Hokkaido Nature Tours and was helping the owners out that weekend. My joy at seeing him tempered my sorrow over saying goodbye to Ido, whom I now considered a true friend.

My dormitory-style room at Shirakaba-so had four bunks. A Japanese woman about my age had already claimed the low bunk farthest from the door, but I happily took possession of the other lower bunk. At dinner, I stretched my growing Japanese vocabulary in a conversation with my roommate, who had also come to see Mount Asahi, though she had gone only as far as the park at the upper ropeway station.

After dinner I went straight to bed. The Asahi Ropeway would cut the next day's climb to about five hours, but I knew better than to underestimate Hokkaido's tallest peak.

In the morning, I woke to find my roommate gone. She had left a note on my suitcase wishing me success on Mount Asahi and a pleasant journey back to Tokyo. Although I came to Japan to climb alone, I also felt as if I'd made a lot of friends along the way—even if our lives connected only briefly, at the edges, like the columnar joints I'd seen in Sōunkyō Gorge.

At breakfast, Takuto told me about the trail up Mount Asahi. He said he thought the route was clear, although it snowed on the mountain two nights before. Between his confident report and the clear blue sky, I felt excited and eager to start the climb.

Mount Asahi, whose name means "rising sun," did not look nearly as intimidating as I expected. I remembered how enormous Mount Bandai had seemed three months before, and how even Mount Yōtei seemed too high to climb. Experience had altered my perspective, even in the past few days. I could not claim to have conquered fear, but our relationship had changed.

A 10-minute gondola ride whisked me to the upper station of Mount Asahi, which sits 1,600 meters above sea level on an alpine plateau known for summer flowers. I detoured into the gift shop for a pair of colorful wool mittens that looked warmer and more durable than the gloves I'd used on Yōtei and Rausu.

With the mittens stowed in Blue, I started up the rocky, 1.7-kilometer hiking trail that loops around the plateau between the upper gondola station and Sugatami Pond, a volcanic pool directly in front of Asahi's summit cone. I stopped on the viewing platform by the pond to watch enormous fumaroles send gouts of steam into the air along the sides of the summit massif. Casual visitors in jeans and sneakers lined the walkway, snapping selfies with the mountain. I walked past them and climbed the rocky stairs that marked the start of the hiking trail, past a sign that warned "Experienced climbers only beyond this point."

A year before, I would have stood among the crowds that strayed no farther than the wooden platform. I would have stared in awe at the boot-and-pack-clad hikers trekking upward, shrinking to the size of ants as they approached the snowy peak. I would have wished for the courage to join them, but believed the challenge was more than I could handle.

Not anymore.

Never again would I sit on the sidelines, watching other people live the life I wanted for myself. With my climbs not even halfway over, I already knew that much was true.

Fumaroles hissed a counterpoint to the crunch of my boots as I started up the trail of dark volcanic scree. The wind hooted faintly, like the ghost of a giant owl. I shivered in the frigid gusts, but in between I sweated as the sun beat down on my winter hiking jacket and the hat my friend Jenny Hansen knitted for me to wear during chemotherapy. Then, it had covered my weakness; now, it would appear in summit photos that proved my strength.

The trail switchbacked up a gravel-covered ridge with steep drop-offs on either side. As I climbed, I reminded myself that I had stood on the summit of harder mountains. I missed Ido, Takuto, and the Yamabushi, but I could do this on my own.

At Station Eight, snow appeared on the sides of the trail, spotty at first but growing deeper and cleaner as I approached the summit. The trail stayed clear until the final push, but the last 100 meters were buried under snow so deep that the dirt beneath did not show through, even though the boots of passing hikers had churned the top to slush. I moved slowly upward, enjoying the softly yielding squish of snow beneath my feet and the realization that I had now hiked "from snow to snow," through all four seasons of the year (even though, by the calendar, autumn had just arrived).

On the summit, I sat on a sunny rock in the middle of the snow and ate a pair of *onigiri* (rice balls) stuffed with *umeboshi* (pickled plums), a sour, salty treat I had grown to love since moving to Japan.

The sky seemed larger on the mountaintop, and impossibly blue and clear. The peaks of Daisetsuzan National Park spread out below me; from that vantage point, I understood why the Ainu called Daisetsuzan "the playground of the gods." In the distance, I saw the distinctive, smoking plume of Mount Tokachi. I found it difficult to believe I had climbed that high—only to realize, with amusement, that I was currently sitting even higher.

As I retraced my steps down the snowy trail, I felt sorry to be leaving Mount Asahi behind. On the descent, I barely noticed the places I had mentally marked as "tricksy bits." I watched my step on the slippery, gravel-covered trail, but even so I reached the lake more quickly than expected. I stopped on the viewing platform once again to watch the fumaroles, impressing them on my memory so I would not forget the sight in the years to come.

* * *

The following morning, I said goodbye to Takuto and boarded a bus for Asahikawa Station, where I caught a train for the three-and-a-half-hour journey to Wakkanai, a port on the northernmost tip of Hokkaido. A storm blew in that afternoon, with gale-force winds and five-foot waves that crashed against the breakwaters on the shore.

I fell asleep to the violent lashing of rain against the hotel window, which did not bode well for my morning plans to ride a ferry to Rishiri Island—or for my planned ascent of Japan's northernmost *hyakumeizan* peak.

33

I LOVE RISHIRI

September 23–24, 2018

The storm, though violent, blew itself out by morning, and September 23 dawned clear and bright. The rising sun tinted the last remaining clouds in rosy hues, and the pink and lavender dawn blossomed into a golden sunrise as I boarded a ferry for the three-hour trip to Rishiri Island. As the ferry left the harbor, I even saw the thin, dark line of Russia's Sakhalin Island on the horizon, 40 kilometers away.

Mount Rishiri (利尻山) (1,720 meters) rises from the sea at the center of the volcanic island that bears her name. The island measures 63 kilometers in circumference; its towns, Rishiri and Rishiri-Fuji, have a permanent population of just over 5,000 people, most of whom work in one of the island's two main industries: fishing and mountain tourism.

True to her namesake, Rishiri-Fuji wreathed herself in clouds as the ship approached, although otherwise the sky was clear. The ferry's 10:10 a.m. arrival left too little time for me to climb Mount Rishiri that afternoon, but I planned to climb the following day if the weather held. I dropped my suitcase at the *ryokan* and headed out to climb Mount Pon (ポン山) (444 meters), a small volcano that rose beside Rishiri's longer flank. Ido had warned me that the weather on Rishiri, fickle at any time of year, could turn on a dime in late September, and Mount Pon would add a mountain to my summit count if inclement weather kept me off Rishiri.

En route to Mount Pon, I stopped at Rishirisan Jinja, a Shintō shrine at the base of Mount Rishiri. The worship hall stood at the end of a long path lined with fir and maple trees. A pair of crows croaked sermons from the branches, and as I left, I accidentally startled a heron fishing at the edge of a nearby pond. He flew to the central island and stared back at me. Though wary, he seemed to understand I was only passing through.

The trail up Mount Pon began at the Mount Rishiri trailhead and followed the same route for the first three stations of the Rishiri hike. The path sloped gently upward through a forest filled with giant trees inhabited by woodpeckers almost the size of crows. Their search for insects filled the air with loud staccato cracks, and their shadows flitted across the trail as they flew from tree to tree.

Near Station Three I saw a hiker returning from Mount Rishiri. He slogged past in muddy boots, clearly exhausted, though he did perk up enough to say, "Good morning," as we passed.

The summit of Mount Pon offered lovely views of neighboring Rebun Island. I sat on a wooden bench near the summit and tried to eat lunch in the open air but discovered I had no appetite. During my time in Hokkaido, I had developed a burning ache on the left side of my chest, not far from the place where the doctors found my cancer. It was also near the spot where my pack straps rested, and I hoped it was only Blue causing the pain. Even so, I was overdue for my first checkup since completing chemotherapy, and I resolved to see a doctor as soon as possible after returning to Tokyo.

The idea of seeing a doctor made me nauseous. I felt healthy, aside from the periodic pains in my chest and knees, but I'd felt healthy when the mammogram revealed my cancer too. Delaying the tests wouldn't change the result (not positively, anyhow), and yet I still felt tempted to put off the day when I would learn if the cancer had returned.

I descended Mount Pon feeling happy to have reached *a* summit on Rishiri Island, and went for a lengthy soak at Rishiri Onsen. The volcanic waters had a near-miraculous healing effect on the soreness in my chest, which made me suspect I could blame the pain on Blue. I returned to my *ryokan*, ate an early dinner, and went to sleep, hoping the weather would cooperate with my plans to climb.

When I woke up at 5 a.m., the rain was pouring down with so much force that it bounced knee-high off the pavement. Rumbles of thunder punctuated breakfast, which I ate while watching the rain-dappled sea. As I drank a second cup of coffee and watched the rain, I remembered the lesson of Mount Hiei.

This was not my day to climb.

By early afternoon the rain had abated—too late for Mount Rishiri but early enough for me to explore the coast. I left the *ryokan* and wandered down the road in search of lunch. Half an hour later, I entered a 10-seat local restaurant and ordered what turned out to be the best *ebi furai* (fried shrimp[1]) on planet Earth. Crispy panko breadcrumbs coated shrimp so soft they melted in my mouth. Their delicate flavor held no trace of fishiness, and the crispy breading held no hint of oil. The shrimp had a mildly salty taste, as if they had lived their lives in a pure, clean sea.

They were the absolute ideal of shrimp—the shrimp all shrimp aspire to be.

All too soon the perfect shrimp were gone, and I continued along the coast.

A few minutes later I reached a hill with an observation platform at the top. I had to fight my way up the slope against the wind that gusted off the sea, but the wooden deck had spectacular views of the crystalline water and the charcoal-colored clouds that continued to wreath Rishiri's summit. The mountain's moodiness reminded me of her cousin Fuji, and inspired similar respect.

The following morning, I walked to the ferry depot with my suitcase and my ticket. As I headed for the boarding gate, I heard a thundering clatter, like a roller-bag stampede. I turned to see a flag-bearing woman in the dark-blue suit and nametag of a tour guide heading toward me with a herd of 50 suitcase-wielding tourists in her wake. Each of her charges had at least one mammoth wheelie bag, and most of them carried giant insulated coolers filled with seafood. At the front of the group, an elderly man wore a sweatshirt that proclaimed *I LOVE RISHIRI.*

I loved Rishiri too. In fact, I loved everything about Hokkaido, even its challenges, and I was sorry to be leaving it behind. That said, Mount Pon was only summit number 30, and the gold and orange leaves of autumn had already started to appear.

The snow would not be far behind.

---

1. I'm allergic to fish, but not to shellfish, a fact that causes no small confusion in Japan and elsewhere.

34

RETURN TO MOUNT KŌYA

September 28, 2018

Before my trip to Hokkaido, I received an invitation to write an article about Kōyasan, so the day I returned from Japan's far north, I packed a bag and headed back to Wakayama Prefecture. While there, I hoped to add the *Kōyasan Sanzan* (Three Peaks of Kōyasan) to my 100 Summits list. Mount Tenjiku (転軸山) (915 meters), Mount Yoryu (楊柳山) (1,008 meters), and Mount Mani (摩尼山) (1,004 meters) rise in an arc around the northern perimeter of Ōkunoin. According to local belief, the sacred mountains stand guard over Kōbō Daishi's eternal meditation and the souls of those interred on the holy plateau. An 8.6-kilometer hiking trail connects the summits of all three mountains, and their thousand-year history as sacred sites made them excellent additions to my 100 Summits list.

Massive typhoons had hammered Kōyasan in August, felling giant trees and damaging the hiking trails. The temples had sent teams to clear the debris and repair the paths, but a through-climb of the sacred mountains was still impossible. Since my writing assignment gave me access to a portion of the trail, I revised my plans and hoped to summit at least one of the sacred peaks.

Before the climb, I stopped for lunch at Kadohama Gomadofu Honpo, a restaurant specializing in *gomadofu*, tofu made from sesame seeds instead of soy. I first tasted *gomadofu* on Kōyasan two years before; the rich taste and creamy texture won me over instantly.

Unlike the many tourist-focused restaurants on Kōyasan, Kadohama sits on a side street near the Daimon, a hidden jewel waiting for people willing to stray from the beaten path. As always, I ordered the special *gomadofu* meal: eight small decorative dishes of *gomadofu* and freeze-dried *kōyadofu*, each prepared in a different way. From crispy tempura-fried *gomadofu* rolls to luscious squares of sesame tofu topped with lime-green *zunda* (soybean paste), every dish was more beautiful and delicious than the last. Each serving was only a few small bites, but by the time I ate them all I barely had room for the *tsukemono* (pickles), savory chest-nut-vegetable rice, and miso soup (without bonito flakes) that rounded out the meal.

Stuffed and satisfied, I shouldered Blue and headed to a side trail near Ōkunoin, where I planned to begin my climb at *Ipponsugi* (the Single Cedar), a massive, 550-year-old tree that originally served as a living landmark. Cedars grow much taller than Kōyasan's native *koyamaki*, and the *Ipponsugi* was planted centuries ago to help travelers find the nearby crossroads from a distance.

From Ipponsugi, the earthen trail paralleled a stream that still ran high from recent storms. The gnarled roots of smaller cedars poked up through the path and rose above the water like tiny versions of the Jizō statues that line so many Japanese roads and trails. Although not native to Kōyasan, the cedars looked at least a century old, most likely children of the *Ippon-sugi* and the other cedars planted at Ōkunoin. Their presence—foreign, yet ancient—made me think about what "native" means. I was not, and never would be, Japanese. Yet I felt happier and more at home in Japan than in the United States. I hoped that, like the cedars, I could put down roots and flourish in this place.

Fallen limbs lay across the path and cluttered the hillsides. I shifted many large ones off the trail as I passed. Twice I climbed over fallen trees whose trunks were as wide as I am tall. A third one left a cavern in the trail that I passed through carefully, testing the water-softened soil to ensure it would not collapse beneath me. The air smelled damp and earthy, filled with the scents of growth and life.

Because of the damaged trail, it took almost an hour to reach Kotsugi Pass, a crossroad where the hiking trail met the *Nyonin-Michi* (Women's Route). A small stone statue of Jizō sat in a wooden shrine where the trails crossed. Although its age remains unknown, an inscription on the Jizō's base suggests it has watched over the path for centuries.

Local histories claim the famous samurai general Toyotomi Hideyoshi (1537–1598) fled through Kotsugi Pass in terror after performing a forbidden tea ceremony on Kōyasan. Legend says the angry gods sent a ferocious thunderstorm to strike the mountain, and Hideyoshi fled on horseback through the pass, not stopping until he reached the safety of Nara, 75 kilometers away.

Whether or not a famous samurai general ever fled through Kotsugi Pass, the route was used for centuries by people bringing agricultural products and religious offerings to Kōyasan. The trail to Nara is now defunct and heavily overgrown, but the pilgrim route along the ridge remains. I followed it up a set of wooden steps toward the summit of Mount Yoryu, which I reached about half an hour later.

A statue of Kannon (the Buddhist goddess of mercy) stood on the summit, beside a waist-high wooden shrine dedicated to the *kami* (Shintō deities) of the sacred mountain. The syncretism seen on Kōyasan was once the norm across Japan. Many of the country's holy sites were long considered sacred by both Shintō worshippers and Buddhists. During the Meiji Restoration, which began in 1868, the Meiji Emperor tried to separate the two religions, viewing Buddhism (and syncretism) as dangerous threats to the indigenous Shintō faith. The effort ultimately failed, but not before making sites like this one, where the two religions exist side by side, significantly rare.

I hiked down the far side of Mount Yoryu through an ancient forest containing a unique mixture of trees from northern and southern Honshu—one of the only places in Japan where the species naturally mingle. A breeze blew through the forest, carrying the scents of earth and musty, fallen leaves, along with a tiny whiff of spicy incense from the temples in the valley far below.

Eventually I reached Kuroko Pass, where another Jizō statue watched over the road from a wooden shrine. Like Kotsugi, this pass once served as a crossroads, connecting the Nyonin-Michi with a trail that led to villages on the far side of the mountain. Another trail led down the mountain toward Ōkunoin. I followed this second route down a heavily forested trail strewn with branches and fallen trees. The autumn temperature felt far more comfortable than summer's heat. Still better, the biting insects that had plagued me in July had disappeared. Twigs and branches snapped beneath my hiking boots. The ground felt spongy underfoot from months of rain.

I stopped and listened to the forest. A bird chirped forcefully from a nearby tree, warning others of my presence in the woods. Breezes rustled through the towering pines. Moss and ferns covered the ground, while taller clumps of *sasa* grew at intervals among the trees. Alone in the forest, I felt both very small and completely safe. I could not finish the Kōyasan Sanzan climbs that afternoon but planned to return to Kōyasan to climb the others later in the year.

For the moment, I had an article to write, a bus to catch, and an appointment with another sacred mountain, hundreds of kilometers to the south.

STATION 6: SURVIVOR
MOUNTAIN TOTAL: 31

Upon my return to Tokyo, I began my search for an oncologist. I soon learned that not many doctors were willing to accept a post-operative breast cancer patient on a post-treatment maintenance basis, particularly when the patient did not speak Japanese. Eventually, I found an English-speaking cardiologist with connections to one of Tokyo's best hospitals. He referred me to a breast cancer specialist, Dr. K., who accepted me as a patient sight-unseen.

I had my first appointment in early October, and the doctor scheduled a follow-up visit a few days later, when I would receive my test results. On that fateful second-appointment day, I approached the hospital with my stomach churning and my nerves in knots.

I struggled not to cry when Dr. K. announced that the MRI and blood test were both clear.

My cancer had not returned.

I finally began to believe, at my core, that the nightmare was over. I had survived.

Literally and figuratively, I had many mountains left to climb.

35

CHICKEN AND TOWELS

October 7, 2018

At 8:30 p.m. on a warm, windy evening in early October, I boarded an overnight "Pirate Bus" for the 10-hour, 788-kilometer journey to Imabari, the second-largest city in Ehime Prefecture, on the island of Shikoku. Once aboard, I tried to fall asleep as soon as possible, suspecting that decent sleep would be hard to achieve on a moving bus.

I slept well for several hours, and dozed off and on for several more.

Somewhere in southern Honshu, as the bus rolled through the night, I had a revelation: I was allowed to enjoy my life. While not precisely news—I had known, and heard, this concept for many years—something in me shifted that night, and I finally believed it.

I was allowed to make the decisions that made me happy instead of always picking the most responsible option available. I had worked hard for 20 years. I was allowed to rest.

And if I wanted to retire from practicing law, I was allowed to do that too.

I fell asleep still processing these heady ideas and woke as the bus arrived at Imabari Station in the cold, gray dawn. I retrieved my suitcase and headed inside to catch the local train to Matsuyama, where I planned to spend the next two nights.

According to the schedule board, the train was supposed to depart in about an hour, but a flashing sign above the departure list read *"All trains subject to cancellation, due to incoming typhoon."*

While I waited to learn the fate of my train (and my climbs as well), I went to the station bakery and bought the breakfast special: a ham and cheese sandwich on toasted bread, a dish of salad, and a steaming cup of coffee. By the time I finished eating and returned my tray to the window near the counter, the warning had disappeared and the typhoon apparently had too. (I never learned what happened to the storm, but my train departed right on time.)

I left my suitcase at the hotel in Matsuyama and boarded a train for Marugame, a town at the base of Mount Iino (飯野山) (422 meters), a conical volcano known as "Sannuki-Fuji" for its striking resemblance to its famous namesake.

I began my climb at noon, feeling much more rested than expected after ten hours on a bus and two more on trains. Unfortunately, my mobile phone—which doubled as my camera—wasn't feeling quite so chipper. I'd forgotten to plug it in on the bus the night before, and by the time I reached Mount Iino, the battery was at 37 percent. I wanted to keep at least 15 percent of the power in reserve for an emergency, which left me with less than a third of the power I normally used to document my climbs with notes and photographs. Iino was a shorter hike than many, though, so I hoped the math would work.

The trail wound around the mountain, slowly gaining altitude as it curved through the deciduous forest that covered the mountain's slopes. Breaks in the trees offered periodic glimpses of the city far below. As I climbed, the sun burned through the clouds, and patches of blue sky appeared.

At Third Station, I saw a large black cat in the center of the trail. It stared at me through bright gold eyes, and though it walked away as I drew close, it seemed more wary than afraid.

Two more cats stared at me from the underbrush above Fourth Station. The first ran off, but the second, a dust-brown tabby, crouched and stared as I walked by.

Just past Fifth Station, yet another tabby—this one gray—sat on the path with a half-grown silver kitten at her side. The mother moved away as I drew close, but the kitten flopped on its side and wiggled its paws as if inviting me to play.

When I tried to pass the kitten, it jumped to its feet and followed, twining its body around my legs and trilling. When I stopped, it flopped on its side and began to purr. I felt sad that this beautiful, healthy kitten, clearly fond of people, lived on a mountainside instead of in a warm, dry home. However, none of the cats I saw on Mount Iino looked sick or hungry. They had the glossy coats, bright eyes, and padded sides of animals that someone cared for. All the same, I thought of Oobie's easy life and wished the silver kitten had a house and family of her own. I even wondered, briefly, what would happen if I tried to take her home with me, but setting aside the logistical challenges that presented, I suspected that Michael might—and Oobie absolutely would—object to my impulsive choice.

When I finished playing with the kitten, it turned and trotted down the mountain, tail high, to beg attention from the female hiker coming up the trail behind me. Just before I walked around a curve in the path that blocked my view, I saw the kitten flop on its side beside the hiker's boots, waggling its paws as it invited her to play.

A little over an hour after leaving the trailhead, I reached the summit. Large stone monuments stood in a clearing on the mountaintop plateau, along with a pair of picnic tables that stood beside a Shintō shrine. A set of wooden stairs led down to a viewing platform with an excellent, if hazy, view of Marugame; beside the platform, a large stone with a roughly foot-shaped indentation supposedly bears the footprint of a giant named Ojomo who, according to local legend, created Mount Iino centuries ago.

As I descended the curving trail, I considered how effortless the climb had seemed. Mount Iino was tiny compared with Hokkaido's peaks, but even its 429 meters would have been too much to handle when I was undergoing chemotherapy six months before. The fact that it had become a pleasant walk in the park reminded me of just how far I'd come.

I reached the trailhead at 2 p.m., but the next bus back to Marugame Station didn't leave until 3:30. I didn't feel like waiting so, with my phone at 9 percent power, I called up the battery-draining GPS and charted a course for the 5.3-kilometer walk to the station. According to the GPS, I would reach my destination at the same time as the bus would leave the trailhead, and the extra hike would bring my total distance to a respectable 10 kilometers, which made the walk a winning proposition from every angle.

Every angle, except for the ones I did not consider: the fact that the route to the station followed roads with no cover and no shade, and the fact that hiking boots were not designed for extended walks on asphalt.

During the third kilometer of the hike, my feet began to ache.

By the fourth, I was hoping to find a taxi.

By the fifth kilometer, the charge on my phone had dropped to 1 percent, and I tried to memorize the rest of the winding route so I wouldn't get lost if the phone gave up the ghost.

I finally reached Marugame Station at 3:25 p.m., five minutes before the bus would have left the trailhead and just in time to catch the 3:30 train to Matsuyama. As the train rumbled back along the coast, I reflected on the fact that my climbs were almost one-third completed. I felt like Odysseus, traveling an uncharted course to find my way back home. Like Odysseus, I began my odyssey afraid that I might not reach my goal. Now I suspected that, like the snails my pace resembled in the mountains, I was already home. In fact, I had carried "home" with me all along.

I desperately wanted home to be a physical location, a place I could put down roots and stay forever. But the more I climbed, the more I began to realize that in life, as with my 100 Summits, the journey itself was home.

36

STONE HAMMER MOUNTAIN

October 8, 2018

Mount Ishizuchi (石鎚山) (1,982 meters), whose name translates "stone hammer mountain," is the highest mountain in western Japan and one of the country's most sacred peaks. The mountain remains a popular training ground and worship site for practitioners of *Shugendō*, many of whom climb to the peak wearing traditional white pilgrim garb with conch shell horns around their necks.

Since the mountain is both a *hyakumeizan* peak and one of Japan's Seven Holy Mountains, it also seemed a fitting place to complete my 33rd climb and mark the official one-third point of my 100 Summits journey.

The forecast promised clear skies, but soft rain was falling as I waited for the early morning bus to the trailhead. I hadn't forgotten Mount Ibuki but decided to trust the forecast, take the bus, and see what happened when I reached the mountain. A dozen other hikers huddled under the covered bus stop with me, which I took as a positive sign, given the number of times I'd ridden the bus alone in bad conditions. If Japanese hikers planned to climb, the weather would probably be okay.

I fell asleep as the bus left Maruyama for the hour-long drive to the base of Ishizuchi, and woke only once—to the chattering of rain against the window. At the base of the mountain, I stepped off the bus into a light but steady rain that seemed unable to decide between clearing up and getting worse. Low-hanging clouds concealed the mountain. I walked to the ropeway station, still undecided about the climb.

I bought a round-trip ticket and joined the other hikers waiting in the chilly ropeway station. The massive cables disappeared into the clouds just meters beyond the gondola loading platform. I didn't want to cancel the climb. I had come so far, and wanted to include one of Shikoku's two *hyakumeizan* in my 100 Summits list. That said, the trail up Mount Ishizuchi was supposedly steep and difficult near the summit, and I did not want to attempt it in the rain.

As I boarded the gondola for the five-minute ride to the upper station, I decided I would climb until I reached the top or it started raining heavily, whichever happened first.

The rain had stopped by the time the gondola reached the upper station. Soupy mist hung over the trail, reducing visibility to less than 20 yards. I followed a wide but spooky path through the trees to the Shintō Shrine that serves as the gateway to the holy peak. After purifying myself at the ritual fountain and offering a prayer for a safe ascent (and descent), I passed through a sacred gate at the far side of the yard and began the climb.

The trail initially led through a heavy forest of beech and maple trees. Their limbs grew over the trail, concealing the sky. The mist that filled the tunnel of trees created the illusion of a mystic portal to another realm. I saw a few other hikers, but most of the time I walked alone, accompanied by the gentle crunch of my footsteps and the rustling of the leaves.

Mount Ishizuchi features three "tests of faith"—large sets of iron chains that worshippers use to scale three nearly vertical cliffs along the trail, the tallest of which is 70 meters high. Modern detours with stairs and handrails let most hikers skip the chains, but those who climb the mountain as a pilgrimage still take the harder route. I thought about trying at least one set of chains, but when I reached the first of the cliffs and saw the thick iron links cascading down its face, I decided not to try. I remembered Ido's comment, back in Hokkaido—here, as there, I had come to climb the mountain and have fun. I decided I would have more fun without the chains, so I happily went around them.

In much of Japan, the summer typhoons had damaged the delicate maple leaves, which browned and fell before their colors showed. Mount Ishizuchi's trees had escaped the storms and painted the mountainside in brilliant shades of orange, red, and gold. When the sun emerged from behind the clouds, the colors grew more vibrant and the trees appeared to glow.

The sun danced in and out of the clouds all morning, transforming two-peaked Ishizuchi into a mountain with two faces. Sometimes I hiked a sunny trail through blazing tunnels of autumn leaves. At other times, I climbed up clouded cliffs past steep drop-offs whose bottoms vanished into the shifting mist.

Every few minutes I passed a white-clad pilgrim wearing woven leather sandals. Most of the pilgrims also wore a conch shell horn on a bright red cord. Their presence served as a reminder that although Ishizuchi has become a popular hiking course, it remains a holy peak.

At the second set of chains, I once again bypassed the test of strength. In doing so, I passed a far more personal test: I felt no guilt or shame about taking the "easy way."

Thirty minutes below the summit, I heard the haunting moan of a conch shell horn. The sound had barely died away when another one sounded, and then a third. The mist ahead of me shifted, revealing a large wooden torii built across a set of steep stone stairs. Above the stairs, the third and final set of chains led to the rocky summit. I turned aside and followed a narrow set of metal stairs to the mountaintop, where I found a Shintō shrine . . . and almost 100 hikers eating lunch on the rocky summit plateau.

I took a picture with the marker and bought a lucky amulet at the shrine. I had originally planned to climb along the narrow ridge to Ishizuchi's second summit, a rocky outcrop called the Tengu's Nose. However, when I saw the dozens of people already navigating the knife-edged ridge and the charcoal-colored clouds on the horizon, I decided the summit I'd already reached was the better part of valor. I found a spot on the rocks and ate my lunch, watching the clouds and crowds that moved across the mountaintop.

As I descended, the sunlight disappeared and the colorful trees took on more muted hues as the clouds closed in. I hiked downward with a spring in my step, happy to have added another *hyakumeizan* to my summit list and to have reached the one-third point of my 100 Summits quest.

Several hours later, I reached the ropeway station and boarded the gondola for the short ride to the bus stop. As the rain began to fall once more, I realized I hadn't spent even a minute of the six-hour hike worrying about the time or weather.

One day did not a life change make, but it was another enormous step in the right direction.

37

ANNAMARIA

October 22, 2018

I hurried home from Shikoku and off to the airport to welcome my friend, fellow mystery writer Annamaria Alfieri, who shared my love of history and natural places and had come to see Japan and join me on the next few climbs. After several days in Tokyo, we headed to Hakone, a place I love so much that I took every one of my visiting friends and hiking companions there. In addition to many beautiful and historically important mountains, Hakone features a sightseeing circuit that begins with a ride on the oldest electric railway in Japan, followed by a cable car, a gondola ride up and across the smoking crater of a live volcano, and, finally, a ride on a "pirate ship" across (landlocked) Lake Ashi. It also has spectacular autumn foliage and magnificent views of Mount Fuji on clear days—though the latter, I knew only from other people's stories. In almost a dozen trips to Hakone and more than a dozen to the parts of the area where Fuji should be visible, she had never revealed herself to me at any of those locations.

I didn't want to spend Annamaria's first day in Hakone climbing— and I'm a sucker for volcanoes and pirate ships myself—so we opted to start with the circuit and leave the climbs for the following day. As our gondola crested the rim of Owakudani, I looked up and saw Mount Fuji rising before me in all her snowcapped glory.

I stared, dumbstruck by her beauty and by the startling realization that I had climbed to the top of such a massive mountain.

Everyone else in the car was looking down into the volcano . . . until I whispered, "Fujisan."

The other women in the car looked up, gave little shouts, and the gondola filled with the click of photographs. Annamaria and I took one another's picture with the mountain, and then simply stared, in awe of Fuji's beauty.

We left the gondola at Owakudani and ate lunch in a restaurant on the volcano. Annamaria insisted I take the seat with a view of Fuji, but I switched with her while we ate dessert so we each had time to gaze at the snowy peak. I could have stayed and stared all day, but after lunch we hurried off to see the sites before the next day's hike.

The following morning, we caught the early bus to the trailhead of the Yusaka Michi, an ancient travel route through the mountains near Hakone. The road fell into disuse during the early 17th century, when it was replaced by the more famous Tokaidō, but the older route has been preserved as a modern hiking trail.

As Annamaria and I started up the tree-lined path, I shared the history of the Hakone region and the Yusaka Michi as well as a little bit about the local plants and trees. We also talked about our lives and the changes we'd experienced since seeing one another last. Annamaria mentioned having made difficult, but necessary, arrangements on behalf of her husband, David, who had suffered from dementia for many years. While the doctors said his health was good enough to live for many more, Annamaria had been advised to make final arrangements for him in case something happened while she was away on one of her frequent trips out of the country.

After about an hour on the trail, we reached the summit of Mount Takanosu (鷹ノ巣山) (833 meters) and the ruins of Takanosu Castle—which turned out to be only a knee-high stone monument bearing an inscription.

From Takanosu we descended through the forest on sun-dappled paths and crossed a ridge covered in wild camellia trees. From there, we climbed another slope to the summit of neighboring Mount Sengen (浅間山) (802 meters).

After taking photos with the summit sign—which was both larger and nicer than the one on Takanosu, we took advantage of the sunny weather and sat down at a nearby picnic table for an ersatz lunch of *senbei* (rice crackers) and mixed nuts. Annamaria expressed relief that her overnight tennis shoe repair—gluing down the sole of a sneaker that was more than 10 years old—was holding. I felt relieved as well. We still had several kilometers to walk, and—barring any footwear-related emergencies— another mountain to ascend that day.

Regrettably, the ancient sneaker did not fare as well on the descent. By the time we reached the base of Mount Sengen, the sole had separated from the toe to the ball of Annamaria's foot, and flapped open every time she took a step. She was adamant that she didn't want to prevent me from reaching the top of every mountain I had planned, so we caught a bus to Lake Ashi and ducked into a *conbini* in hopes of finding something we could use to repair her sneaker. None of the glues looked promising, but I found a ball of plastic twine in the kitchen aisle. Ten minutes later we started off around the lake toward Mount Komagatake (駒ヶ岳) (1,356 meters), with Annamaria's sneaker wrapped like the foot of a plastic mummy. It wouldn't work for a lengthy hike, but the Komagatake Rope-way would carry us almost all the way to the summit, and we hoped the twine would hold long enough to get there.

According to my GPS, the ropeway lay a short distance around the lake, past Hakone Shrine.

Thirty minutes after we set out along the asphalt road beside the lake, the GPS claimed we had covered only half the distance. With the hour growing late, and Annamaria's sneaker once again in flapping rebellion (the twine kept slipping off), we watched the deserted road and hoped for a taxi. The chances of finding one were worse than slim, since the road led only to the ropeway and a few high-end hotels. As we soldiered on, I began to think I had made a mistake dragging Annamaria so far around the lake, on a road with no bus stops and essentially no traffic, with no contingency plan to get us back to our hotel if things went wrong.

My anxiety increased. I didn't believe Annamaria or I would come to any physical harm, but I didn't want this afternoon to become a miserable slog. I thought about turning back. With only an hour left until the rope-way closed for the afternoon, we might not arrive in time to catch the final gondola to the summit anyway. That said, turning back would mean a long hike back around the lake with nothing but aching feet and a flapping sneaker to show for all our time and effort. As I wobbled be-tween perseverance and turning back, I heard the rumble of an approach-ing engine.

A taxi appeared around a bend in the road, and it was vacant—but not for long.

We flagged the taxi down and gratefully piled in for the five-minute ride to the Komagatake Ropeway, where we arrived with barely 45 minutes left to reach the summit and return before closing time. We bought our tickets and climbed aboard the third-to-last gondola of the day. As it rose toward the summit, Mount Fuji rose slowly into view behind a line of mountains to the north.

A thin white cloud stretched across Fuji's neck like an accent scarf. The setting sun bathed her peak and sides in rosy alpenglow. I had imagined a moment like this for decades, and the reality exceeded all my expectations. She was one of the most beautiful things I had ever seen.

The gondola reached its upper station with only fifteen minutes left until the last return trip of the day. Annamaria and I looked at the sloping, rocky trail reinforced with inset wooden logs. I didn't know if we had time to reach the summit and return.

"Go," Annamaria said. "You can make it."

I was not so sure. More importantly, I didn't want to leave her behind. We had already reached two summits that day. A third one felt too greedy if it meant abandoning a friend.

Again she urged me, this time adding that she wanted to remain behind to photograph Mount Fuji. That, I could understand. In fact, I felt equally tempted to forget the peak and simply bask in Fuji's sunset-painted glory.

But you came to climb.

And climb I did.

I ran along the path and up the stairs to the high point of Mount Komagatake, claiming my 36th summit. Although we mostly "climbed" the peak by gondola, I later learned that the distance Annamaria and I had walked on the road around the lake was almost equal to the length of the hiking trail. Even without that knowledge, we returned to the gondola thoroughly satisfied with the day's achievements and looking forward to a relaxing evening at the hot spring baths, as well as the next day's journey to Kyoto.

38

FLYING FREE

October 23–24, 2018

The day after our three-summit adventure, Annamaria and I decamped from Hakone and rode the *shinkansen* two hours south to the former Japanese capital of Kyoto. We arrived too late to climb, so we indulged our mutual love of history with a visit to Nijo Castle, once the palace of Shogun Tokugawa Ieyasu (1543–1616), and celebrated the previous day's mountain victories with a dinner of enormous ice cream parfaits.

In the morning, we prepared to climb again—but this time, the Angry Sneaker did not join us. After many years and many miles, its sole had finally fled for good, and it landed in the refuse bin.

Our hike began at the north end of the Philosopher's Path, a famous tree-lined route along the Lake Biwa Canal in Kyoto's northeastern Higashiyama district. Although the path dates only to the Meiji Period (1868–1911), the Buddhist temples and Shintō shrines along its course are many centuries older. Our starting point, Ginkaku-ji, was originally constructed as a retirement villa for shogun Ashikaga Yoshimasa (1436–1490) but was converted to a Buddhist temple after his death. After touring the grounds, Annamaria and I hiked up a road behind the temple to the trailhead of Mount Daimonji (大文字 山) (467 meters), which rises directly behind Ginkaku-ji.

For centuries, Daimonji has played an important role in Obon, a three-day summer festival honoring the spirits of departed ancestors. Each August, volunteers drag and carry enormous logs to a clearing two-thirds of the way up Mount Daimonji, where the logs are arranged in the shape of the Chinese character 大, pronounced "Ō" or "Dai" in Japanese. As darkness falls, the logs are set ablaze. The flaming 大 on the mountainside is visible all the way across Kyoto, and its appearance marks the moment when the ancestors return to the spirit world for another year.

The start of the trail up Mount Daimonji bore witness to the destructive power of the huge typhoons that ripped through the region during the summer months. Although the path itself was clear, broken branches littered the mountainside, along with dozens of fallen trees—some almost a meter in diameter.

The air carried the pleasant scents of damp earth and fallen leaves, along with a hint of incense from the nearby temples. Rays of sunlight pierced the trees as the morning clouds began to burn away.

Crows traded insults overhead as Annamaria and I climbed upward through the forest beneath a tunnel of branches that grew across the trail. Some of the trees had begun to show autumn foliage, though many of the leaves had already fallen, casualties of the summer storms.

An hour after leaving the trailhead, we arrived at the famous clearing where the "Dai" burned every summer. Along with the famous "iron cross" that held the logs in place at the center of the fire zone, the clearing held a shrine dedicated to Kōbō Daishi, who apparently studied on Mount Daimonji during his time in Kyoto.

Groups of schoolchildren played and picnicked on the cement platform at the center of the clearing. Overhead, a raptor soared on the thermals, wings spread wide. The city of Kyoto spread out beneath us, ringed by mountains and slightly fuzzy through the morning haze.

Given that she was hiking in slip-on loafers, and seeing the steepness of the trail beyond the clearing, Annamaria decided to remain behind to enjoy the view and watch the children play while I continued to the summit. Her goal, upon arriving in Japan, had been to climb two mountains with me. She had managed three already (with another planned for the following day, on Kōyasan) and she was more than satisfied.

I scurried up the trail—which did indeed become not only steep but muddy and slippery on the slopes above the clearing—tagged the summit, and returned to the clearing to find Annamaria sitting happily in the sun, shooting videos on her phone. We sat together and enjoyed the view. My heart felt full.

After climbing back down the mountain, we spent a pleasant afternoon in Kyoto and returned to the hotel after dinner to prepare for the next day's trip to Kōyasan. A few hours later, as I was getting ready for bed, my phone buzzed with a text from Annamaria, asking me to come to her room.

Given the hour, I knew something was wrong.

When I reached her room, Annamaria told me her husband had passed away. She had just received a telephone call from her brother, letting her know that David had died peacefully in the night. In some ways, she had lost him gradually—Alzheimer's had stolen his mind and identity, transforming the gentle man she loved so deeply into a blind, uncomprehending shadow of his former self. However, his body had remained strong enough that his passing now came as a sudden shock.

I felt devastated on her behalf. I could not make things "better" but wanted to support her any way I could. I gave her a hug and asked what I could do—and, more importantly, what she wanted to do. She had been looking forward to seeing Kōyasan for several years—ever since I first blogged about it at the *Murder Is Everywhere* blog where we were both contributing authors—but I expected she would probably want to head back to New York as soon as possible.

She replied that she had been thinking about the issue for several minutes before she texted me, and had discussed it with her brother back home. She was in shock, and understandably conflicted about what she should do. She told me that David—though not specifically religious— did believe in reincarnation and a peaceful afterlife. The fact that he had died the night before our departure for Kōyasan—a holy Buddhist site with a heavy focus on death and the afterlife—struck Annamaria as a sign. She decided that she was meant to go to Kōyasan. I felt humbled and honored that she wanted to accompany me. I also felt the weight of responsibility: I would be sharing Kōyasan with Annamaria not as a friend and a mountain climber, but as a pilgrim, joining her trek to the sacred mountain on a search for enlightenment, as well as to honor David and his memory.

Annamaria was raised a devout Catholic, but in her adult years she had fallen away from the Church. On Kōyasan, we visited sacred sites, lit candles, and burned incense in front of Kōbō Daishi's tomb. I could tell the entire experience had a profound impact on Annamaria, but did not know quite how profound until later, when she told me, "As the smoke from the incense rose, I realized that David's soul was free—returned to its pure and original state, without the scars inflicted by his miserable childhood, free of the body he could no longer use. Just him, his kind, sweet and funny, energetic and curious self."

That realization freed Annamaria too. She was still mourning, but her grief grew lighter knowing that David's suffering—not only from childhood trauma, but from the disease that took him from her, and from himself as well, was over.

Later that day, we visited the Otake Jizō, a large copper statue of the Bodhisattva Jizō that stands across the street from the Women's Hall. A widow donated the statue to Kōyasan in 1745, after coming to the holy mountain to pray for her husband, who was recently deceased. While she was staying at the Women's Hall, Jizō appeared to her in a dream, and she had the statue made to honor both the Bodhisattva and her husband's spirit. As I explained the history of the Jizō, Annamaria said that she knew she had made the right decision in coming to Kōyasan.

"If there was ever a place for a woman to contemplate a loss like mine," she later said, "Kōyasan was it."

We climbed no physical mountains on Kōyasan, but—as I learned before my climbs began—life's most challenging summits are not made of dirt and stone. Annamaria reached an important one that day. I will always be honored, and humbled, that I had the chance to climb it at her side.

39

INJURY

November 12, 2018

During Annamaria's final day in Japan, I tripped and fell on a sidewalk in Osaka. I landed directly on my knee, and although I escaped with only a painfully bruised kneecap, the injury kept me off the mountains for several days.

I stayed in Tokyo to recover, spend time with Michael, and work on my next mystery novel, which was due to the publisher shortly after Christmas. One evening, I walked to the *conbini* with Michael—ostensibly for a cup of coffee, but more to enjoy his company and the pleasant autumn evening. Ten yards from home, I tripped on a crack in the pavement and twisted my right ankle hard. The burning, tearing pain that followed made me forget my nearly-recovered knee. I knew at once I had reinjured the ligaments I tore in a different clumsiness-related incident during high school. I iced my ankle as soon as Michael and I returned from the *conbini*, but the damage was done. I could only hope my need for a few days' rest hadn't just turned into weeks.

And resting wasn't easy. The temperate autumn mornings made for perfect climbing weather. Every day, I heard the mountains calling.

The only thing that kept me off the trail was my concern about recovering in time to make the seven-day, 100-kilometer hike of the Kumano Kodo that I'd also booked during chemotherapy. I was scheduled to depart for the hike on November 24, and although I had originally planned to reach the 50-summit mark before I left, I now just hoped my ankle would allow me to make the extended hike at all.

Historically, pilgrims prayed and meditated on their lives while walking the mountainous trails connecting the three Kumano Grand Shrines on the Kii Peninsula. In addition to enshrining powerful Shintō deities, the shrines corresponded to the past, the present, and the future. I'd planned the trip as a chance to reflect on what I'd learned in the first half of my 100 Summits journey, and although the halfway point was now unreachable before the Kumano Kodo trip, I decided to attempt another set of hikes to see if my ankle could handle the strain it would face in the mountainous Kii Peninsula.

The closest place without significant snow was Hakone, which also had the advantage of familiarity. Although I planned to climb mountains I had never hiked before, knowing the area well would make it easier for me to avoid getting lost or in trouble if my ankle wasn't quite as healed as I believed.

I set an aggressive two-day goal—too aggressive, in retrospect—but I was determined not to let injury slow me down. I planned to spend the first day on a three-peak traverse through the mountains north of Lake Ashi. If my ankle didn't hurt too badly afterward, I would attempt a second three-peak climb the following day.

I left Tokyo at 6:45 a.m. and reached the trailhead at 10:30, later than I'd hoped. With sunset only six hours away, and the climb requiring multiple ascents, I'd have to move quickly to reach the end by dark. My ankle and knee felt strong as I started up the forested, earthen trail. I felt confident I could finish the hike in the five-hour standard trail time, as long as my ankle and knee held up and nothing unexpected happened.

The lower portion of the climb wound upward through a forest of maples and old-growth pines that towered above the trail. Beyond the split, the trail cut a narrow tunnel through dense fields of *sasa*—broad leaf bamboo—whose finger-width canes grew eight to 10 feet high. They rustled in the breeze and blocked the sunlight, leaving the trail in shadow.

Although the trail was not as steep, my progress slowed because large portions of the trail were covered in patches of deep black mud. Even at the edges of the path, where the mud was shallowest, my boots sank deep into the sucking mire.

Eventually I left the mud behind and my pace increased. The bamboo that lined the trail filled the air with the dusty, sweet scent of drying grasses. My knee felt good as new. My ankle was stiff, but thankfully didn't hurt. My spirit soared like a falcon that slipped its jesses and flew to freedom in the mountain air.

The summit marker for Mount Hiuchi-ishi (火打石山) (989 meters) took me by surprise when I encountered it at the top of a forested slope covered in colorful maple trees. The summit had no view (unless you counted trees), no benches, and no place to rest, so I stopped just long enough to take a picture with the summit sign before hiking on.

Two hours later, I reached the summit of Mount Myojingatake (明神ヶ岳) (1,169 meters), a flat-topped mountain with multiple benches arrayed in a semicircle on its small summit plateau. Yet even with all the benches, I couldn't find a place to sit. I'd seen only two hikers on the trail, but more than a dozen people were sitting or standing on the summit of Myojingatake, most of them enjoying lunch. I wove through the groups of picnicking hikers and waited my turn for a picture with the summit sign.

Afterward, when I checked the photo, I noticed a snowcapped photo-bomber in the background: Mount Fuji, rising above a ridge of mountains to the north.

It was supposed to be Mount Myojingatake's moment in the sun, but if Mount Fuji wanted to crash the party, that was more than fine with me.

As I descended the far side of Mount Myojingatake, a shift in the wind carried the sulfurous smell of Owakudani across the valley. The scent of the volcano grew stronger and more pungent until it seemed as thick as it did beside the crater, even though I was several kilometers away. I thought of all the volcanoes I had climbed in the past few months, and how much I loved their compelling landscapes and challenging terrain.

The sun sank out of sight behind the mountains in the west, and the temperature dropped as well. Ninety minutes remained until dark, but I couldn't tell how much trail remained before the top of Mount Myojin-gatake (明星ヶ岳) (924 meters), my final summit of the day. My ankle had begun to ache, and I hoped I hadn't tried to attempt too much. I slowed my pace despite the fact that time was growing short.

Ten minutes later, I emerged into a clearing that looked like a summit but had no marker. The trail split; one portion continued across the mountaintop, while a branch trail to the right led down the mountain. I stood at the place where the trails crossed, confused. If I could not confirm that I'd reached the summit, the mountain didn't count.

I reached for my phone, opened the YAMAP hiking app, and established that I wasn't on the summit. The tiny flag on the in-app map that marked the true high point lay just to the east of the dot that indicated my position. I walked toward the flag, using YAMAP to track my progress, and with the help of the app I found the summit marker—behind a tree a little farther down the path.

With the summit confirmed, I retraced my steps to the split and followed the descending trail through a forest of colorful maple trees. I tried to watch my step, but five minutes down the path, I twisted my ankle on a rock.

Stabbing pain shot through my ankle, followed by a looseness in the joint that scared me more than pain. I stopped to examine my ankle, which hurt so badly I suspected I had not only reinjured it but done more damage than before. The initial pain and weakness faded quickly, but the ache that remained confirmed that I had pushed too hard, too soon—with two kilometers of rocky trail still to go.

An excruciating hour later, in which I twisted my ankle two more times, I reached the end of the forested trail and started down the asphalt road to the bus stop. Stabbing pain shot through my ankle with every step, despite the ibuprofen I had taken on the trail.

A well-dressed couple in their 20s stood beside the bus stop sign. They gave me looks of ill-disguised concern as I limped across the street to join them, but said nothing. I queued behind them and stared up the road in the direction from which the bus would come, filthy, sweaty, hurting, and attempting to distract myself by visualizing a soak in the steaming waters of the *onsen* at my *ryokan*. After 10 minutes that felt like 40, the bus pulled up, so crowded with tourists that the doors would barely open.

The driver raised a hand and shook his head. "Too crowded. Please wait for the next bus."

The doors slid closed and the bus rolled off, leaving both the couple and me behind.

The sky had begun to change from blue to lavender. In less than half an hour, it would be dark. I wondered what I'd do if the next bus also had no room. There were no taxis out this far, and the bus stop didn't even have a bench.

Ten minutes later, another bus arrived—almost equally full, but the driver allowed the couple and me to cram ourselves aboard. I squeezed into the narrow space between the fare box and the doors and shifted my weight away from my injured ankle. I could feel the swelling straining the laces of my high-top hiking boot. The pain grew worse as the bus rolled slowly down the hill to Hakone-Yumoto Station.

* * *

A soak in the *onsen* and a good night's sleep reduced the swelling in my ankle, but the ache remained. In place of the scheduled hike, I spent the day riding pirate ships across Lake Ashi and taking the ropeway to Owakudani, where I saw Mount Fuji before the clouds rolled in.

As I rode another pirate ship back across the lake to my *ryokan*, I gazed at the colorful trees that lined the shore and wondered why I'd spent so much of my life worrying about things I could not change, and why I'd tied myself to so many places and jobs that did not bring me joy. I wondered why it had taken me so long to find the courage to change my life—and although I had no answers, I was grateful I had made the change before it was too late.

By evening, the ache in my ankle had not subsided, and I made the decision to abandon the second climb and return to Tokyo in the morning. I felt like a quitter, but I didn't care. At that point, I simply hoped I could recover in time to make my planned Kumano Kodo pilgrimage.

40

CORINNE

November 15, 2018

My resolve to stay off the mountains and let my ankle heal lasted just three days.

Two days after I left Hakone, another of my best friends, fellow author Corinne O'Flynn, arrived from Colorado for a visit. I couldn't wait to see her and to show her my beloved mountains. In fact, I'd planned our first climb for the morning after she arrived.

In my excitement, I overlooked the fact that not everyone bounces off a day-long trans-Pacific flight—with a 13-hour time change—prepared to head directly to the mountains. To her credit, Corinne did not complain. She even seemed eager to hit the ground running on my aggressive schedule.

On November 15, we traveled three hours west by train to Mitakesan Station in the city of Ōme. From there, we hopped the first bus of the day to the base of 929-meter Mount Mitake (御岳山), a sacred peak in Chichibu Tama Kai National Park.

It's possible to hike the heavily forested slopes of Mount Mitake from base to summit, but most visitors—including Corinne and me—opt to skip the first half of the hike and ride the Mitake Cable Car, the steepest funicular in the Kantō area. The upper station sits about an hour's hike from the top of the mountain. Mount Mitake is sacred to both the Shintō and Buddhist faiths, and en route to the top we hiked beneath a vermilion torii and along a paved path through a forest of enormous trees. Beyond the forest, we walked through a little village of *shukubo*, small Buddhist temples that offered overnight lodging to hikers as well as pilgrims.

The sun shone brightly overhead as we reached the entrance to Musashi Mitake Shrine and started up the dozens of flights of stairs that led to the mountaintop worship hall. Stone benches with finials carved in the shape of animals—real and mythological—offered several places to stop and rest, but the climb was neither long nor unreasonably steep, so Corinne and I continued up until we reached the shrine.

The various buildings of Musashi Mitake Shrine cover the entire holy summit of Mount Mitake. Its primary guardian statues are shaped like wolves—a rarity in Japan, where most such statues take the form of lion-dogs or foxes. The shape pays tribute to a first-century legend in which the deity of the mountain took the form of a large white wolf and led the legendary prince Yamato Takeru to safety. The shrine itself is even older, dating to the late first century BCE.

Corinne had never visited a Shintō shrine, so when we arrived, I gave her a tour of the grounds, from the brightly painted worship hall where the *kami* of the mountain is enshrined to the secondary shrines honoring other local deities. We also visited the Inari sub-shrine, where another rare set of guardian wolves take the place of Inari's customary foxes.

Afterward, we descended to a trail just below the shrine and hiked around the side of the mountain to a set of picnic tables, where we stopped for an early lunch.

Corinne's visit, like Annamaria's, filled a hole in my spirit. Between 2003 and 2017, my closest writer friends and I attended at least two writers' conferences (sometimes as many as five) each year. That time together recharged our mental batteries and left us all inspired and energized. In the 12 months since my cancer diagnosis, I had not attended a single conference or spent any significant time in the company of my friends and writing peers. As I sat beneath Mitake's towering cedars "talking shop" with Corinne, it occurred to me that although I loved the mountains, I missed professional interaction. I could feel my creative spirit charging as I heard about her works in progress (which I couldn't wait to read) and asked for her advice about my own.

After lunch, we hiked along a forested trail to the Tengu's Seat, a famous cedar whose giant, U-shaped branches curve away from the trunk, providing a perfect resting place for the legendary long-nosed *tengu* (Japanese mountain spirits). Beyond the tree, the trail curved steeply upward through the pines to the forested summit of Mount Okunoin (奥の院山) (1,077 meters). After taking our second summit photos of the day, Corinne filmed a short video for her social media feed. She looked a little tired, but in my eagerness to share the mountains and my joy at seeing her again, I didn't process the fact that she was suffering from a combination of jet lag and the change in climate between her arid home in Denver and the heavier, more humid air of Japan. A kinder and more attentive host would probably have suggested turning back. But I was not an attentive host that afternoon, and Corinne was far too supportive of my quest to request a reprieve, so on we went.

A short but steep descent led down to a forested ridge between Okunoin and neighboring Mount Nabewari (鍋割山) (1,082 meters). The hike across the ridge and up the shady slope to the summit took just under half an hour, and by 1:40 p.m. we had completed three summits in a single day. My ankle didn't hurt, and I felt euphoric. (I will note that, as between us, Corinne's achievement was by far the greater one, given the circumstances in which she climbed.)

The descent led us past—but not back over—the top of Mount Okunoin and around the side of Mount Mitake to the cable car. As we hiked back through the forest, it finally dawned on me what I'd put her though. I felt terrible. Even worse, the train was so crowded that we didn't have a place to sit and had to stand in the aisle for several stops.

Halfway to our destination, I checked my phone and found an upcoming station where we could ditch the crowded local train for an express with reserved seating that would get us back to Tokyo in half the time.

Best of all, it had a green car.

Fifteen minutes later, Corinne and I settled into a pair of plush reclining seats in the first-class car. As the train pulled out of the station, bound for Tokyo, we propped our feet on the drop-down rests and settled in for a comfortable ride. When the snack cart wheeled by, we purchased drinks and a package of the same potato sticks I ate on Mount Amagi during my very first 100 Summits climb. I ordered them primarily because I thought Corinne would like them, but also from a perverse sense of irony. I had learned a lot in the past six months, but in some ways—the interpersonal in particular—I still was woefully unprepared.

Fortunately, Corinne was an excellent sport and kind enough not to hold the adventure—or my blind enthusiasm—against me.

We had originally planned to make two more climbs together, including the last two peaks of the *Kōyasan Sanzan* (Mount Mani and Mount Tenjiku) that Annamaria and I had chosen to forgo. Regrettably, circumstances required Corinne to return to the United States ahead of schedule, and once again I deferred the climbs on Kōyasan for another day.

On November 24, with my ankle mostly healed and the trees exploding with glorious autumn colors all across Japan, the time had come for me to undertake the longest continuous hike of my 100 Summits year—a 100-kilometer pilgrimage along ancient trails through the sacred mountains of Wakayama Prefecture.

41

LIFE AND DEATH
ON THE KUMANO KODO

November 24–27, 2018

The sacred history of the Kumano Kodo dates back more than a thousand years. During the sixth century, the mountainous Kumano region was a popular site for ascetic training, and considered particularly holy to the Shintō faith. Between the 11th and 13th centuries, members of the Japanese imperial family made the month-long pilgrimage from Kyoto to the three Kumano grand shrines more than 100 times, seeking blessings from the powerful *kami* (deities) believed to inhabit the Kumano region.

By the 15th century, the Kumano Kodo had become a popular pilgrim trail; people of all ages, genders, and social classes made the arduous journey through the mountains to pray, meditate, and visit the three Kumano grand shrines: Kumano Hongu, Kumano Hatayama, and Kumano Nachi. Today, the Kumano Kodo is one of only two pilgrim trails in the world to be designated a UNESCO World Heritage Site (the other is Spain's Camino de Santiago).

My pilgrimage began at the village of Takijiri, near the western coast of the Kii Peninsula. Before hitting the trail, I visited the nearby Pilgrimage Center and acquired a small wooden amulet with the kanji for "Kumano Kodo" burned into one side and the character for "reborn" on the other. My excitement, already high, mounted as I fastened the amulet to Blue and crossed the street to Takijiri-Oji, the Shintō shrine that marked the traditional starting point of the Nakahechi, or "Inner," Kumano Kodo route.

I had studied the history of the Kumano Kodo in college, and had longed to hike the sacred route for more than 20 years. I could barely believe the time had come. I stopped at the shrine to pray for the strength to make it safely through the many kilometers ahead and for the wisdom to emerge from the trail more at peace and more enlightened than I was when I began.

When I finished, I walked around the shrine and began the steep climb upward through the forest. Woodpeckers flitted through the trees, and holes along the sides of the trail marked the hunting spots of wild boars. The air smelled fresh and clean, and except for another hiker I met briefly at the trailhead (and outdistanced as soon as we left the shrine), I was completely on my own.

Ninety minutes into the hike, I reached the site of a sutra mound at the summit of Mount Tsurugi (剣山) (371 meters). Many centuries ago, wooden gates representing the virtues pilgrims had to obtain to ensure safe passage into eternity stood at intervals along the Kumano Kodo. Historians believe the first of these gates stood on top of Mount Tsurugi, and that pilgrims placed handwritten sutras (Buddhist scriptures) in protective sheaths and buried them in a sutra mound near the gate on the mountaintop. The mound was raided during the 19th century, and most of the artifacts were lost, but a monument marks the mound's location near the summit marker.

I hiked down the far side of Mount Tsurugi, across a forested ridge, and up a narrow trail to the summit of Mount Meshimori (飯盛山) (341 meters), where I got my first clear look at the surrounding Hatenashi Mountains. Peaks spread out around me in all directions, receding toward the horizon like the swells of a dark green, gold, and orange sea. Small clusters of traditional houses huddled in the valleys, but the tree-covered mountains showed no signs of human interference.

I descended from the summit of Mount Meshimori and followed the forested trail over ridges and down rocky slopes for another hour until I emerged from the trees near the village of Takahara, the first of the traditional overnight stops on the Kumano Kodo pilgrim trail.

Thanks to the miracle of modern luggage transfers (and the assistance of the company that helped me book accommodations for the six-night trip), my suitcase was waiting when I arrived at my *ryokan*, a traditional inn called Kirinosato. I soaked in the *onsen* and sat on the balcony outside my room watching the mist roll in and the sun go down in a blaze of color over the Hatenashi range.

The next morning at breakfast, I noticed a woman at one of the other tables speaking English with the staff and wondered if she had booked her trip the same way I had—through a company called Walk Japan, which handled all the reservations and provided detailed maps and historical information, letting me enjoy the hike with no logistical concerns. The other woman left before I had the chance to say hello, but I figured if she *had* booked through Walk Japan, we'd meet again.

An hour into the second day on the trail, I met a married couple named David and Yoko (he was American; she was Japanese) and stopped to chat. They were on vacation from their home in the United States, hiking parts of the Kumano Kodo and visiting Yoko's parents. I told them about my 100 Summits project, and we visited as we hiked along the trail. Eventually, our paces diverged and I continued on alone, stopping to visit the many historical and religious sites along the earthen trail.

At lunchtime, I met a young couple from London and an Australian ecologist at a roadside shop where we all stopped for lunch. The English couple was hiking a three-day course that covered half the Nakahechi Route, as part of a year of backpacking around the world. The Australian planned to hike the entire route, but when we compared itineraries, we learned we were overnighting in different villages. After lunch, we all set out—again, at different paces—and I hiked alone again until I caught up with David and Yoko about an hour later, and the three of us walked together for a while.

Late that afternoon, and once again alone, I crossed the final mountain ridge of the day, on a trail that wound through peaceful forests and over ridges with views of misty peaks.

The innkeeper at Kirinosato told me that the three Kumano Grand Shrines represented the past, the present, and the future, as well as life, death, and rebirth. In light of that, I had decided to meditate on my past until I arrived at the first major shrine, Kumano Hongu, and then shift to the present and then the future as I hiked to each of the other shrines in turn.

It was almost impossible for me to meditate on the past in isolation. My thoughts kept moving to the future—specifically, to what I wanted from my life—and I had to keep forcing myself to consider who I *was* and where I came from.

At the far end of the final ridge, I reached Tsugizakura Oji, an ancient Shintō shrine with a famous grafted cherry tree that appears in an account of the Kumano Kodo pilgrimage written in 1109. The shrine was beautiful and would have been peaceful too, but for the three exquisitely odoriferous American backpackers bathing in the purification fountain. A braver person might have explained that the fountain was not a public bath, but there were three of them and I was alone, so I decided silence was the better part of valor.

As I descended the rocky mountain slope toward my *ryokan*, I heard macaques calling in the forest and raptors shrieking high above the trees.

That evening at dinner, I met the woman I had seen at breakfast. Her name was Karen, and she was a trail runner from Hong Kong. As I suspected, she had also booked through Walk Japan, and though she finished the routes much faster than I did, we ate breakfast and dinner together every evening for the rest of the hike, and our conversations grew into a friendship that lasted beyond our seven days on the Kumano Kodo trail. We both enjoyed having someone to share the experience with, while still being able to hike at our own (wildly divergent) paces.

Less happily, my ankle had begun to hurt in a way that suggested my tendons had not healed. I had packed compression tape and a brace, and had no plans to quit the hike regardless of the pain, although when I learned that landslides (triggered by the summer typhoons) had closed a portion of the trail, I decided to take a bus around the closed-off section the following day. The decision would save me seven kilometers' worth of walking, take a little pressure off my ankle, and let me take my time on the remaining 10 kilometers of trail between the bus stop and the first Grand Shrine: Kumano Hongu Taisha.

At first I felt guilty about the decision to take the bus, but just before I fell asleep, it occurred to me that living with guilt about doing things "the easy way" was a hallmark of my past. One point of the Kumano Kodo pilgrimage was dying to that past, which meant I had to put my shame and fear to rest.

In the morning, I woke before dawn, taped up my ankle, and ate breakfast with Karen before she jogged off toward the trail. Half an hour later, I walked in the opposite direction beneath a brilliant silver moon that was just setting as the sun came up. The air smelled cool and clear, and my heart felt light. I tried to consciously forgive myself for expecting too much of myself for so many years.

The "bus boost" left me with an entire day to walk just 10 kilometers. I settled into a pace that didn't push my ankle and enjoyed the spectacular mountain views as I hiked along a ridge past rows of carefully tended *Camellia sinensis*, the shrubs whose leaves and leaf buds produce tea. I had never seen it growing—yet another exciting "first" in a year that overflowed with unique experiences.

At midmorning I stopped for coffee and homemade donuts at a shop beside the hiking trail. While eating, I visited with a Japanese teacher and two hikers he was guiding on this section of the Kumano Kodo trail, as well as a pair of women from the Netherlands who were hiking "only the interesting bits."

Two hours later, while hiking alone, I reached one of the most spectacular sights in Japan: a high cliff overlooking the largest torii (sacred Shintō gate) in the world. The enormous steel gate, which stands almost 34 meters high and weighs 172 tons, marks the original site of Kumano Hongu Shrine. After a massive flood destroyed the shrine in 1888, the buildings were reconstructed on an adjacent, higher site, but the original grounds remain a holy place.

It took almost an hour to descend from the cliff to Kumano Hongu Shrine. When I arrived, I offered prayers of thanks for my safe arrival, as pilgrims have done for centuries, and bought an amulet emblazoned with Yatagarasu, the three-legged crow whose image appears at thousands of Kumano shrines across Japan—all of which are subsidiaries of the three Grand Shrines on the Kumano Kodo. I felt a special connection to the shrine, and to Yatagarasu, and I lingered beneath the massive trees, aware that when I left, I would die to my past and enter the "present" phase of my pilgrimage.

An hour's hike still separated me from my *ryokan* at Yunomine Onsen, so as the sun began its journey toward the mountains in the west, I left Kumano Hongu Shrine and began the next phase of my journey along the Kumano Kodo.

42

REBIRTH

November 28–30, 2018

Two of the many trails that make up the Kumano Kodo meet at Yuno-mine Onsen, a place so rich in volcanic hot spring water that a steaming river runs through the center of the town. One of its oldest public baths, called Tsubo-yu, is a UNESCO World Heritage Site, and the same spring that feeds Tsubo-yu provides the water to all the *ryokan* in the town.

That night, I bathed and soaked my ankle twice. It had swollen underneath the brace and tape, but the pain and swelling responded well to a combination of volcanic water, ice, and ibuprofen. I elevated the ankle when I went to bed and taped it up again in the morning.

Injured or not, I had no intention of canceling the hike.

My itinerary called for me to take a bus from Yunomine to the town of Ukegawa. There, I would begin the lengthy hike to the even smaller town of Koguchi, where I had reservations at a once-abandoned high school that the villagers transformed into a *ryokan* for pilgrims walking the Kumano Kodo. My ankle hurt worse than ever, but I thought I could tough it out for the few days that remained.

Clouds rolled in and blocked the sun as I hiked up and over the mountain passes between Ukegawa and my first milestone of the day, a famous overlook that ancient travelers claimed had a view of 1,000 mountain peaks.

As I walked through the silent woods, I considered my present state. I felt fortunate. I had spent almost half a year traveling across Japan, and just as many months still lay before me. The cancer was gone. Except for my ankle, I was in the best shape of my life.

Wood pigeons wandered across the forest floor as other birds sang in the trees. Gentle breezes rustled through the branches and set the ferns in the undergrowth to bobbing. In the distance, I heard the territorial shriek of a macaque. A second answered, and a screaming match ensued.

By the time I reached the overlook, the monkeys and the birds had all gone silent. I didn't try to count the peaks, but the sea of mountains spreading out beneath the cloudy sky made even the spectacular views in Takahara pale by comparison.

The sight was too spectacular to hurry past, so I stopped for lunch—a sandwich spread with "peanut butter whip" that reminded me of the peanut butter and honey sandwiches my mother made me every day in elementary school. As I prepared to continue hiking, an Australian couple—Ron and Linda—arrived at the overlook. We hiked on together, talking, as Kumano Kodo pilgrims do, until we reached the remains of a famous teahouse. The clouds had darkened and it smelled like rain, so I stopped to put a rain cover on Blue as Ron and Linda continued down the trail.

Precisely at noon, I reached the top of Sakura-toge, a pass named for the many cherry trees that line its slopes. On the far side, I faced a steep descent to Koguchi, my stopping point for the night, so I swallowed some ibuprofen and took it slow.

Enormous ferns grew up on both sides of the narrow, sloping trail. Beyond them, ancient trees towered high overhead. The muggy air smelled rich with the primeval scents of damp earth and wet foliage.

I saw this movie. Any minute now, the velociraptors eat the novelist.

The writer-eating dinosaurs apparently had other plans that day, and I reached Koguchi without incident. Better still, I reached the doors of the converted school-turned-*ryokan* just as the first fat drops of rain began to fall.

I had planned to spend the time between check-in and dinner writing and meditating on the hike, but the next thing I remember, I was waking up with a writing pad beneath my hand and lines from the tatami floor embedded in my cheek. Outside, the rain poured down in sheets.

At dinnertime, I met up with Karen and the Australians, Ron and Linda, who were also spending the night at the *ryokan*. We ate together, comparing notes about our experiences on the trail.

At 10:30 that night, with rain still pounding down, I began to have concerns about the trail. The next day's hike would take me over Echizen Toge, the highest pass on the Kumano Kodo. The first part of the hike, known as the *dogiri-zaka* (belly-cutting slope) gains 800 vertical meters of altitude in a kilometer and a half of trail distance, a brutally steep ascent that acquired its name because travelers would supposedly rather commit seppuku (a form of ritual suicide involving a slit across the belly) than climb it twice. The trail was treacherous even in dry weather; I had no desire to climb it in the rain, with or without an injured ankle. There was a bus from Koguchi to my end point at Kumano Nachi Shrine, but I didn't want to ride a bus. I had come to climb.

I reminded myself that morning was still several hours in the future and that this was the *present-only* portion of my pilgrimage. Instead of making backup plans, I made the decision to see what dawn would bring.

I woke to a misty, dripping dawn. My ankle hurt, but the swelling had gone down again, and I didn't want to miss the *dogiri-zaka*. I hadn't reached any summits on the Kumano Kodo after my first day on the trail, and the reason was as obvious as the mountains all around me: the original journey from Kyoto to Takijiri-Oji and then across the Nakahechi to the end point at Kumano Hatayama Shrine took 40 days, entirely on foot, and ancient pilgrims did not hike to unnecessary summits when the mountain passes offered a (slightly) easier route to the destination.

I left the *ryokan* at 7 a.m., intending to test the route and loop back for the bus if the rain left things too slippery. Water dripped from the massive cedars, but their branches had sheltered the trail from the worst of the downpour. Wispy mist lingered in the valleys; overhead, the sky was pale blue. Birds sang in the trees to greet the dawn, and I chose to make the climb.

At 7:55 the sun appeared above a line of mountains to the east. I greeted it with a shout of joy. I hadn't seen another hiker since leaving the *ryokan*—and wouldn't until Karen passed me at the bottom of the *dogiri-zaka* 30 minutes later. We said a brief hello and she continued up the trail. I took my time, letting my ankle set the pace.

The guidebooks said, "There are no words to describe" the *dogiri-zaka*'s brutal incline. Having climbed it, I beg to differ. There are several words—all of which would have gotten my mouth washed out with soap if I had said them as a child.

An hour's hard climb put me up and over the massive pass ahead of schedule. I took my time on the descent, which wound down a stony mountainside before taking a lengthy detour around the site of yet another summer landslide. The detour followed an unpaved logging road through the mountains. Along the road, the trees grew straight and tall, and a river sang a splashing song as it tumbled through a nearby gully.

At midmorning the road rejoined the Kumano Kodo at Jizōchaya, the site of a former teahouse where a group of ancient Jizō statues watched over pilgrims walking the sacred trail. According to my hiking plan, I remained almost an hour ahead of schedule and was almost halfway to the second Kumano Grand Shrine, Nachi Taisha.

From Jizō Chaya, the trail gained yet more altitude, zigzagging upward until it seemed my life would consist of nothing but up . . . up . . . up through giant trees on sunlight-speckled trails lined with ferns. The scenery was relaxing, the air was fresh, and but for my aching ankle, the walk would have been among the most beautiful of my life.

I still found it hard to believe how far I'd come in the six months since chemotherapy: from a weak, bald woman who removed her cap to prove her identity at immigration to a curly-haired hiker climbing the passes of the Kumano Kodo faster than the posted times. I had returned from the dead, and I felt truly blessed to be alive.

Shortly after noon, I entered a forest of even more massive cedars, with *sasa* growing higher than my head on either side. At a split in the trail, a sign indicated the left-hand fork led to a historical overlook with a view of the Pacific Ocean. Ignoring my ankle, I hurried upward, extending my hike by half an hour but unwilling to miss the famous view. When I reached the coast, I would have walked across the entire Kii Peninsula—almost 100 kilometers in six days—and I wanted to see the famous ocean view.

At the overlook, I gazed down across the mountains to the sparkling blue Pacific. I couldn't see Kumano Nachi Shrine, which sits a short way inland, but did spot a number of small volcanic islands off the jagged coast. One of them, though I didn't know which, was home to the *onsen ryokan* where I would spend my last night on the trail.

The thought of soaking in an island *onsen* with sea caves and views of the Pacific sent new energy through my tired limbs. I barely noticed the ache in my ankle as I hiked back through the forest and down the trail to

Kumano Nachi Shrine, a highly sacred site that's also home to Japan's tallest uninterrupted waterfall.

Nachi Falls drops 133 meters down a vertical cliff in a glittering bridal veil. It's justifiably considered one of Japan's most beautiful waterfalls—a significant achievement in a country with hundreds, if not thousands, of breathtaking falls. I stood and stared at Nachi Falls from the public viewing platform and from the top of the Nachi Shrine's five-story pagoda before making the long trek down many stairs to the base of the falls themselves. A wooden torii stood before the pool at the base of the falls. I stood beside it, reveling in the cool, refreshing mist that filled the air. Water over rock on a massive scale—my reward for finishing the second portion of my Kumano Kodo pilgrimage. I ended my meditation on the present with the joyful realization that my life had become everything I hoped that it would be.

From the falls, I took a bus to the coastal town of Kii Katsuura, followed by a shuttle boat to Hotel Urashima, which stood on a volcanic island in the bay. Natural hot springs welled up from the ground beneath the island, creating freshwater sea cave *onsen* with wide views of the Pacific Ocean.

I met up with Karen, Ron, and Linda at the restaurant for one last happy dinner reminiscing about the Kumano Kodo. In the morning, we would go our separate ways, but the friendships we forged on the pilgrim trail felt solid, real, and permanent.

The following morning, I woke at dawn and took the boat to shore as enormous kites swooped and cried in the pale sky. The raptors flock to Kii Kaatsura because of the fishermen—tuna and squid have been the backbone of the area's fishing industry for centuries—and the giant birds roosted on telephone poles across the town like pigeons do in Tokyo.

A train ride and one last short walk took me to the final Kumano Grand Shrine, Hatayama Taisha, and nearby Kamikura Shrine—where I climbed one final long, steep hill to see the Gotobiki-Iwa, a massive stone where legend says that Shintō deities once came to earth. I had only that single morning to meditate on my future self, but my future didn't need much thought. More accurately, I had thought about it plenty in the last few months and already knew what I wanted it to be.

When I finished climbing the 100 Summits, I would find a way to make Japan my long-term home.

43

OVER BYOBU

December 19, 2018

Upon my return from the Kumano Kodo, I spent two weeks in Tokyo resting my ankle and trying to recover. The pain stopped after the first few days, but the tendons needed much more time to heal. In truth, they needed longer than the time I could afford to give, if I wanted to complete a hundred mountain climbs before May 19. Still, I thought a judicious mix of activity and rest would let me finish the climbs without any lasting damage.

I visited with Michael, worked on my novel, and took short trips to visit Tokyo's celebrated "winter illuminations" and Christmas markets. Although Japan has very few Christians, the country celebrates Christmas as a secular, cultural holiday. Tokyo, in particular, indulges in a veritable orgy of twinkling lights, decorated trees, and lovely gifts.

As lovely as the city was, by December 19 I had rested as long as my wanderlust could handle. Most of the mountains over 1,000 meters were buried under several feet of snow. However, Hakone's peaks were accessible all year, so on a clear but chilly morning a week before Christmas, I boarded the *shinkansen* and headed south. Mount Fuji was visible as the train approached Odawara, her sloping sides almost completely covered in pale white snow. My heart swelled with love for the beautiful mountain, which now also held memories of Mom, Annamaria, Kaitlyn, and Laurie. I understood and shared the Japanese fascination with Mount Fuji, and she *almost* felt as if she was my mountain too. The thought of moving back to the United States, where I could not see her regularly, felt like a punishment my heart could not endure.

From Odawara I caught a local train to Hakone-Yumoto and then a bus to Lake Ashi, arriving just after 11 a.m. My goal for the day was Mount Byobu (屏風山) (948 meters), a haystack-shaped mountain that rises behind the famous Hakone Barrier.

During the 17th century, Shogun Tokugawa Ieyasu built the barrier to serve as a strategic checkpoint on the Tōkaidō, a major travel road that connected his new capital of Edo with the former capital city of Kyoto. The barrier sits in a natural bottleneck between Lake Ashi and the surrounding mountains. Mount Byobu, in particular, would have been extremely difficult to climb without the wooden steps set into the modern trail.

The air in Hakone smelled of wet earth and recent rain. Gentle breezes rustled through the bamboo canes and fluttered the final maple leaves that clung to the trees along the trail.

Mount Byobu hadn't looked like much of a challenge from the base, but I had no idea how cruelly steep the climb would be. Narrow steps of earth and wood led up the mountain, each at least knee-high and many higher. In places, the steps were so steep and tall that I had to climb them on my hands and knees.

My pants grew muddy, but my ankle held up even better than I'd hoped. It ached at first but loosened up enough to make me hopeful about the longer climb I'd planned for the following day.

The climb to the wooded summit only took about an hour. I had hoped for a view of the Hakone Barrier and possibly Mount Fuji, but the trees were too high and close together; the only thing I saw was the summit sign.

On the descent, the trail wove downward through a forest of maple trees whose leaves still burned with autumn's reds and golds. On the lower slopes, pine trees outcompeted maples, and the deciduous trees soon disappeared. Pine boughs littered the ground, along with several enormous fallen trees—more victims of the summer typhoon season.

As the ground grew level, the trail curved around a fallen pine and disappeared. I stopped and looked around. The trail curled up the mountainside behind me, so I hadn't wandered off the path. I walked slowly toward the place where the trail disappeared and discovered that the missing trail was an optical illusion. A wooden bridge that I'd mistaken for another fallen tree ran across an almost-dry riverbed; the trail continued on the other side.

A few minutes later, I reached the trailhead and an asphalt road that led to nearby Amazake Chaya, an 18th-century teahouse that was once a popular resting point for travelers on the Tōkaidō. The teahouse is preserved in its original condition and still serves *amazake*, a sweet, fermented rice-based drink, as well as traditional mochi (cakes of pounded glutinous rice) topped with *kinako* (roasted soybean powder) and *kurogoma* (black sesame). My ankle didn't need a rest, but I stopped for a cup of tea and a plate of chewy sweetened mochi. The teahouse smelled of wood smoke from the fire in the traditional hearth. The fire's warmth felt good on my chilly skin.

That night, I soaked in the *onsen* and went to sleep much earlier than normal. In the morning, I planned to tackle yet another three-peak climb, and the bus to the trailhead left at 6 a.m.

44

ALIVE AND FREE

December 20, 2018

Dawn came and went, and I remained in bed. I wanted to climb, but my ankle felt too weak, so December 19 became a rest and writing day. The following morning, I woke at 5 a.m. to a brooding sky. Taking a page from Ido's book on Rausu, I rolled over for another three hours' sleep and gave the weather time to clear.

At eight o'clock the clouds remained, but looked far less foreboding, so my doubly-rested ankle and I caught the 9 a.m. bus to Otome Pass. Half a dozen other hikers boarded the bus as well, which reinforced my confidence in the weather and the climb.

As the bus approached the tunnel at Otome Pass, a recorded message cautioned us—in Chinese and English as well as Japanese—to remain seated when the bus emerged from the tunnel. I barely had time to wonder at the unusual warning before daylight appeared again—along with Mount Fuji in all her snowcapped majesty. The open, elevated road gave us an unimpeded view of the mountain, from base to summit. An audible gasp went through the bus—including one from me.

Two seconds later, the bus stopped at the trailhead. All of the hikers disembarked, but instead of the usual flurry of checking gear and heading for the trail, we all stood and stared at Fujisan. This was the first time I had clearly seen, from a distance, the face I climbed, and it looked impossibly high. I stared, mesmerized by the snow that now reached halfway down the cone. I took several dozen pictures—all essentially identical, but the need to freeze that moment in time, to save it forever, felt almost overwhelming.

The temperature hovered only a degree above freezing, so after only a couple of minutes I put the camera in my pocket, shoved my rapidly-numbing fingers into gloves, and followed the other hikers toward the trail. Towering pine trees covered the mountainside, obscuring my view of Fuji, though I caught occasional glimpses of her snowy flanks between the trees. My breath plumed out in thick, white clouds. My woolen gloves did little to block the chill. The rising sun broke through the clouds and sent bright beams between the trees, but they seemed to give no warmth.

Instead of stopping every hundred meters for pictures as I usually did, I debated the value of every shot against the pain of exposing my hands to the cold. My fingers never really recovered between the photo stops, and they burned fiercely as I climbed.

Two deep booms and a resonant rumble echoed through the silent air. I stopped and listened. The sound seemed far away, but remained loud enough that it would have been almost deafening at the source. Silence returned, and I hiked on. A few minutes later, I heard the noise again—a booming report, like cannon fire, that came from the direction of Mount Fuji: the sound of avalanches thundering down her massive slopes.

Near the top of Otome Pass, small patches of ice appeared beside the trail. Underfoot, the mud had frozen, preserving the footprints of hikers who passed before. As my boots crunched along the trail, I wondered how many of the people whose steps I shadowed had also climbed the other mountains I had climbed and whether I had stepped on their foot-prints before. I felt connected to them, even though I would never meet them face to face.

At the top of the pass, Mount Fuji reappeared through a gap in the trees. Foliage blocked her lower slopes, but I stopped for pictures any-way. After waiting so long to see her, I felt compelled to document every sighting.

Four trails converged at Otome Pass, including the one I had just ascended. Straight ahead through the crossroads, a narrow trail descended into Hakone, while to my left and right, a mountain trail followed an undulating course along a ridge of mountains that ran along a roughly north-south axis.

I turned right, planning to snag the summit of 1,154-meter Marudake (丸岳)—40 minutes south along the ridge—before backtracking to the pass and heading north toward 1,212-meter Mount Kintoki (金時山) (1,212 meters), my ultimate goal. The rising sun had finally started giving noticeable warmth as well as light, and I hiked along the rolling ridge, ascending and descending over little peaks and passes. All the time, I watched Mount Fuji through the trees.

An hour and 15 minutes later, I suspected something had gone wrong. The trail signs no longer mentioned Marudake. Instead, they pointed to Nagaotoge, a mountain pass much farther to the south.

I opened YAMAP to check my position with GPS, and discovered that I had overshot the mountain without noticing. I doubled back, embarrassed, and took a photo on the summit as I passed.

After a quick lunch break at Otome Pass, I continued north, climbing a short but very steep trail to the summit of Mount Nagao (長尾山) (1,144 meters), which had no view but did have two large summit markers, one on either side of the small mountaintop plateau. I took pictures with both and then began the steep descent to the ridge that connected Mount Nagao with the lower shoulder of Mount Kintoki.

As I reached the ridge, I met an older man approaching from the opposite direction. He wore hiking boots with gaiters and a pair of blindingly white short-shorts that made him look like an aging Japanese Freddie Mercury. The hiker stopped to say hello and ask where I was from.

His face lit up at my answer. "I've been to California!" he exclaimed. "I visited a friend and saw the oldest church in California."

We talked about Mount Fuji, which he urged me to climb again via the longer Gotemba trail, adding, "I've climbed that route five times."

I expressed surprise—and admiration. "You must really like to climb!"

He said he climbed Mount Kintoki four or five times every week—and that he had climbed it over 200 times since his retirement six years before.

"You must love these mountains very much," I said in Japanese.

He switched to English. "I am not rich, but here, I am alive and free."

His words stuck with me long after we went our separate ways, and I summited Mount Kintoki for the first (but hopefully not the only) time.

I understood precisely what he meant.

45

HAPPY NEW YEAR, FUJISAN

December 31, 2018

I wanted to end 2018 with a special mountain—preferably one of the *hyakumeizan*—to mark the halfway point of my 100 Summits quest and the end of my "cancer year."

I also wanted to spend my first Japanese New Year in Tokyo with Michael, which meant I needed a mountain close enough to climb and return in a single day.

Mount Tsukuba (筑波山) (877 meters) was made to order.

The twin-peaked "purple mountain" sits on the northern end of the Kantō plain, 90 minutes from Tokyo. In addition to appearing on Fukada's *hyakumeizan* list, Mount Tsukuba is famous for its (one-sided) rivalry with Mount Fuji, which rises from the opposite end of Japan's largest plain.

According to legend, thousands of years ago the creator deities Izanagi and Izanami descended from heaven in search of a place to spend the night. Mount Fuji refused them shelter, believing in her arrogance that she did not need the *kami*'s blessing. Mount Tsukuba humbly welcomed the deities as honored guests, and while Mount Fuji remains a cold and barren mountain to this day, Mount Tsukuba bursts with life and color.

The deities are still enshrined and worshipped on Mount Tsukuba's twin summits: Izanagi on the lower, male peak called Mount Nantai, and Izanami on Mount Nyotai, the higher, female peak.

New Year's Eve dawned cold but clear. I headed for the train just after dawn and walked through the silent streets as the sun came up.

Although I was not Japanese, I felt more at home in Japan than I had in any other place. The moment I stepped off the plane in 2015, on my first trip to Tokyo, a pilot light ignited in my spirit. Even then, I knew I had come home—albeit to a place I'd never been.

In the years since then, I had fallen ever more deeply in love with this land of mountains, rivers, waterfalls, towering forests, and rice fields glowing green and gold in season. I loved the food, the culture, and the towns and cities resonating with a soul that was both modern and as ancient as the rising sun.

Mount Tsukuba had a gondola that carried visitors almost all the way to the summit, but as the bus to the trailhead rolled across the plain, I decided to forgo the ride—despite my rule—and hike the entire way from the trailhead to the peaks.

Rules were made to be broken, after all.

Before the hike, I visited Tsukubasan Shrine at the base of the mountain. A crowd had already arrived to get a jump on *hatsumode*, the traditional New Year's visit to a Shintō shrine, believed to ensure good fortune in the coming year.

Sunbeams filtered through the cedars as I started up the trail. The enormous trees grew straight and tall, their trunks far broader than my outstretched arms. The trail wove around the trees and over giant stones. It gained altitude gently, as if giving hikers time to enjoy the forest. I heard the ululating cry of a raptor overhead and the rustle of a squirrel in the underbrush. The periodic thump of footsteps heralded the approach of trail runners, mostly solo or in pairs, descending from the summit. I admired their fortitude, not only for running up and down the mountain but also because the length of the trail meant that they must have started before dawn.

Fifteen minutes from the trailhead, the real climb began. Large stones and occasional flights of earthen steps reinforced with logs curled up the mountainside. Here and there a step had worn (or been washed) away, and I had to strain to reach the next step up. Despite the chilly air, I quickly broke a sweat—and the trail remained steep for the rest of the climb.

Two hours after leaving the trailhead, I emerged on the saddle-shaped plateau between Tsukuba's peaks. My guidebook warned that the football field–sized saddle looked more like a mini-mall than a mountaintop, and it hadn't lied. Souvenir shops and restaurants filled the area. On either end of the saddle, trails continued to the summits, which rose above the plateau like the horns of a giant ox.

Mount Nantai was closer and lower, so I headed that way first. On my way, I passed a souvenir shop with a display of summit pins, including one that had the mountain's name (in Japanese) and a small enamel frog—a reference to the famous *gama ishi* (frog rock) near the summit of Mount Nyotai. I wanted the pin but forced myself to wait. Throughout my journey, I had held to one absolute rule: I could not buy a summit pin before I reached the summit.

Ten minutes later, I earned my pin—along with one of the loveliest and longest views of my climbs to date. The Kantō Plain spread out beneath the mountain, a checkerboard of brown and golden winter fields punctuated by villages and, in the hazy distance, the skyscrapers of To-kyo. I lingered on the summit, thinking about the dying year and how happy I was not to be dying with it.

As I descended to the saddle (and my summit pin), I passed a pair of brothers, the younger three or four years old and the older nine or ten. With every step, the toddler gleefully chanted, *"Abunai desu"* (It's dan-gerous). His bouncing steps and joyful tone reminded me of the way my son had bounced with similar joy (and infinite phrase loops) through his toddler years. Inspired, I hopped from stone to stone all the way to the saddle, where I bought my summit pin and then headed off in search of the *gama ishi*. According to legend, the frog-shaped rock brings great fortune to anyone who successfully pitches a coin or a stone into its open "mouth," but my personal interest ran deeper than superstition. As a child, I often visited Santa Monica's Douglas Park and hunted for tad-poles in the lake. I fed and cared for them, eagerly watching their trans-formation into frogs. Forty years later, my fondness for frogs remained, and I looked forward to seeing the famous *gama ishi*. To my delight, it did, indeed, look like an open-mouthed frog large enough to swallow a person whole.

Two dozen fruitless attempts to pitch both coins and stones into its mouth left me no more fortunate than before, but I felt exceptionally fortunate anyway.

Ten minutes after leaving the *gama ishi*, I arrived on the rocky summit of Mount Nyotai, the high point of Mount Tsukuba and the official halfway point of my 100 Summits. I had heard that on a clear day, it was possible to see Mount Fuji from the summit of Mount Nyotai, and sure enough, a hazy but instantly recognizable blue pyramid rose through the clouds on the southern horizon. It was the first time I had seen Mount Fuji from a different prefecture, and I smiled so much my cheeks began to ache. Despite the three-hour climb, they were the only things that hurt.

With the upper ropeway station just ten minutes below the peak, I decided to follow the "ropeway rule" after all and rode the gondola back down. As I watched the hazy orange sun sink toward the horizon for the final time in 2018, it occurred to me that I was now on the downhill side of my climbing year, and with all the visa-, housing-, and weather-related challenges, the time had passed much faster than expected.

It had taken more than seven months for me to finish the first half of my climbs, and the bulk of the winter snow had yet to fall. If I wanted to finish all 100 by May 19, I would have to pick up the pace in the new year.

STATION 7: HELP WANTED
MOUNTAIN TOTAL: 50

Just after New Year's, I saw an online listing seeking an experienced English-language editor in Tokyo. The position required no Japanese and offered visa support for successful candidates—which meant, if I got the job, the company would sponsor my visa.

Although I saw the ad by chance, and hadn't planned work (aside from writing) until I finished the 100 Summits climbs, the opportunity seemed too serendipitous, and the job too perfect, for me to ignore. I dusted off my resume and sent it in.

I wanted the job, but after I sent my resume, I didn't fret about the outcome. If the opportunity was meant for me, I would get the job. If not, something else would come along.

In the meantime, I had 50 mountains left to climb.

46

THAT'S NOT THE SUMMIT

January 10, 2019

On January 10 I woke at dawn, rolled over, and almost chose to stay in bed. My schedule called for a climb of Nokogiriyama (鋸山) (330 meters) in Chiba Prefecture, northeast of Tokyo, but the cloudy, chilly day felt better suited to sleeping in. I huddled under the covers, thinking about the history of "Sawtooth Mountain," whose quarries played a major role in the construction of Edo-period castles and fortifications. In the end, my curiosity proved too great. I dressed and headed for the train.

Due to a geographical quirk, the fastest way north to Chiba involved an express train south, followed by a ferry ride across the Tokyo Bay. On board the ferry, I wandered through a souvenir-and-coffee shop that sold everything from coffee and "cheesy potato wedges" to towels emblazoned with Chiba-kun, the bright-red cartoon dog who serves as Chiba Prefecture's official mascot. I had plenty of towels, but since I've never met a fried potato I didn't like, I bought the wedges and a cup of strong, dark coffee, which I took to a table beside the window just as the ferry started across the bay.

Large white gulls swooped through the air like pilots guiding the boat to sea. The fresh, briny smell of the ocean filtered in through a nearby window, mingling pleasantly with the fragrance of my coffee.

An hour later, I disembarked from the ferry and hiked to the trailhead of Nokogiriyama. The mountain towered overhead, a series of jagged ridges half-covered in trees. Here and there, a vacant quarry gaped like the socket of a missing tooth.

The forested limestone trail dates to the 18th century and still bears the marks of its history as a quarry. Unlike many Japanese mountain trails, it runs almost directly up the mountain, cutting through any obstacles in its path. Several enormous boulders along the route still bear tool marks showing where the trail was cut through them.

At various points along the route, signs in English and Japanese explained the history of Nokogiriyama. During its days as an active quarry, most of the workers who dragged the heavy stones down the mountain's slopes were women. As I climbed, I imagined repeating the process two to three times every day while hauling a cart loaded high with massive stones. After fifty mountains, I was in the best shape of my life, but I wasn't strong enough to work a quarry on flat land, let alone on mountain trails. My admiration for Edo-period women rose with every step.

Two-thirds of the way to the summit, I reached the first of the quarry sites. Rectangular vacancies in the rock showed where the blocks of stone had been removed. Some gaps were only one block deep, but others looked as if someone had carved a four-story building from the rock.

It took me only an hour to reach the summit—45 minutes less than the posted time. Most of the benches on the small plateau were already claimed. Two men stood near the summit marker, carrying on an intense debate about the view. I couldn't grasp the details of their argument, but it seemed to involve how much they could have seen on a clear day.

I took pictures of the slate-gray sea as I waited for the men to vacate the summit marker. Eventually they moved away, and I discovered—to my intense embarrassment—that I wasn't on the summit. The sign I'd taken for a summit marker was merely a description of the view from this observatory platform.

That does explain how I reached the "top" so quickly.

The map revealed that I had inadvertently taken a wrong turn at a split in the trail. In my defense, I had followed the branch that continued climbing, not realizing that the trail to the summit made a brief descent before ascending the final ridge.

I retraced my steps to the fork in the trail and continued toward the summit. The forested trail offered no views of the mountains or the ocean, and also did little to block the freezing winds that swept in off the sea. I hiked as quickly as I could to fight the cold. It didn't help as much as I would have liked. My nose began to run.

A gap in the forest at the summit revealed a lovely view of the surrounding hills and the sea beyond. The summit marker stood in precisely the right position to create a photogenic backdrop—a standard on Japanese mountain trails—and I braved the cold just long enough to get a good picture before I started down.

When I returned to the turnoff for the observation platform, I faced a choice. A secondary trail led from the observation deck down into the massive, defunct quarry that covered the mountain's spiny upper ridge. If I followed it, a winding trail would lead me through the quarry to a ropeway that would take me to the trailhead. If I returned the way I came, I could take a different side trail to a famous statue of Kannon, the Buddhist goddess of mercy, and an overlook known as the View of Hell. With the afternoon half spent, I could take one path or the other but not both.

Hell and Kannon were the greater draw.

On the way to the Kannon statue, I passed another quarry site. The hiking guide described it as a small one, but it towered overhead, an empty, echoing box of stone. Wind whistled eerily through the man-made caves, and dead vines clung to the cliff face, creating a post-apocalyptic atmosphere.

I stood beside the caves, amazed at the strength it must have taken to cart the quarried stones down the mountain from this height.

A little farther along the path, I stopped at another overlook and stared across the hazy bay. Despite the clouds, I could see Mount Fuji rising, blue and beautiful, on the far side of the water. To her left, the smaller cone of Mount Amagi rose above the Izu Peninsula, looking like Mount Fuji's lesser twin. I felt a thrill at the sight of the famous mountains. One, I had climbed already, and the other I hoped to climb in the next few weeks.

The sky was growing dark with approaching rain, so I tore myself away from the mountain overlook and hurried up the steps to the Hyaku-Shaku Kannon, a 30-meter-high carving of the goddess of mercy. The statue was created in 1966 and dedicated to those who die from wars, sickness, or accidents. A set of wooden steps led up from the ground to a shrine near the feet of the goddess. Wooden benches at ground level provided a place for people to sit and pray, meditate, or simply enjoy the view.

After leaving Kannon, I climbed one final set of steps to the famous *Jigoku Nozoki* (Hell Overlook), an outcropping of stone shaped like a long, narrow nose that hangs out over a high, sheer cliff. A railing surrounds the overlook, and I walked out all the way to the farthest point.

That afternoon, hell had an excellent view of Mount Fuji and Mount Amagi.

I originally hoped to continue down the far side of the mountain to Nihonji, a Soto Zen Buddhist temple founded 1,300 years ago, which is home to a famed *daibutsu* (giant Buddha) and 1,500 *rakan* (statues of Buddha's disciples) that line the slopes of Nokogiriyama. But between the gathering clouds and my growling stomach, I decided to hike to the gondola instead. I would return to Nokogiriyama when the 100 Summits climbs were through.

47

TOPS AND TOFU

January 14, 2019

In Japan, the second Monday in January is a public holiday celebrating people who reached adulthood during the previous year. On the Sunday before the Coming of Age Day holiday, I headed to Isehara, 90 minutes south of Tokyo, for a holiday climb of Ōyama (大山) (1,252 meters), a mountain famous for its wooden tops, and for tofu created using water from the mountain's many springs.

In the hotel the night before my climb, I studied the hiking map and tried to ignore the way my climbing time was slipping away. Instead, I focused on a comment Christopher made when I mentioned the problem to him the week before: "When will you figure out that this isn't about the numbers?"

He was correct; at its core, the 100 Summits journey was about experiencing the mountains and becoming the best possible version of myself along the way. By now, the changes were obvious: I no longer worried about everything, and I hadn't had a nightmare since the night before Mount Shari—the longest stretch of sound sleep in my adult life.

Even so, I wanted to climb 100 mountains before May 19.

On Coming of Age Day, I woke at dawn and arrived at the bus stop 30 minutes before the 8 a.m. bus was due to depart for the trailhead. Several trail guides warned that the infrequent buses to Ōyama often filled to capacity, especially on holidays, forcing latecomers to wait well over an hour for another bus. At 7:37 a.m., I began to think the guides were wrong. I was third in a line of 10 people at the bus stop, only three of whom looked mountain-bound. The early departure had forced me to skip the breakfast buffet at my hotel, and the bakery buns in Blue seemed a poor substitute.

I changed my tune at 7:43, when a horde of people flowed out of the station and the bus line swelled to 10 times its former length.

More than half of those people were left behind when the bus departed at 8 a.m., crammed to the gills with people in hiking gear. Thanks to my early arrival, I was not only aboard but in a seat.

The bus let us off at the bottom of a famous set of stairs—362 stairs, to be exact—that led to the cable car station. As I climbed them, I considered skipping the cable car (despite my personal rule that I had to take them whenever possible), but the trail map looked as if the climbing trail bypassed the Shintō shrine near the upper cable car station (near the middle of the mountain), so I bought a ticket and climbed aboard. Once again, my early arrival paid high dividends: as the crowded cable car began its journey, I looked out the window at the lengthy line of people left behind to wait for the gondola's return.

The upper cable car station sat at the base of a flight of steep stone steps that led to Oyama Afuri Shrine, a Shintō holy site that honors deities associated with the weather, particularly rain. An enormous wooden torii stood at the top of the stairs, at the entrance to a courtyard. On the far side of the yard, a worship hall with a sloping roof backed up against the mountainside. A large metal incense burner stood directly in front of the worship hall and a bonfire burned at the center of the yard.

Beyond the shrine, another set of even steeper stairs led up to the hiking trail, which curled up the mountain beneath massive cedars that cast the path in shadow.

A sheen of sweat soon covered my face and neck, and I stopped to remove my jacket. As I did, I noticed a wiry man approaching quickly from behind. He wore a pair of Day-Glo bicycle shorts and leaned heavily on walking sticks that helped him balance the four full cases of bottled soda and drinking water he carried on his back. The boxes rose almost a meter above his head, and I estimated he was carrying 54 kilograms (120 pounds) of beverages up the mountain. I stared, mouth open in awe at the feat, which I wouldn't have believed if I hadn't seen it.

I remained at the side of the trail to let the porter pass because his climbing pace was faster than mine. He strained beneath his burden, calf muscles bulging, and I thought about all the times I had purchased drinks on mountain climbs. More specifically, I thought about the fact that every one of those precious, refreshing bottles had gone up the mountain on someone's back. I had known this before, but seeing it gave me new appreciation—and respect—for the porters who carried them. (It also made me remember, with a twinge of shame, that I sometimes groused about carrying a two-liter bottle from the 7-11 to my apartment—a distance of only 100 meters across flat ground.)

After 90 minutes on the trail, I loved and hated the mountain simultaneously. On the best of days, mountain climbing was an exercise in pain control and tolerance. Put simply: mountain climbing hurts. And yet, the pain—more accurately, learning to enjoy the climbs despite it—was as critical to the experience as the beautiful, often unexpected sights I saw along the way.

Near the summit, patches of ice and snow appeared along the sides of the path. I felt a flicker of concern, because I'd left my ice spikes back in Tokyo, but mostly, I found the prospect of a snowy hike exciting.

Snow frosted the red torii that marked the entrance to the summit shrine and lay in deeper drifts beneath the pines on the mountaintop plateau. Recently-melted snow and many boots had churned the sunny portions of the summit into a quagmire. The view was lovely, but the slippery mud and the presence of many other hikers on the summit sent me scurrying back to the trail after only five minutes on the mountaintop.

It took me 90 minutes to descend to Ōyama Afuri Shrine, where I noticed that the stand selling *omamori* (charms and blessed objects) near the worship hall still had two *hamaya* on display. *Hamaya* (demon-breaking arrows) are traditionally sold at Shintō shrines during the first few weeks of each new year and displayed in Japanese homes to protect the family against evil, illness, and bad fortune. The blunted arrows have feather fletching and often include an *ema* (small wooden plaque used for writing prayers) with the Chinese zodiac symbol for the year. The new year—2019—was the Year of the Boar, which was also the symbol for 1971, the year I was born.

When I boarded the cable car, one of the last two *hamaya* went with me.

I disembarked at the base of the mountain with one last goal in mind: eating some of Ōyama's famous tofu. A sign outside one restaurant proclaimed that it had specialized in Ōyama tofu for more than 100 years. I went inside and took a seat at a low, traditional table in a room with a tatami floor. The seven-course meal that followed was one of the best I have ever eaten in Japan. Ōyama tofu was the star of every delicious dish. My favorite—a ramekin of tofu gratin—featured chunks of firm tofu baked in a velvety Parmesan cream sauce, with a crispy crust on top. After a dessert of soft tofu mixed with fruit that reminded me of ambrosia salad, though not as sweet, I paid the bill and left the restaurant, satisfied not only with my meal but with the entire day.

Outside, an elderly woman was sweeping the walk with a traditional Japanese broom. She smiled at me and gestured to Blue. *"Did you climb Ōyama?"*

"I did!" I replied, also in Japanese.

"Sugoi!" She gestured to the restaurant. *"Do you like tofu?"*

"I do, and it was delicious."

"You liked it!" She looked genuinely happy (and a bit surprised).

I wished my Japanese was good enough to tell her how well the silky tofu complemented the crispy vegetables and how much I enjoyed the contrasting textures, colors, and flavors that transformed the meal into an exciting sensory experience. Instead, I simply repeated, *"It was delicious."*

She noticed my feathered burden. *"You have a hamaya! Where are you from?"*

"America—but I live in Tokyo now."

"How wonderful!" She smiled. *"You must come back again."*

"I will," I promised—and I meant it from the bottom of my heart.

48

THESE MOUNTAINS WON'T CLIMB THEMSELVES

January 15, 2019

The morning after Ōyama, I woke up early but wanted to skip the climb. I wasn't sore or pressed for time. I simply didn't feel like pushing through another 10-kilometer hiking day. I rolled over to go back to sleep, but my inner critic had other plans.

These mountains won't climb themselves, you know.

I got dressed and headed for the city of Hon-Atsugi, where I planned to catch a bus to 284-meter Mount Hakusan (白山), a mountain famous for the many *sakura* trees that cover the slopes in blossoms every spring. Forewarned by the internet that there were no shops or restaurants near the trailhead, I planned to buy lunch before I caught the bus.

The bus stop sat directly in front of a *conbini*, and the bus was already there when I arrived, its doors wide open (but without a driver at the wheel). According to the schedule, I had either nine or 39 minutes before it departed—the schedules changed on different days and in different seasons, and I couldn't tell for sure which one applied.

I ducked into the convenience store and grabbed the first semi-suitable things I saw: a pizza bun, a rice ball, and a can of café latte.

I heard the bus rumble to life as I waited in line to pay the clerk. It seemed to take forever for him to return my change and place my purchases carefully in a plastic bag. I hurried outside as the front door of the bus swung closed. I jumped in the back door just in time, and the bus pulled out before I could even take a seat.

According to the articles I'd read online, the trail up Hakusan began behind a Buddhist temple famous for its statue of Iiyama Kannon, an 11-headed avatar of the goddess of mercy. I left the bus at the proper stop but saw no sign of the temple. In fact, the surrounding trees prevented me from even seeing the mountain I'd come to climb. The GPS on my phone didn't help, but in a flash of inspiration I opened YAMAP, hoping the trail map for Hakusan might help me find my way. Within moments, I knew which way to go.

Hakusan features two hiking trails. The shorter, steeper "men's route" heads directly up the mountain, while the "women's route" involves a longer trail with a less aggressive grade. I hadn't made up my mind which one I planned to take as I walked through the temple heading for the trailhead. In the woods behind the worship hall, a three-meter fence topped with curls of razor wire ran away through the trees as far as I could see in both directions. As far as I knew, it might encircle the entire mountain.

It reminded me of the raptor fences in *Jurassic Park*—and the towering trees, huge ferns, and overcast skies did nothing to disabuse me of the notion that something wild and dangerous might be lurking on the far side of the fence.

Directly ahead of me on the path, a gate led to the "women's trail." A sign indicating the "men's trailhead" sat at the top of a nearby slope. Gender biases aside, I decided to hike the women's trail, primarily because it would be easier if it rained. Another brightly-colored sign requested that I use the gate "with care" and showed a variety of overexcited cartoon forest creatures surging past a horrified hiker (who clearly had not used sufficient care).

Having no desire to release a flood of wildlife—animated or otherwise—I looked around before opening the gate and closed it carefully behind me. To my mild disappointment, not even a moth attempted to escape.

Beyond the fence, a forested trail paralleled a gully bursting with oversized, feathery ferns. The damp, cold air smelled fresh and clean, with an undertone of pine and fallen leaves.

My phone pinged with an incoming text—a friend and fellow author checking in on me from the states. We visited via text as I walked along, but when the trail grew steep I put the phone away and enjoyed the trail.

As I climbed higher, I caught a whiff of wood smoke in the air. My boots crunched over fallen leaves. Overhead, birds sang and flew among the trees. I hadn't seen another person on the trail. Apparently, I had Hakusan completely to myself. Six months before, that would have frightened me, especially given the rising scent of rain. That day, I found it exhilarating. I loved that I lived in the world's sixth-largest city, and yet was still only an hour from unspoiled nature. I loved the towering trees and the clean, cold air. I loved that the stress that once hung over me like a thundercloud had disappeared, leaving me relaxed and free.

A peaceful, solitary hour after leaving the trailhead, I reached the summit of Hakusan, which sat in a wooded glade. Not far from the summit marker, I found the small wooden worship hall of Hakusan Shrine. Beside the hall, a slender, snakelike dragon statue guarded an unmarked hole in the ground about the size of a child's wading pool. Small stone steps led into the hole, which was empty except for a few dead leaves. I looked around for a sign, hoping to learn about the dragon, but found nothing; the statue and its pool would remain a mystery.

Raindrops pattered the trees above my head as I began a steep descent down the far side of Hakusan. The rain remained light, but the smell of dampened leaves soon filled the air. I stopped to slip a bright yellow rain cover over Blue, but had only a sweater for myself. The forecast had not called for rain, so I'd left my own waterproof jacket back in Tokyo.

With Blue protected from the rain, I hiked across a ridge and began the ascent to the summit of neighboring Mount Sakura (桜山) (280 meters). Cherry trees covered the mountain's slopes. In a few short months they would burst into puffy pink and white bloom, but that day their branches were stark and bare, and gave no shelter from the rain. I stopped only long enough for a rain-spattered summit photo before starting my descent. The trail switchbacked down a mountainside strewn with last autumn's fallen cherry leaves, which crunched underfoot like thousands of boxes of stale breakfast cereal. In places, my boots sank ankle-deep in leaves, and I walked slowly to avoid a twisted ankle or a fall. The rain fell harder, and though the path was slippery and often steep, I felt happy and at home on the forest trail.

A little less than an hour after leaving the summit of Mount Sakura, I reached another massive fence. I felt a quiver of nerves as I approached. The rain had flattened my mop of curls (an unexpected gift from chemotherapy) to my skull, and it would be a long, wet hike back over the mountains to the temple if the gate was locked.

I held my breath, but the gate latch yielded beneath my hand. Once more, I exercised the requested caution, though no hordes of wildlife—cartoon or otherwise—rushed the gate as I passed through. I followed my GPS to the nearest bus stop, which I reached exactly two minutes before the bus arrived. I was soaked to the skin by the time I climbed aboard, but I considered that a worthwhile trade for overcoming my fear of hiking in the rain.

49

EXPERIENCED HIKERS ONLY

January 20, 2019

On the morning of Sunday, January 20, I crawled out of bed at the seldom-pleasant (if often beautiful) hour of 5 a.m. and boarded an early train for the 150-kilometer journey to Kawaguchiko, the second-largest lake in the Fuji Five Lakes region.

My train rolled southwest through the dawn. Everyone on board was either a mountain climber, a teenage girl in a sports team uniform, or a suit-wearing businessman nursing a vicious hangover. Only those of us in category 1 looked happy.

I closed my eyes, enjoying the warmth of the under-seat heater on my calves and listening to the muted whispers of the teenaged girls, whose uniformed numbers increased at every station.

I felt entirely content with both my circumstances and my life. In the mountains, I was learning how it felt to live for experiences instead of goals. I still had goals (and I doubted that would ever change), but they now felt more like station markers on a mountain trail—gauges of progress, but neither the purpose of the climb nor its destination.

As I changed trains for the final leg of my journey to Kawaguchiko (Lake Kawaguchi), I noticed a colorful flyer advertising New Year's fireworks at the lake. The final show took place that night, directly in front of the *ryokan* where I was staying. Once again, unplanned circumstances ruled in my favor.

Freezing winds blew in the open doors of the railway car as I waited for the train's departure. The under-seat heater was set to "magma" and roasted the back of my calves even as the rest of me shivered from the draft. Eventually, the doors slid shut and the train rolled out toward Kawaguchiko.

The Fuji Five Lakes region sits in a mountainous area northeast of Mount Fuji and includes Lakes Motosu, Kawaguchi, Saiko, Shoji, and Yamanaka. Lake Kawaguchi is the easiest to access, making it an ideal "base camp" for my initial climbs in the Five Lakes area. My train arrived at 9:30 a.m., but by the time I checked into my *ryokan* and hiked to the base of the nearby Kachi Kachi Ropeway to begin my hike, it was almost ten.

I planned to climb several mountains in the Mitsutoge Range, northeast of the lake. I doubted I had time to reach Mount Kaiun (1,785 meters), the high point of the range, because I had to begin my return hike by 1:30 p.m. if I wanted to be off the trail before dark. However, the route crossed over several other mountains on the way to Mount Kaiun, and I planned to see how many I could reach.

At 10 a.m. on a Sunday morning, the ropeway's tiny gondola was crammed to capacity. I clutched Blue to my chest, crammed in between a pair of women in voluminous winter coats with collars so fuzzy they could have passed for feather boas.

The observation platform at the top of the ropeway was crowded too. Dozens of tourists squeezed against the railing, taking selfies with the bottom half of snowy Fuji. A hood of clouds obscured her upper slopes, but even the sight of her lower half made me smile. I bought a stick of grilled *tanuki dango* (balls of chewy mochi coated in a sweet soy glaze) branded with an image of the grinning tanuki mascot of the Kachi Kachi Ropeway. As I ate, I watched the clouds cascade down Fuji's snowy flanks like snowboarding ghosts. After finishing my snack, I walked beneath the wooden torii that marked the entrance to the hiking trail. A nearby red-lettered sign read: "HIKING COURSE: PREPARED AND EXPERIENCED HIKERS ONLY."

I marched smugly past. After eight months and 54 summits, including massive Fuji, I felt prepared and experienced enough to handle whatever these mountains had in store.

The ropeway had done the initial heavy lifting for my first ascent, and I reached the summit of Mount Tenjo (天上山) (1,140 meters) only 20 minutes after leaving the trailhead. Skeletal trees covered the mountain-top, their wintery branches devoid of leaves. The view from the summit was not as good as the one from the viewing platform, so I took a picture with the marker and began the steep descent toward the ridge that led to neighboring Mount Shimo.

The clouds that rolled down Fuji's slopes soon covered Lake Yamana-ka and the surrounding mountains. Overhead, the sunlight faded as the sky turned gray. The temperature dropped below freezing, making me glad I had brought my heavy gloves and warm knit cap in addition to the down jacket that had served me well since Hokkaido.

Scattered raindrops pattered on my head and pack but stopped as quickly as they began.

Like Mount Tenjo, the forested summit of Mount Shimo (霜山) (1,302 meters) had no view except for obstructed glimpses of Lake Yamanaka through the leafless trees. The wind blew hard across the valley, rattling the barren branches. I took my summit photo and contin-ued on my way.

Forty-five minutes later, as I climbed the steepest, rockiest ridge of the day, a small white speck appeared on my left mitten. A second one followed, and then a third. I looked up. All around me, tiny snowflakes fell from the cloudy sky. They melted almost instantly when they landed, but they filled my heart with joy and made my chest feel warm and tight.

For the first time on my 100 Summits journey, I hoped for *more* precipitation—and I got my wish. By the time I reached the summit of Mount Kenashi (木無山) (1,732 meters) 45 minutes later, those first few tentative flakes had become a dense snowfall, bordering on a blizzard. Snowflakes swirled through the air, heavy enough to obscure the trail ahead. Pure white snow began to coat the ground. Between the heavy snowfall and the time, which was approaching 1 p.m., I decided to end my climb at Mount Kenashi. In decent weather, the summit of Mount Kaiun was only 30 minutes farther up the trail, but I didn't see any reason to push myself, or my luck. I would rather just enjoy this perfect day.

The snowfall gradually slowed, then ceased, as I retraced my steps back up and over Mount Shima and Mount Tenjo. As I rode the ropeway back to the lakeside station, golden rays from the setting sun broke through the clouds.

That evening, after dinner and a bath, I stood beside Lake Yamanaka and watched as brilliant fireworks lit the sky with showers of blue and purple fire. They whistled upward and exploded in glittering, multicolored blooms. Smoke and gunpowder added a slightly acrid tang to the freezing air. As the show came to an end, dozens of pure white rockets filled the sky with sparks the color of falling snow.

A perfect end to another perfect day.

50

BENCHED

January 21, 2019

The morning after the fireworks, I slept until the luxurious hour of 8 a.m., a rarity on a day when I had more than 10 kilometers to hike. After breakfast, I boarded a westbound bus toward Lake Saiko. The sun shone brightly overhead, but the air was only one degree above freezing. The heater on the bus did nothing to assuage the bitter cold, and I shivered in my mittens and down jacket as the bus made its slow circuit around the southern shore of Lake Yamanaka.

More people climbed aboard at every stop, none of them dressed for hiking. When the bus stopped at the trailhead for Mount Haneko (羽根子山) (930 meters), it came as no surprise that I left alone. No reasonable human went for a hike on a day that cold.

I stopped to review the trail map and check the time—9:35 a.m.—before starting up the trail. An enormous crow gazed down at me from a barren ginkgo tree, gave a derisive cry, and flew off toward Lake Yamanaka. Part of me wished I could follow him and settle down to enjoy the view with a cup of coffee instead of spending the next six hours on freezing mountain trails.

I started upward through an ankle-deep carpet of golden ginkgo leaves. Twice, my boots slipped off the wooden logs installed to support the trail, and I almost fell. I regained my balance just in time, but my knees felt weak and wobbly when I considered the consequences of a fall.

At the summit of Mount Haneko, large trees ringed a small plateau. A wooden shrine sat on the near end of the clearing, beside the trail. On the far end of the summit, a pair of benches sat in the shade of the giant trees. They were on the wrong side of the clearing to see Lake Yamanako, and as I walked toward them, I wondered what kind of fool put benches on the side of a mountain that had no view.

Ten steps later, I realized *I* was the fool.

The benches had a perfect, unobstructed view of Mount Fuji's northeast face. The snowy mountain rose against a clear blue sky, looking larger than she had ever seemed before. A line of wispy clouds trailed off her summit like a lace scarf fluttering in the wind.

The view was infinitely better, and more intimate, than the one from the ropeway platform, and not only due to the lack of tourists. The mountain seemed both closer and larger when viewed through the surrounding trees, and the silence made the view feel sacred.

Beyond the summit of Mount Haneko, the trail grew even steeper, though still covered with a deep, often slippery, carpet of fallen leaves. Eventually, the deciduous forest gave way to cultivated pines as I entered one of Japan's many timber groves. I increased my pace as the trail—no longer covered in fallen leaves—grew easier to see and hike.

A faint buzzing sound I'd mistaken for seasonally-challenged cicadas grew louder and more distinct, and I realized that I was hearing chainsaws. Pine branches covered the forest floor. Here and there, an entire tree lay felled. Many of the other trees had fluttering strips of colored tape or pale chalk symbols on their trunks.

Despite the piles of prunings, the forest felt unusually neat and orderly. The trees grew straight and tall, at precise distances from one another (doubtless calculated to ensure their ideal growth).

When I reached the pair of helmeted forest workers, I hurried past. They had their backs to me, and the chainsaws growled loudly. I don't think they even knew that I was there.

I spent another hour climbing upward through the manicured forest along a well-marked trail that eventually joined an unpaved logging road. A few minutes later, the road emerged from the forest, revealing yet another panoramic view of Mount Fuji—if possible, even more impressive than the one from the summit of Mount Haneko.

I stopped and stared. Without the crunching of my boots, the only sounds were the whistling of the wind and the rustling pines.

Thousands of people saw Mount Fuji on that clear, cold winter day, but as I stood alone on that mountain trail, I felt as if she was mine, and mine alone.

Above the overlook, the forest closed in once more, but without the carefully manicured pruning and calculated spacing that marked the trees on the lower slopes. Here the forest grew natural and wild. Branches cluttered the ground, but these looked old—most likely wreckage from the summer's strong typhoons.

As I climbed toward the summit of Mount Danwa (段和山) (1,233 meters), the forest grew so wild and thick that no sunlight reached the ground. The temperature had fallen below freezing, and although my down jacket cut the chill, my lightweight hiking pants were no defense against the cold. I added heat packs to my gloves and slipped one into every pocket of my pants. They didn't help. I hiked faster, hoping to generate some warmth.

My legs went numb. My nose ran from the cold and wind. I didn't care. The mountains felt real, and challenging, and I loved that I could make my body respond to that challenge, mentally and physically.

A few minutes after noon, I arrived on the summit of Mount Ashiwada (足和田山) (1,535 meters), which meant I'd hiked right over the top of Mount Danwa without noticing. I checked YAMAP and, sure enough, the app claimed I had reached the summit of Mount Danwa half an hour earlier.

It felt like cheating to claim a summit I hadn't known I reached. Since I planned to follow the same trail off the mountain, I decided to "count" the summit when I hiked back over it on the descent.

The summit of Mount Ashiwada offered yet another view of Fuji, though only her upper third was visible above the trees. I sat in a clearing beside the summit marker and ate my lunch as I watched the wind blow snow off the top of Fujisan. The sun shone brightly, but did little to alleviate the chill.

On the descent, I paid unusually close attention to the GPS, trying to solve the mystery of the missing mountaintop. Half an hour later, I had my answer: Mount Danwa's summit looked as if a bomb had gone off among the trees. Pines lay scattered across the ground like enormous pick-up sticks. Sticks and branches littered the summit area, and in places the debris was almost knee-deep. Even with the assistance of GPS, it took almost 10 minutes to find the survey marker in the ground at the high point of the mountain. I never found the summit marker—if one existed, it had become a casualty of the summer storms.

An hour and a half—and two more stops to stare at Mount Fuji—later, I returned to the bus stop, arriving six minutes before the bus was due. I wished I could have spent more time at Lake Kawaguchi, exploring the nearby caves, museums, and hiking trails. But, as usual, other mountains called, and I had barely enough time to return to Tokyo, wash my clothes, and pack for a week-long trip to the southernmost major island of Japan.

51

THE KINDNESS OF STRANGERS

January 28, 2019

On January 26, with a blizzard dumping snow on northern Japan, I rode the *shinkansen* to its southernmost terminus on the northern tip of Kyushu—a five-hour journey south from central Tokyo. I hoped to climb at least four mountains during my week in Kyushu but, regardless of the numbers, I planned to enjoy my first experience on Japan's fourth major island.

My *shinkansen* arrived at Hakata Station just after 11 p.m., and although my hotel was technically within walking distance, it was late and I planned to take a taxi.

As I started toward the taxi stand, a silver-haired man in a business suit approached me and asked where I was heading.

"To the taxi," I replied in Japanese.

He switched to English. "Come with me." He wheeled his little suitcase toward the exit.

I followed, touched by his desire to lead me to the taxi stand.

Outside the station, he waved me away from the line of waiting taxis. "My wife is over there, with the car. She will drive you to your hotel!"

In a radical breach of all my childhood training (and every established rule for women traveling alone at night), I decided to follow him.

As we approached the car, a Japanese woman emerged from the driver's seat. She looked a little alarmed to see me, but when her husband explained the situation, she immediately echoed his offer to drive me to my hotel. On the way, we discovered that our sons were exactly the same age. In fact, the man in the business suit was just returning home from a two-week trip to see their son, who was living and working in Las Vegas.

Our conversation made the world seem very small.

After a restful, if brief, night's sleep I checked out of the hotel and stashed my suitcase in a locker at the station before traveling 90 minutes south to Kamado Jinja, a Shintō shrine at the base of Homanzan (宝満山) (829 meters), a popular mountain on the Kyushu Nature Trail.

On the way from Dazaifu Station to the shrine, my taxi driver pointed out the cap of snow that frosted the top of Homanzan, several centimeters of which had fallen the night before. The fact that I had traveled 1,100 kilometers south to avoid a blizzard, only to end up climbing in the snow, felt both absurd and entertaining.

It would have been funnier, however, if I hadn't left my ice spikes in my suitcase at the station.

Sparkling ice and clumps of snow coated the trees at Kamado Shrine. More snow covered the yard beside the path, where groups of children were building knee-high *yuki daruma* (snowmen) with sticks for arms and tiny pebble eyes.

Wisps of mist rose from the roof of the worship hall like spirits rising into the morning sun. The trees dropped clumps of melting snow, which thumped as they struck the ground. As I entered the forested trailhead, a fist-sized lump of snow fell from a tree and splattered on the head and shoulders of a hiker just ahead of me on the trail.

Moments later, another one hit me. A rivulet of icy water ran down my back beneath my light wool shirt. After that, I kept an eye on the trees as well as the trail.

The route led steadily upward through a tall, dense forest of pines and leggy maples. Most of the snow had melted off the path, but drifts remained beneath the trees.

Higher up, the earthen path gave way to flights of long stone steps and then to rocks piled stair-step fashion up the mountainside. Rays of sunlight pierced the trees and dotted the trail with golden light. The rising sun continued to melt the snow in the canopy, filling the forest with constant dripping punctuated by periodic thumps.

Halfway to the summit, I stopped at a small rest area for a snack. An older Japanese man arrived a couple of minutes later, and offered me a small, soft roll filled with adzuki paste. The hiker introduced himself as

Hide, and we struck up a conversation in a mixture of English, Japanese, and charades.

When I started up the trail again, Hide-san went, too. We chatted as we climbed up the increasingly snowy trail. It took me almost half an hour to realize that Hide-san—whose children were my age—had appointed himself as my guide and guardian for the remainder of the climb. He pointed out the important sights and told me about the various landmarks visible from the overlooks on the trail.

We reached the snowy summit at 1 p.m. to find a dozen other hikers (and two Shiba Inu dogs) already resting and eating lunch on the small plateau. Since I planned to continue to the summit of neighboring Mount Buccho (仏頂山) (869 meters), I thanked Hide-san for guiding me this far and started off.

He followed, looking as excited as a kid on Christmas morning. *"Bucchosan? Let's go!"*

I felt guilty about dragging this kind, retired man up another mountain, but he was already pointing out the two trails down the back of Hakusan. The first involved a 30-meter vertical descent down a set of massive iron chains reminiscent of the ones on Ishizuchi. Given the snow—and my desire not to plummet to my death—I opted for the second route.

As it turned out, that "trail" was not much better. I followed Hide-san down four aluminum ladders that were secured to the snowy cliff with climbing ropes. Hide-san slid down the ladders with the speed and confidence of experience. (I later learned that he climbed these mountains twice a week "to get some exercise.") I descended much more slowly, trying not to think about whether I could get back up when we returned.

From the base of the ladders, Hide-san led me along a snowy trail through the trees. Unlike the more-traveled trail up Hakusan, this path was completely buried under several feet of snow. Hide-san seemed as surefooted as a *kamoshika* (Japanese mountain serow) in the snow. I followed tentatively, wishing for my crampons.

A minute later, my feet slipped out from under me. Both my legs shot into the air and I fell backward, feet above my head. I landed on my tailbone, which in turn landed directly on a pointed rock that stuck up through the snow.

A painful shock went through my legs. For an instant, I couldn't feel anything below my waist. As I registered that horror, sensation returned. Sharp pains stabbed through my hips, down both my legs, and up my spine all the way to my shoulders. I could barely breathe. I wasn't sure I could even move my legs.

Hide-san bent over me, concerned. *"Are you okay?"*

I drew a breath and forced a smile. *"It's okay,"* I said. *"I'm fine."*

I didn't want to let him know how much it hurt. He had been so kind, and he would feel responsible for my injury. Instead, I willed myself to my feet. Waves of pain coursed down my legs. My tailbone hurt so badly that I knew I had bruised it—if not worse.

"I am okay," I repeated, *"but I think I should go down, and not to Bucchosan."*

The thought of re-ascending those metal ladders made me want to cry. I wasn't certain I could do it.

Instead of reversing course, though, Hide-san led me farther down the snowy path. I hid my pain behind a pretense of moving slowly on the snow. As we walked, Hide-san explained that the path we were on made a descending loop and rejoined the main trail halfway back to the trailhead on Homanzan. I wouldn't have to climb back up the ladders after all.

I just hoped I had the strength to make it down.

A hundred yards farther along the snowy trail, which mercifully became both flat and slushy enough for my boots to get reasonable traction, Hide-san paused beside a trail sign.

"We are here." He indicated our location and then touched a spot nearby. *"Bucchosan is fifteen minutes more."*

Each step brought a wave of pain, but I didn't think I had any serious injuries. It also occurred to me that if I toughed it out and reached another summit, I would add another mountain to my total without having to make another full-day climb.

"Okay, let's go."

I followed Hide-san along a steep, snowy trail to the summit of Bucchosan. Sunlight filtered through the trees, making patches of the snow glow brilliant white. Occasional drips of water spattered my head and sent trickles down my back. At the top, Hide-san took my picture with the summit marker. Looking at the photo now, I see the pain behind my frozen smile.

I struggled to keep up with Hide-san on the descent, and not only because of my injury. Forget "when I reached his age"—I wished I had his strength and agility *now*.

A kilometer from the trailhead, the route cut through a tiny parking lot at the end of a service road. Hide-san gestured to a white, four-door sedan. *"That's mine. I'll drive you to the station."*

I tried to refuse, but Hide-san persisted. *"It's no problem! Today is my wife's birthday. I have to buy a present at a shop right by the station."*

He unlocked the rear passenger door and held it open.

For the second time in as many days, I got into the back of a stranger's car.

And once again, I lived to tell the tale.

When Hide-san left me at the station, I watched him drive away with a pang of sorrow. Like so many other wonderful people I had met on this odyssey, I would not see or hear from him again, except in memories.

By the time I retrieved my suitcase in Hakata and boarded a southbound train for Kumamoto, I had accepted that my plan to climb Mount Aso was off the table.

With my own ass so painful, there was no way I could climb.

52

SEVEN LUCKY GODS
January 30, 3019

After a rest day in Kumamoto, I dragged my aching butt to Beppu, a famous *onsen* resort on the northern coast of Kyushu, in Oita Prefecture. As a special treat, I'd booked a suite at a beachfront *ryokan* that featured private *onsen* tubs on balconies overlooking the Seto Inland Sea. It proved a fortuitous splurge. The steaming volcanic water soothed my injured tailbone, though the pain returned in force when I left the tub.

The following morning, my tailbone ached so badly that I wasn't certain I could climb. My original plan called for a full-day climb of Mount Tsurumi (鶴見岳) (1,375 meters) and neighboring Mount Yufu. Due to my injury, that now seemed like a bad idea. Still, I was going to hurt no matter what I did (or didn't do), so I packed my snow spikes into Blue and headed for the bus to the Beppu Ropeway.

As I rode the bus across Beppu, I noticed columns of volcanic steam rising up from the ground on almost every street. The city is home to more than 1,000 volcanic springs, including seven celebrated "hells" where water emerges from the ground in vibrant colors, too hot for bathing but so cool to look at that the "Hells of Beppu" are a major tourist draw. (Despite my aching tailbone, I had toured them myself the day before.)

After an excruciating hour in which I noticed every painful bump in the road, I disembarked at the lower ropeway station. Mount Tsurumi rose before me, tall and brown, without a drift of snow. The sight made me feel foolish about carrying the snow spikes. They added a pound of weight to my pack, and I felt every ounce of it on my aching backside as I climbed the steps to the ticket counter.

The 1,816-meter Beppu Ropeway is the longest ropeway on Kyushu. It has a total elevation gain of 800 meters, and each of its two enormous gondolas holds up to 100 passengers; the day I visited, there were 12 of us aboard.

Halfway up the mountain, I saw patchy drifts of snow beneath the trees. As we approached the upper station, the gondola crested a ridge, and the summit of Mount Tsurumi came into view.

The upper slopes wore a dazzling coat of fresh, white snow—and I suddenly felt much better about carrying my spikes.

At the upper station, I stepped outside into a freezing wind that made me glad I'd also packed my hat and gloves. I squinted in the brilliant glare of sun on the glittering snow until I remembered I had brought sunglasses too.

The upper slopes of Mount Tsurumi feature a unique pilgrimage route. A hiking trail winds around the mountain's upper reaches, passing small shrines dedicated to the Gods of Fortune, also known as the Seven Lucky Gods (七福神). Many Japanese people make special pilgrimages to visit these deities during the New Year's season, to pray for good fortune in the year to come. Since the hike to the summit was relatively short, even in the snow, I decided to climb up via the normal route and descend by the circuitous pilgrim trail that passed by each of the special shrines.

All the other tourists on the gondola were wearing jeans and sneakers, which proved woefully insufficient for the biting wind and slippery snow. They managed well enough on the wide, flat area around the ropeway station, but the path to the summit was steep, and the snow grew deeper as the climb progressed. Narrow footprints marked the trail, but their numbers revealed that very few people had made the climb since the last snow fell.

Five minutes up the slope from the trailhead, I stopped at a bench to strap the snow spikes on my boots. Nearby, a pair of teenaged girls clung to the metal handrail, giggling and shrieking as their sneakers slipped over the icy ground. They made it only five more meters up the path before abandoning the climb and turning back.

As I stood up, I felt the metal snow spikes bite securely through the upper ice into the snow beneath. I felt better balanced and more secure than I did on packed earth trails.

Sunlight sparkled on the snow and transformed the icy trees to glittering crystal.

Once again, I felt as if I had the trail entirely to myself. I thought back to my snowy climbs in Tōhōku eight months before. Back then, I would have panicked at the steepness of the slope on Mount Tsurumi. I would have worried about my ice spikes slipping and whether I had time to reach the summit and return before the final gondola descended. (I wouldn't have dared to try for the shrines at all.) Since then, I had learned that worry wasted time and energy that I would rather spend on curiosity and happiness.

From the point where I put on my spikes, it took almost an hour to reach the mountaintop. An enormous radio tower on the summit marred the view but not my mood.

A trail led down the back of the summit toward Mount Yufu, whose snowy slopes looked alluringly close. Despite my plan to take it easy, I considered trying the traverse. The snow spikes made me feel secure and the pain in my tailbone, though constant, didn't seem so bad. I started across the summit to take a closer look at the Yufu trail. Halfway there, I slipped on a patch of ice. I managed to regain my balance, but the effort sent stabbing pains through my back and legs.

Point made. No Yufu today.

I retreated from the summit and followed the pilgrim trail through groves of icy trees and clearings covered in virgin snow. I took my time, enjoying the views and the crisp, cold air.

The shrines near the top of the mountain showed no signs of recent visitors, but lower down, offerings of coins and tiny *yuki daruma* sat around the bases of the statues that depicted the seven lucky gods. I saw people, too, including a few who had come prepared for the snow on the upper slopes.

Back at the *ryokan*, I spent a final evening in the balcony tub, doing my best impression of a crab in a peaceful tide pool.

The next morning, I bid farewell to Kyūshū. I hadn't reached as many summits as I hoped for in Japan's far south, but I didn't care. I had fallen in love with hiking in the snow (even if it didn't always love me back) and hoped I would have the chance to see even more in the mountains close to Tokyo.

STATION 8: *SHODŌ*
MOUNTAIN TOTAL: 63

Between my climbs, I began to pursue another lifelong dream: studying *shodō* (traditional Japanese calligraphy) with a master in Tokyo. The history of *shodō* as an art form goes back centuries, and it remains (along with poetry and flower arranging) a highly traditional and respected practice. I had long admired the flowing characters on Japanese scrolls and wished that I could write them too.

When I arrived at my first lesson, my *sensei* (teacher) looked at me and gently explained, "There are no left-handed Japanese calligraphers."

I got the point. I—a lifelong southpaw—would have to learn this complex art right-handed. That seemed impossible, but I chose to embrace the challenge as yet another way to reinvent myself.

Shodō is a difficult but meditative art, and every time I took the brush in hand, the rest of the world disappeared. The level of concentration required left no room for worrying or fretting, and every time I practiced, the calm and peace *shodō* inspired remained with me longer than it had before.

53

PEEPING FUJI

February 10, 2019

After my calligraphy class on Saturday, February 9, I traded my brushes and inks for Blue and traveled two hours west to the city of Hachio-ji. Snow was falling through the midnight sky as I left the train, though the forecast promised it would clear by morning.

Sure enough, I woke to see Mount Fuji rising against a cloudless sky. An excellent omen, especially since I hadn't even known Mount Fuji was visible from Hachioji, let alone the hotel where I spent the night. I hopped a train to nearby Hinode, a town on the edge of Chichibu Tama Kai National Park. From there, I'd hoped to catch a bus to the trailhead near Shiraiwa Falls (白岩滝), but the posted schedule (which did not match the one online) said the first bus to the trailhead didn't leave for another hour.

I hadn't skipped the free buffet at my hotel to wait an hour for a bus.

There were taxis waiting at the stand across the street, and my taxi driver didn't bat an eye when I asked to go to Shiraito Falls, so I settled back for what I thought would be a 15-minute ride. However, my calcula-tions omitted a critical detail. The closest *bus stop*, also called "Shiraito Falls," was a kilometer from the waterfall. However, there was also a narrow, unpaved road that coiled past the bus stop and through the forest all the way to the trailhead at the falls.

I had asked to go to Shiraiwa Falls, and my intrepid taxi driver took me literally.

Twenty-five minutes later—the final ten a wild ride through the icy woods that would have done a theme park proud—we pulled into the snowy clearing at the trailhead. I thanked the taxi driver, whose decision saved me almost an hour's hiking time, and he wished me a successful climb before he drove away.

The trailhead sat in a narrow canyon within earshot of the waterfall. The sun had not yet crested the eastern ridge, and the previous night's snowfall covered the ground in a layer of untouched powder several centimeters deep.

My breath plumed out in front of me as I climbed the wooden stairs to the lower falls.

Tarukubo Stream flows down the side of Mount Aso (麻生山) (794 meters), creating 18 waterfalls along the way. The final three, which are also the largest, are collectively known as Shiraiwa Falls. For centuries, people have visited these waterfalls to pray for rain, and climbed neighboring Mount Hinode (日の出山) (902 meters) to pray for good fortune and watch the sunrise on the first day of the year. I was too late for New Year's, as well as dawn, but I looked forward to seeing waterfalls in snow.

Two sets of footprints marked the trail ahead of me—one large, the other small. At a split in the trail where a bridge led to the lowest tier of Shiraiwa Falls, the footprints continued up the mountain, but I left the hiking trail and headed for the falls.

On the far side of the bridge, a viewing platform offered an unimpeded view of the largest waterfall, which tumbled 15 meters down a rocky cliff and splashed into a snow-rimmed pool below. Dark trails of ice showed where the falls would spread across the rocks like a fan when both the stream and the temperature were higher.

A breeze blew snowflakes off the trees. They swirled around me, mimicking a snowfall. I listened to the chattering of the falls and the rustling trees, the only sounds in a world that seemed entirely unspoiled.

I retraced my steps across the bridge and up a tree-lined switchback to the next tier of the falls, a narrow bridal veil that fell through a narrow gap in the snowy rocks. At its base, the water was so clear that I could count the rounded tawny stones that covered the bottom of the pool.

The sun appeared above the ridge, transforming the snow on the west side of the canyon from pale blue to sparkling white.

As I continued upward on the snowy trail, I thought about how radically my life had changed since my cancer diagnosis. Before cancer, I had focused on the things I could not do and why I could not do them. I did not believe an adventurous life was possible for me.

But once I made the decision to reject those old, false narratives, this year had exceeded my wildest expectations. I did not truly believe in magic, and yet that was the word that sprang to mind each time I thought about the many serendipitous events that shone like diamonds in my memories of the previous nine months.

Best of all, it didn't have to end. I had seen what life *could* be, and I chose to grasp it.

Above the waterfalls I passed a Japanese couple and their Shiba Inu heading down the mountain. Ten minutes later I reached their high point on the trail; after that, my footprints were the only ones that marked the snow.

Just after 10 a.m., I reached an overlook at a snowy pass. The mountains of Chichibu Tama Kai National Park rolled away to the south like white-capped swells on a deep green ocean. The tracks of rabbits crossed the path, along with those of hikers who began the ascent along a different route.

Above the pass, the pine trees wore a dusting of snow that reminded me of a winter scene on a Christmas card. The trail grew noticeably steeper, and the snow covered my boots with every step. I considered retrieving the snow spikes from my pack, but didn't want to sit in the snow while I put them on, and since I saw no other option I continued in the boots alone.

Eventually, the trail grew so steep that I could touch the ground in front of me without bending over. I did not let myself look down and, though I mentally marked the trail as a "tricksy bit," I didn't fret. By then, I knew that worry sapped my energy, broke my focus, and created a higher risk of a dangerous fall.

Eventually, I emerged atop a narrow ridge where an easy trail led upward to the summit of Mount Aso. There, I sat on the summit bench and ate an enormous cookie, enjoying the view of the nearby mountains. My tailbone injury—now fully healed—had kept me off the summit of Mount Aso in Kyushu, but I'd now climbed another Aso in its place (a smaller and less famous one, but when life gives you lemons, a little glass of lemonade is better than none at all).

I wondered whether the baker who made my cookie ever thought about who might eat it or the places the cookies might end up. That, in turn, made me consider how many people my life touched in ways that I had never thought about. As I started down the trail toward Mount Hinode, I resolved to make a positive impact on other people's lives whenever possible.

As I started down the trail, I checked YAMAP and realized the trail to Mount Hinode continued along the ridge, which meant I wouldn't have to descend the steep slope after all. Had I worried about it earlier, it truly would have been a waste of time.

Another hour of snowy hiking, almost half of it on thigh- and soul-crushing "stairs" of earth and wood, brought me to the summit of Mount Hinode. While taking pictures of the view, I noticed the topmost sliver of Mount Fuji peeking above a distant ridgeline, instantly recognizable despite the haze and partial view. She reminded me of the pigeon on Mount Yōtei—but this time, I got to keep my pants on.

I descended along a trail that led to Tsuru-Tsuru Onsen, a famous hot spring bath near the base of Mount Hinode. A soak in the steaming water chased the cold from my core and left me feeling relaxed, renewed, and ready for the two-hour train ride home.

54

YAMANAKA-KO
February 12–13, 2019

The following week, just hours before I was due to leave for a series of climbs near Lake Yamanaka in the Fuji Five Lakes region, I felt a lump beneath the scar where my left breast used to be. I wanted to see Dr. K. as soon as possible, but the receptionists at the hospital where she worked spoke only Japanese, so I sent an email to an NGO in Tokyo that helps with scheduling medical appointments and explained my need. Even if the NGO moved quickly, I doubted my doctor would have an appointment available in the next three days (the planned duration of my climbing trip), so I decided to leave town as scheduled. At best, the mountains would distract me while I waited to hear about the lump. At worst, I would get closer to my 100 Summits goal before the time for hard decisions came.

Yamanaka-ko (Lake Yamanaka) sits at the base of Mount Fuji's northeast slope. Other mountains also rise around the lake, and I had my eye on a lengthy traverse that, if successful, would boost my summit count by a whopping nine peaks in a single day.

On the morning of February 13, I caught the earliest possible bus to the east end of Lake Yamanaka. The temperature hovered just below freezing. I was hoping to climb in snow again, and my spirits soared as tiny flakes began to spiral downward through the air.

My hike began at the base of Mount Ishiwari (石割山) (1,412 meters), where I passed beneath a red metal torii hung with sacred Shintō ropes called *shimenawa*. The heavy, twisted ropes are used for spiritual protection and to further emphasize the sacred nature of the trail, which began with a climb up a long flight of stairs (I lost count when the number passed 100). Falling snow frosted the leaves of the waist-high *sasa* beside the trail. Above the stairs, an earth-and-gravel path wound up the mountainside to Ishiwari Shrine, the holy site for which the peak is named.

A massive, 15-meter boulder stood in a clearing next to a wooden altar. The largest *shimenawa* I had ever seen dangled across the stone like a giant necklace, half a meter thick. Hemp tassels hung from the rope like giant pendants.

The boulder had a lengthwise split with just enough space for a person to walk through it. According to Shintō belief, walking through the gap in the stone two times in a row will give good fortune, and the water that drips from the boulder after a rain can cure diseases of the eyes and skin. I wondered whether anything would help the lump in my chest, and what its unwanted presence meant for my future. Thick ice made the steps to the crack in the rock impassable, preventing me from putting its healing powers to the test, so I continued up the trail.

The snow fell heavier than before, in granules so fine and hard that they made a sound like bacon frying. I stopped and listened, previously unaware that snow could *sizzle* as it fell.

I had not seen another hiker on the bus or on the trail. I was entirely alone in a peaceful world of dense white clouds and falling snow.

Above the shrine, the path grew steep. In places where the trail made short but steep ascents up rocky faces, lengths of climbing rope had been installed on metal posts or tied to trees to serve as climbing aids.

Two hours of steady climbing brought me to Mount Ishiwari's summit. A sign on the mountaintop displayed a photograph of the view from the mountain on a sunny day, with snowcapped Fuji rising on the far side of a deep blue lake. The day I climbed, the world beyond the peak held only colorless clouds and swirling snow. Biting winds blew hard enough to bend the trees, and though my jacket kept me warm when moving, it was far too cold to stop for lunch, so I took a summit photo and started my descent down a frozen gully on the far side of the summit.

Waist-high lines of climbing rope acted as guidelines for the steep descent, but even with their aid I slipped and almost fell. My heart hammered in my chest, and I did not relax until I reached the place where the fixed ropes ended and the trail flattened out.

A pleasant walk down a forested ridge through a tunnel of leafless maple trees led to another steep ascent which ended on the summit of Mount Ichinosunanosawanoatama (1,318 meters), the mountain with the longest name of any peak on my 100 Summits list. (It was also the only mountain whose name I never saw written in Japanese script—even on trail maps, its name is written in English letters, known as Romaji).

With snow still falling and the wind still blowing hard, I hurried down the far side of the mountain and along another ridge, through a tunnel of barren trees whose branches stretched like skeletal fingers toward the sky. I expected the trail to rise again before the summit of Mount Hirao (平尾山) (1,290 meters), so it surprised me when the summit marker appeared through the mist. The wooden marker stood alone in a clearing ringed by chest-high golden grass that made the air smell faintly sweet, as if the ghosts of summer lingered on the mountaintop.

On the far side of Mount Hirao, the trail descended along a flight of earthen steps reinforced with wooden logs. Three-toed footprints on the steps announced the recent passage of a crow, who apparently trusted feet more than wings in the cold, thin air.

At the base of the steps, the trail flattened out along a narrow ridge that sloped slightly downward before altering its course and climbing steeply to the summit of Mount Okubo (大窪山) (1,267 meters). The trail and I continued on to Mount Imo (イモ山) (1,280 meters), and Mount Ohira (大平山) (1,296 meters), both of which looked much the same as the mountains that came before them—a descent from the summit, followed by a hike along a misty, forested ridge that descended slightly before renewing its ascent to the next cloudy mountaintop. I began to feel like an ant walking up and down the teeth of a giant saw.

Through it all, snow fell, wind blew, and the trees reached barren limbs toward the cloudy sky as if praying for the return of spring.

By the time I reached the top of Mount Ohira, I was ready for a little warmth myself. I was drawn to the stark beauty of the snowy trail, but the unrelenting cold crept through my clothes, my nose was running, and my stomach growled.

An octagonal gazebo stood on the summit of Mount Ohira, and its wooden roof offered a little shelter from the driving wind and snow. I hunched on a bench and devoured a half-frozen ham and cheese croissant and a bag of trail mix so quickly that I barely tasted them. As I finished eating, another hiker appeared through the fog and swirling snow. She was alone and looked as surprised as I was to see another hiker on the mountain.

After we greeted one another in Japanese, I added, *"It's quite snowy."*

"And cold." She blinked against the snow. *"The forecast said it would be sunny, but I think the weather report was wrong."*

We left the summit separately but passed one another several times on the way to Mount Iimori (飯盛山) (1,191 meters) as one or the other of us stopped for photographs. Around us, woodpeckers flitted through the trees and hammered on the trunks in search of insects.

The snow stopped as I passed Iimori and continued toward Mount Nagaike (長池山) (1,178 meters). The mist receded, revealing Lake Yamanaka far below. The lake looked gray and cold, and the line of storefronts on the western shore—all closed for the winter—was dark and uninviting. I looked for Fuji, but the clouds still hung too low to see her.

After leaving Mount Nagaike, I hiked for another hour along a saw-toothed ridge that rose and fell, at times quite steeply, as the sun attempted to burn through the heavy clouds. The first pale golden rays appeared as I reached the summit plateau of Odeyama (大池山) (1,102 meters), where the trail split. One branch led down to a bus stop on the shore of Lake Yamanaka, while the other crossed the plateau to Hotel Mount Fuji, where I had reservations for the next two nights.

The hotel had a reputation for delicious food, spectacular views, and an outdoor *onsen* with a view of Mount Fuji (when she wanted to be seen). I walked into the marble lobby, feeling out of place in my grubby, mud-stained clothes. At the registration desk, my embarrassment increased. I had finished the hike significantly faster than expected and arrived twenty minutes before the check-in time.

The clerk suggested I wait in the coffee shop. A cup of coffee sounded excellent (better still, if it came with cake), so I took the elevator two floors down to the restaurant level.

My embarrassment deepened into mortification as I followed the server across another marble floor to a window table next to a pair of women in expensive business suits. As I lowered my eyes to avoid their gaze, I saw the crumbs of dark-brown earth my boots had shed across the polished floor.

To their credit, the restaurant staff behaved as if they didn't notice my grime-streaked face and clothes. My coffee arrived with lightning speed, and the first taste of that rich, dark brew—among the best espressos of my life—made me forget both my humiliation and the lingering cold from the windy hike.

Best of all . . . the coffee came with cake.

55

WHERE THERE IS NO TRAIL

February 14, 2019

The morning after my nine-summit climb, I woke to another cloudy day.

It didn't bother me that I was spending Valentine's Day alone. Michael and I had never gone in for the hearts-and-flowers holiday. In fact, for years we celebrated Cheap Chocolate Day (February 15) instead.

My distaste for manufactured holidays aside, Valentine's did seem an appropriate day to dedicate a climb to my beloved grandmother Margaret, known to everyone as Peggy, who died of breast cancer 35 years before. The terrifying lump in my chest added fuel to my determination to make the climb—my 75th—in Mama Peggy's honor.

I had chosen Mount Teppouginoatama (鉄砲木ノ頭) (1,291 meters), on the south side of Lake Yamanaka, because in clear weather the mountaintop supposedly offered an unobstructed view of Mount Fuji from base to summit. The forecast didn't call for snow but also held no hope for sun, so my chance of seeing Fuji wasn't good.

Both Teppouginoatama and neighboring Mount Mikuni (三国山) (1,343 meters) were visible from my hotel room, and they looked more brown than white. I hadn't needed snow spikes on the trail the day before, so I made a judgment call and left them in my room.

I waited in the cold beside the bus stop as the scheduled departure time came and went with no sign of the bus. Minutes ticked by, and I wondered whether Valentine's was a transit holiday in Japan. The trailhead was 20 minutes away by bus—too far to walk—and I hadn't seen a taxi since arriving at Yamanaka-ko two days before.

As I prepared to scrap the hike, the bus appeared—a shocking (and extremely unusual) 20 minutes late. As I climbed aboard, the driver apologized profusely. Apparently the money for the on-board change machines had not arrived at the bus depot on time, so the buses were delayed.

I was just thrilled that he showed up at all.

At 11 a.m., I disembarked at the trailhead, tied one of Mama Peggy's large silk scarves around my neck, and hiked through the forest toward a scenic overlook called Panorama Dai. As I hiked, it occurred to me that I was not only wearing Peggy's scarf but using the hiking poles my mother had used to climb Mount Fuji. She had left them in Japan, and I started using them several climbs before, when the hinge on one of my poles jammed.

I arrived at Panorama Dai to find the overlook deserted. Pale clouds concealed the upper half of Fuji. I took a few pictures and then continued up the side of Mount Teppouginoatama. Crystalline "flowers" made of ice bloomed all along the black earth trail where water had extruded from the soil as it froze. On either side, enormous fields of pampas grass grew higher than my head. Now dormant, it had taken on the pale hue of straw.

Though steep, the frozen earth offered good purchase underfoot, and the trail was almost free of rocks. I had nothing to fear from a fall but getting dirty.

When I crested the final rise and saw the summit marker, I turned around and looked across the lake. In the time it had taken me to climb from Panorama Dai, the clouds had lifted . . . and there was Fuji.

I burst out sobbing, as instantly and uncontrollably as I had on Mount Tokachi. I could feel Mama Peggy's presence, and I knew she was there with me. Mom had climbed with me on Fuji, and now her climbing poles had helped me reach summit number 75.

Just then, a dozen crows flew out of the trees on the far side of the summit. They called to one another—and, I felt, to me—as they circled overhead.

I still had 25 mountains left to climb, but in that moment, I felt that I had already reached my goal. I no longer wasted my energy, or my life, worrying over things I could not control. I had learned to accept myself, and to find fulfillment in the journey, instead of racing headlong for the goal.

I thought of the unknown lump in my chest. I didn't want to learn these truths only for cancer to return and kill me.

Isn't that how these stories always end? The hero dies?

"This isn't a story," I said aloud, "and the hero does not die today."

As I took my photo with the summit marker, I noticed the name on the post didn't match the one on my trail guide or YAMAP. They all agreed that the mountain's height was 1,291 meters, and the GPS said I was on the proper mountain, but while YAMAP and the trail guide referred to the peak as Teppouginoatama, the summit sign read "Mount Myōjin (明神山)." The mountain apparently had two names, likely because the first one was so difficult to read and to pronounce.

When my tears had dried and I had taken at least two dozen pictures of Mount Fuji, I tore myself away from the view and started the descent toward Mount Mikuni. On the way, I checked my email and learned that the NGO had scheduled an appointment with my Japanese oncologist on February 22. I felt queasy about waiting another week, because the lump was growing.

I filed the lump under "things I cannot change today" and continued down the dark earth trail through a forest of cherry trees that grew at the base of Mount Myōjin. The cherry orchard ended at a two-lane asphalt road. On the opposite side, the trail continued up the side of Mount Mikuni.

Which was also where the snow began.

When I looked at the mountains from my hotel room that morning, I forgot to consider that while the trail up Teppouginoatama/Myōjin ascended the mountain's southern slope—the one that faced the hotel—I planned to climb the north side of Mount Mikuni, which I could not actually see until I reached the trailhead. I also failed to take into account (although I knew) that the north face of a mountain receives the least sunshine and, thus, has the most accumulated snow.

The snow at the base of Mount Mikuni measured almost half a meter deep and obscured the path completely. Pink tape flashes on the trees gave me a rough idea where to climb, but the slippery snow presented a complication, since I'd left my snow spikes in my room at the hotel.

So much for experienced hikers only.

"You shut up," I said aloud.

Spikes would have helped, but the snow looked fresh and my boots had decent traction if a route was not too icy. As for the fact that there was no obvious trail . . . I chose to see that as the chance to make my own.

I had a GPS. I had YAMAP. And nine months of climbing mountains had given me the highly technical knowledge required to find the top of Mount Mikuni: *Go up until the mountain doesn't go up any more. When you find that point, you're probably on top.*

More than once, I lost track of the pink tape flashes that marked the route, but when that happened I followed the path of least resistance through the trees, continuing upward until I found a flash and returned to the "real" trail. I slipped on the snow a couple of times but didn't fall.

Forty-five minutes later, I crested a rise and found the summit marker. No words could express my overwhelming joy. I had blazed a trail up a mountain through snowy woods, entirely alone, and I enjoyed every minute of the climb.

For those few, precious minutes, I even forgot about the lump.

As I started my descent, I saw a set of tracks in the snow and followed them. The route was steep, and I felt safer following someone else's trail back down. I descended quickly, hopping down the path with confidence as I enjoyed the views and the cool, crisp air.

It took me only twenty minutes to reach the bottom of the mountain—less than half the time it took me to ascend. I felt grateful to the unknown hiker whose prints had been so easy for me to follow.

As I looked at the tracks more closely, it slowly dawned on me that they were pointing up the slope, not down—and that the tracks I had been following *were my own.*

It had snowed the night before. There were no other trails.

Without knowing it, I had trusted *myself* enough to follow the path I blazed back down the mountain at full speed and without fear.

A valuable lesson I planned to use far past the end of Mount Mikuni's snowy slopes: where there is no trail, it's time to trust yourself and make your own.

56

COCK-A-DOODLE DELICIOUS

February 22–23, 2019

The lump on my chest did not go away before my appointment with Dr. K. on February 22. After an examination and an ultrasound, she said she did not think the lump was cancer, but she couldn't tell me what it was with certainty. If it didn't go away before my April checkup, she would perform a biopsy; until then, she wanted me to track its progress and return if anything seemed unusual.

Everything about it seemed unusual already.

Still, I trusted her opinion, and I tried to trust her diagnosis too. Relieved that she didn't think the lump was cancerous, I headed out to climb again—this time, in Gunma Prefecture, where I planned to ascend another "Hometown Fuji."

The "Hometown Fujis" are a group of more than 400 Japanese volcanoes, each of which has a perfect (or nearly perfect) conical shape. Although they also have unique, individual names, these mountains acquire the nickname "[Something]-Fuji" in recognition of their resemblance to Japan's most famous peak. I had already climbed Ezo-Fuji (Mount Yōtei) and Sannuki-Fuji (Mount Iino), along with several others, and was heading for "Haruna-Fuji," also known as Mount Haruna (榛名山) (1,449 meters), a dormant volcano on the shore of Lake Haruna, whose ropeway guaranteed access to the summit all year long.

Most people visit Mount Haruna in the summer, when the lake draws droves of fishermen, or in midwinter, for its famous *onsen* and the chance to drive a go-kart on the surface of the frozen lake. I hoped the February chill would keep the crowds away and planned to climb both Mount Haruna and at least one other nearby peak in a single day.

Events began to conspire against me at Tokyo Station, where I learned that every reserved seat on the morning *shinkansen* to Takasaki City was already sold. I bought a non-reserved ticket and went to the platform, where the lines for non-reserved cars were more than 50 people long. Most of the travelers wore heavy winter gear and carried snowboards (here and there, somebody carried skis).

When the double-decker *shinkansen* pulled in, I started grinning. I'd forgotten double-decker bullet trains existed, and that winter trains to popular ski areas used two-story cars to accommodate the crowds. I also felt better about the chance to find a seat, despite the line.

The doors swung open and the line of people filed aboard. Most went upstairs for the better view, but I hurried down to the lower level, where I snagged a window seat and settled in for the 60-minute, 125-kilometer ride.

The train arrived in Takasaki just in time for me to catch the first bus to Lake Haruna. I climbed aboard and fell asleep as soon as the 90-minute trip began. Before beginning the 100 Summits project, I wondered how Japanese people managed to fall asleep on trains and buses, but it was a mystery no longer. Without anxiety running my mind at a fever pitch, I found it easy to let purring engines soothe me into sleep. Although I didn't understand exactly how or why, I also always managed to wake up precisely when I needed to in order not to miss my stop and overshoot my destination.

When the bus arrived at Lake Haruna just before 11 a.m., I stepped out into the coldest weather I had yet experienced in Japan. Ferocious winds blew off the lake, so cold they took my breath away. The sun shone, but it seemed to provide no heat. My nose hairs prickled each time I inhaled, and the icy wind blew through my pants as if I wasn't wearing pants at all.

The bus to the ropeway didn't leave for over half an hour, but I had no intention of waiting in the cold, so I started walking. Not that it helped. My hands went numb inside my gloves. My nose began to run, and my head soon ached from the cold that leached into my ears through my knitted hat and earmuffs.

On the lake, the ice had begun to melt. A flock of ducks stood on the ice and paddled in the leads between the floes. I knew their feathers kept them warm but wondered why their webbed feet didn't freeze.

I could see how beautiful the lake would be when spring had filled the trees with bright green leaves and revived the dormant grass. Part of me wished I had waited to come and climb, but that ship had sailed.

When I reached Haruna Ropeway, I had to remove my gloves to open my wallet and buy a ticket. In the seconds it took to complete the transaction, my hands turned red and began to burn from cold. I tucked the ticket in my pocket and shoved my hands into my gloves, curling my fingers into fists in the hope it would generate warmth. Five minutes later, the ropeway staff opened the gates and waved me toward the small round gondolas, each of which could carry 15 passengers. As I stepped into one, the only other visitors—a Japanese couple who looked as miserable as I felt—stepped into the second gondola, leaving me to ride alone. The red-cheeked staff secured the doors, and the gondolas began the five-minute trip to the upper station, which sits 10 minutes' walk below the summit of Mount Haruna.

No snow remained on the mountain, but patches of viscous, icy mud suggested the final drifts had melted recently. The wind blew harder, and my legs chafed painfully against my pants. I gave up even trying to get warm.

An aging, faded Shintō shrine sat on the mountaintop—a rarity, given the Shintō custom of keeping shrines pristine to show respect for the *kami*. A sign on the summit displayed a map of the local mountains with a large red arrow and the words "You Are Here" pointing to the top of Mount Haruna.

I removed my gloves to take a summit photo—silently chastising myself for not investing in smartphone-friendly gloves—and promptly dropped my brand-new phone in an ankle-deep puddle of sticky mud.

I retrieved the phone and wiped it off with the linen handkerchief I'd planned to use to wipe my freezing nose. Thankfully, the phone seemed none the worse for the experience. I took my summit picture and hurried back to the ropeway station, arriving just in time to catch the noon gondola off the mountain.

As the gondola descended, I used YAMAP to help me find the trail up nearby Mount Temmoku. The upper portion wasn't hard to spot; it curled across the mountainside precisely where the app said it would be. The trailhead proved more difficult to see, but both the app and my online guide said the trail began behind a shop near Lake Haruna.

Thirty minutes of futile searching later, I suspected the trailhead was either closed or blocked off for the winter. I couldn't find it, even with the assistance of YAMAP and GPS, and my fingers were so numb I wasn't sure I could grip my poles securely enough to climb the mountain anyway. I surrendered the search and felt no disappointment. While I would have liked to claim a second summit, the walk around the lake had already given me a six-kilometer hike, and in the cold those six felt more like 10.

En route to the bus, I stopped at one of two open restaurants beside the lake, hoping to try the local chicken specialties called "cock-a-doodle dishes." The proprietor met me at the door and led me to a table with a glowing heater underneath. Before I could remove my hat and gloves, she brought me not only a steaming cup of tea but an enormous, insulated thermos full of refills.

To my gastronomic joy, the menu offered several "cock-a-doodle dishes." I ordered a set that included thinly sliced tempura chicken breast, mountain vegetables, rice, and sliced konjac (a starchy corm-based vegetable popular in Japan)—the latter, doing a far-too-persuasive impression of raw squid.

The chicken breast was cooked to order and arrived almost too hot to touch. It was crispy on the outside, juicy and perfectly cooked within. The delicate coating added texture but allowed the lightly seasoned chicken to shine through.

As I boarded the bus for Takasaki, I felt a twinge of loss at seeing Mount Haruna and the lake in such an inhospitable season—like visiting the Louvre when all the paintings were away for restoration. Even so, I was glad I had climbed Haruna-Fuji, and even happier that I had the chance to follow the climb with such a cock-a-doodle-delicious lunch.

57

SHORT-SLEEVED SAMURAI

February 24, 2019

After freezing my tail off on Mount Haruna, I took an evening train to Ashikaga City in neighboring Tochigi Prefecture, where I spent the night before the next day's climb. Today, Ashikaga City is perhaps best known for the spectacular wisteria at Ashikaga Flower Park, whose dangling blooms draw visitors from across Japan and around the world. Historically, the city was also the ancestral home of the Ashikaga clan, a noble samurai family that held the shogunate (and, essentially, ruled Japan) during the 14th and 15th centuries.

I had set my mystery novels in the waning years of Ashikaga rule and knew their history in Kyoto well but had never been to the city that bears their name. It was too early in the year for the famous wisteria, but I had heard about a famous *ume* (Japanese plum) grove in the mountains near the city, and I hoped to see the *ume* trees in bloom.

My hike began at the entrance to Gyōdōzan Jyoinji, an esoteric Buddhist temple founded in 713 and later immortalized in a famous woodblock print by Katsushika Hokusai. A pilgrim trail of steep stone stairs wound up the side of Mount Gyōdō (行道山) (442 meters) toward the temple and the summit. Ancient, waist-high statues of Buddhas and bodhisattvas stood on both sides of the path—a few of the 33,000 holy statues that line the mountain's slopes.

As I climbed the ancient stairs, I thought about the effort it had taken to construct them centuries ago. Esoteric Buddhist teachings speak of work as a form of meditation.

Clearly, the priests who built Gyōdōzan Jyoinji were meditative men indeed.

Enormous pine trees shaded the stairs and filled the air with the scents of pine and vanilla. Sunlight filtered through the trees, speckling the path and warming the air to the point where I removed my jacket and hiked in my wool T-shirt for the first time since Hokkaido.

Halfway to the summit, I stopped to visit the famous "bridge of clouds" and, just beyond it, a tiny Shintō shrine tucked into a cul-de-sac high on the cliffs.

Above the shrine, a steeper section of trail led to a rocky overlook where dozens of knee-high Buddhas looked down on Ashikaga city far below. The statues were carved from dark gray stone of a different color from the surrounding rocks, revealing that the statues were made elsewhere and carried up to the holy site. I lingered on the overlook, enjoying the hazy view of the city. Sunshine warmed my shoulders and, although the trees were bare, the air smelled faintly of new growth, the cold of winter giving way to spring.

At the summit of Mount Gyōdō, the ancient pilgrim route through the temple joined the Tochigi Prefectural Hiking Trail, a scenic route through the mountains that supposedly led past the former site of Ashikaga Castle and the trail to the famous *ume* grove. As I followed the Prefectural Hiking Trail off the summit, I passed an older couple hiking in the opposite direction. The husband grinned at me as he tapped his arm at the place where a T-shirt would have ended and said, "Samurai!"—a reference to the fact that I was hiking in short sleeves while everyone else was bundled up in winter hiking gear.

Half an hour's descent and another ascent along a steep, rocky ridge brought me to the summit of Mount Oiwa (大岩山) (417 meters), whose name means "Big Stone Mountain." Trees shaded one side of the summit, while the other had a view of pale brown mountains rolling off toward the horizon. They lacked the majesty of the snowcapped alps but possessed an austere beauty that made me feel at peace.

Hiking on toward Mount Ryogai (両崖山) (251 meters), I reflected on the lessons I had learned since my first climb on Mount Amagi nine months before. That period seemed fitting; I'd begun the hikes like a baby: bald, afraid, and unaware of the person I would become. Since then, I had grown hair and confidence. My feet, which once minced timidly over the mountain trails, now moved with a full, sure stride. I had grown to understand that bravery was not the lack of fear, but the choices I made in response to it.

I was brave now, because I chose to be.

I decided to embrace the flight of fancy that occurred to me on Mount Nasu and attempt to climb 1,000 Japanese mountains, but not on a timer or to set a record. Just for me. I wanted to consciously and consistently experience the beauty of these mountains, to watch the seasons turn at altitude, not just this year but in every year to come.

My pensive mood dissolved into amazement as a group of climbers approached me on the ridge. The elderly woman in the lead walked with a cane. Her husband, who appeared to be completely blind, held her shoulder with one hand. In the other, he gripped a long, red-tipped white cane. Four other hikers walked around them, though the woman and her husband moved with the confidence of long experience. All six members of the group wore happy smiles, and the "support team" bowed as I stepped aside to let them pass. Their presence on the mountain confirmed yet another lesson I had learned this year: the transformative power of focusing on "can" and "will" instead of "can't" and "won't."

Another half hour on the ridge brought me to the forested summit of Mount Ryogai and the ruins of Ashikaga Castle. I stopped for a brief, celebratory lunch near the castle site. Not much remained, but I felt a connection to the Ashikaga clan that made me glad I had chosen this for my 80th summit.

As I hiked down the far side of Mount Ryogai, I watched for the side trail to the famous plum grove, which supposedly contained more than 200 *ume* trees. Forty-five minutes later, I found myself in a sea-level park with signs heralding cherry blossoms and autumn foliage, but not *ume*. YAMAP and my smartphone's GPS agreed I'd overshot the mark by at least a kilometer, though I couldn't understand how I'd missed the trail.

At that point, I faced a difficult decision. The park sat only an easy kilometer's walk from the station where I planned to catch a train to Tokyo. If I wanted to see the *ume*—which might not even be in bloom—I would have to climb back up the trail and search for the path I'd missed on the way down. I had the strength, but the afternoon was growing late and I didn't want to climb back up a mountain—even a little one—if I didn't know for sure it would pay off.

Ume blossoms precede *sakura* (cherry blossoms) by about a month, and last much longer than their world-famous counterparts. For centuries, traditional Japanese art and culture have celebrated *ume* as the first official harbingers of spring, and I had come to Japan with the express intention of experiencing every season on the mountain trails. Two hours earlier, I had committed myself to continuing that plan for years to come.

But was I serious enough about the experience to climb back up a mountain looking for a trail that might be gone or closed and trees that might be bare of blooms?

I was, and I did.

I retraced my steps to the summit of Mount Ryogai but saw no evidence of the elusive *ume* trail. The 45-minute climb merely confirmed what I remembered: I had paid attention and there was no trail. As I started to descend the mountain for the second time that day, I noticed a tiny opening in the trees on the left side of the path. A long, flat piece of wood the length of a ruler, and twice as wide, was tied to one of the trees with fraying twine. Someone had written tiny Japanese characters on the wood. They were too small to read until I stood directly in front of them, but as I drew close I recognized the kanji for "Ume trees."

I had walked right by the narrow trail twice, each time mistaking it for nothing more than a gap between the trees.

An overgrown path wound down the mountain through a stand of barren maples, before entering a tunnel of smaller, gnarled trees whose branches twined together overhead. Their rough bark and twisted branches made me think of the ancient apricot tree that grew in the backyard of my childhood home in Southern California. I used to climb and read in its branches, and my mom made jam from the fruit it grew.

As I thought about that tree, it occurred to me that *ume*—although normally translated "plum"—is also known as the Japanese apricot.

I looked more closely at the trees. Their upper branches were filled with puffy blossoms the same color as the clouds that floated in the deep blue sky. A gentle breeze ruffled the petals and filled the air with the faint, sweet scent of apricots.

I had arrived in the famous grove without even realizing I was there.

Fat bees flew from tree to tree, tasting as many blossoms as they could. I strolled beneath the blooming trees and felt like I was blooming too. The strength and perseverance I had gained on 80 mountains also paid huge dividends in joy and memories. I spent an hour wandering the grove, and headed home that night still feeling like I walked on air. I had grown strong in the summer heat, gained wisdom as I watched the autumn leaves turn red and gold, and found lighthearted joy in winter snow. As winter bowed to spring, it now seemed possible that I might reach my 100th summit by the time the cherry blossoms fell.

58

INTO THE WOODS
March 10, 2019

The first week of March brought a series of storms to Japan, with rain in Tokyo and snow in the nearby mountains. The forecast for March 10 looked clear, so the night before, I hopped a westbound train to Hachioji, where I spent the night before traveling on to Ōtsuki, in Yamanashi Prefecture. Ōtsuki is home to more than 80 archaeological sites that date to the Jōmon period (14,000–300 BCE), when Japan was home to a hunter-gatherer civilization whose cord-marked pottery (*jōmon*) is responsible for the era's name.

I originally planned to begin my walk at the station and hike to the trailhead on Mount Ougi (扇山) (1,138 meters) but, on impulse, I climbed into the only taxi waiting just outside the tiny station. The trailhead lay at the top of a curving road, past groves of *ume* trees covered in blossoms that ranged in color from snowy white to shocking fuchsia. As the kilometers ticked by, I grew increasingly pleased with my choice to take the taxi. Even at my fastest pace, the walk to the trailhead would have taken me at least two hours.

The trail began in a grove of fragrant cedars. Birds sang in the branches, and the rising sun sent rays of light between the trees. I saw no hikers ahead of me, but a college-aged trio followed me up the path, talking in loud voices that shattered my meditative mood. I slowed down to let them pass, and a few minutes later silence reigned once more.

I caught up with the young hikers at a fork in the trail. They clustered near the split, consulting their maps as if confused.

Yellow nylon rope blocked off the left branch of the trail. A sign on the rope declared the path off-limits. The other side of the trail continued upward for another 20 yards and then dead-ended at a fallen tree.

I opened YAMAP and zoomed in on the trail. The red line that represented the route up Mount Ougi didn't show a closure, and the GPS showed me in the proper place. I walked up the trail toward the fallen tree. When I reached it, I noticed another trail that was invisible from below.

I beckoned to the younger hikers. *"Come on up."*

They looked surprised. *"The trail is open?"*

"Yes, right here." I continued up the mountain, leaving them to follow.

I might not be the fastest hiker on the mountain, but I did know how to find a trail.

The lines on the topographical map had warned me Mount Ougi would be steep, but knowledge didn't help the burning in my calves and thighs as I climbed the narrow switchbacks through the forest. The slope's steep angle made the mountain prone to landslides, and I passed by strips of barren earth with piles of fallen trees and other debris at the bottom. The slides looked old, and the ground felt stable beneath my feet, but I remained alert.

Woodpeckers hammered on the trees. A crow announced his territory to the world, and another distant corvid jeered in answer. I couldn't hear the college hikers talking—they had fallen far behind when the trail grew steep—but periodically I heard the tinkle of their bear bells, like a softer, ghostly echo of my own.

The summit of Mount Ougi had a postcard-worthy view of Mount Fuji rising above a ridge of mountains in the distance, which gave the famous peak another chance to photobomb my picture with a summit sign. I didn't mind; Mount Fuji can share my summit photos any time.

I descended from Mount Ougi along a ridge and then made a brief ascent to the summit of nearby Mount Okubo (大久保山) (1,109 meters). The mountaintop was surrounded on all sides by trees that blocked the view, so I didn't stay there long. Dead leaves crunched beneath my boots as I climbed slowly down the far side of the mountain on a trail that wound through a forest of pines and maple trees.

Eventually the trail leveled off along a ridge so curved it looked like a giant letter *C*. At its far end, I climbed to the summit of Mount Kanbano-kashira (カンバの頭) (818 meters), a mountain distinctive mostly for its *lack* of distinctiveness. The summit had no view, and the trees that covered the mountaintop looked just like all the rest I had seen that day. Even so, I took a picture with the summit marker, increasing my total to 83, and then hiked on toward Mount Nagaomine (長尾嶺) (803 meters).

I soon learned that the trail did not go over the summit of Mount Nagaomine. Instead, it cut around the side of the forested peak, 50 meters below the top.

I wasn't having that.

I left the trail and climbed the slope, boots crunching through the ankle-deep debris that covered the forest floor. It didn't take long to reach the leaf- and branch-strewn summit, but I saw no sign or wooden pylon at the top. I shuffled through the fallen leaves and branches, looking for the survey marker at the true high point. When I found it, I confirmed my position by GPS and took a picture before blazing another trail down the far side of the mountain to rejoin the hiking path.

My last peak of the day, Mount Momokura (百蔵山) (1,003 meters), lay another hour down the undulating trail, which followed a forested ridge until it reached the sharp incline that led to the summit. There, the path became both steep and narrow. I barely had to bend forward to touch the trail, which wound between the trees like a long, thin snake. A carpet of dead leaves covered the trail. My boots slipped on them more than once, and I clutched at trees to keep myself from falling.

Eventually I emerged atop the slope, where the path crossed one last tree-lined ridge and through a field of pampas grass before emerging into the summit clearing. Once again, the summit marker stood in an open area with a view of Mount Fuji rising up beyond the nearby mountains.

It occurred to me that I hadn't seen or heard the college hikers in over four hours. I didn't worry about their safety; they had good gear and looked experienced (map-reading skills aside). But when I started my 100 Summits climbs, everyone else on the mountain, from teens to 80-year-old grandmothers, hiked faster than I did. Now I stayed ahead of people half my age, even when I wasn't hurrying. As a person who had spent most of my adult years more fat than fit, I found my new strength gratifying.

I descended Mount Momokura by another trail, which proved even steeper and slipperier than the one on which I ascended. In several places, I found nylon climbing ropes fixed to the trees. I found them fun to navigate, especially where they allowed for short rappels.

The trail ended at an asphalt road, two miles from Saruhashi Station—one stop down the railway line from the place where I had disembarked that morning. Clouds had covered up the sun and the wind blew hard, suggesting an approaching storm. I thought I could reach the station before it rained, but it didn't matter much. The route to the station followed asphalt roads, and after four hours in the mountains I could use a shower anyway.

A few minutes later, I rounded a curve and saw a small park full of *ume* trees in bloom. Each one looked like a giant fuzzy cotton ball, and they filled the air with the heady scent of apricots. I stood admiring them until I felt fat drops of rain on my head and shoulders. The shower trailed off quickly, but I took the hint and didn't stop again until I boarded a train for Tokyo and headed home . . . with only 15 mountains left to climb.

59

FAREWELL TO SNOW

March 16, 2019

The range of mountains collectively known as Mount Amagi (天城山) is the highest point on the Izu Peninsula. Its highest peak, Mount Banzaburo (1,406 meters) is on the *hyakumeizan* list, and I originally planned to climb it—along with neighboring Mount Banjiro (1,295 meters)—directly after my Fuji climb. When that didn't happen, I decided to return and climb them later.

On St. Patrick's Day I finally got my chance.

I left directly after calligraphy class on Saturday evening, March 16, taking only the clothes on my back and some snacks in Blue, and arrived in the coastal town of Ito, three hours south of Tokyo, at 9:25 p.m. Before I made the short walk to my *ryokan*, I checked the schedule for the bus I planned to take to the trailhead in the morning.

According to the posted sign, the first bus left at 7:55 a.m.—on April 1.

Yet again, the posted sign conflicted with the online information, which claimed buses ran to the trailhead all year. In a fit of inspiration, I called up my GPS and asked it for a course to the trailhead of Mount Amagi. Google said there *was* a bus at 7:55, so I decided to come back in time for the morning bus, and hoped the bus would also come for me.

The following morning, I returned to the station at 7:35 a.m. and approached the open door of an idling bus to ask the driver about the bus to Mount Amagi. She confirmed that the bus to the trailhead would leave in 20 minutes, and that the sign reading "April 1" was merely a confirmation of the summer route.

As I waited for the bus, I realized I'd left my sun hat back in Tokyo. I had my winter hat in Blue, but a knit cap wouldn't help against the bright March sun.

At least I'd packed my sunscreen.

The bus pulled in at 7:53 a.m., and I climbed aboard. I settled into an empty seat, prepared for yet another lonely ride, but then—exactly one minute before the bus was due to leave—a river of hikers in colorful gear flooded out of the station and onto the bus, packing it completely to capacity.

Mountain season had begun.

The bus left Ito and began a long, slow climb up a winding mountain road past forests of blooming *ume* and budding maple trees. The sun shone brightly in the sky, and the world seemed full of light and life.

It occurred to me that, except for the terrifying lump on my chest, which had gotten larger since my visit to Dr. K. the month before, my life was perfect.

Maybe it's your definition of "perfect" that wants adjusting.

I had spent the greater part of 50 years viewing my life through the lenses of "if not for . . ." and "if only . . . ," but life is *never* perfect. There would always be a "but for" if I let there be. Viewed in that context, life was perfect now.

I was still pondering that truth when the bus arrived at the forested trailhead.

The lower portions of the trail meandered through a forest that smelled of mud and pines. The soil felt marshy underfoot, and I hiked slowly to avoid a slip.

Farther up, the trail carved narrow switchbacks in the mountainside, gaining altitude with every turn. About an hour into the hike, patches of ice appeared along the trail. In place of the drifts I'd seen on other mountains, here the ice formed piles of tiny balls, like miniature hailstones.

At 10:15 a.m. I reached the top of a rocky slope and saw the summit sign for Mount Banjiro (1,295 meters). The mountain overlooked a nearby valley, where a row of massive windmills turned atop a line of hills. In the distance, the coast of the Izu Peninsula met the Pacific in a jagged line of volcanic rock created by an ancient lava flow.

The wind blew cold across the mountaintop, and stopping would have required me to put my jacket on, so I took a summit photo and continued on my way. On the far side of the summit, the trail descended a steep, forested slope lined with massive stones. I hopped from stone to stone, glad that my original plans for the Amagi range had changed. This mountain, which was proving fun to hike in spring, would have been torturous in the summer heat.

I also felt grateful that delays had forced me to keep hiking through the winter. I had loved the snowy days, and looked forward to more snowy hikes next year—especially without the pressure of needing to complete a certain number of mountains by a specific date.

A dome-shaped hump called the *umanose* (horse's back) rises between Mount Banjiro and neighboring Mount Banzaburo. It looked more like a dromedary's hump to me, but the people who named it—centuries ago—most likely had never seen a camel. The muddy, slippery ascent proved much more challenging than I expected. In places, little landslides had collapsed the wooden trail supports installed along the route to prevent erosion. The angle of the trail and the heavy foliage made detours impossible. I climbed through the eroded areas, pulling myself through the steeper ones by hanging onto trees beside the trail.

At the top of the *umanose*, I passed through a forest of bushy evergreen *asebi*, an indigenous plant containing a toxin capable of making horses sick. Although it doesn't usually kill them, horses that consume *asebi* stagger as they walk, which earned the bush the nickname "drunken horse tree."

The descent from the *umanose* proved just as steep as the ascent, but at least this side had suffered fewer landslides. I reached the base of the hill in half an hour, but the achievement earned me no reprieve. The push to the summit of Mount Banzaburo, highest peak in the Mount Amagi range, began directly from the base of the *umanose*.

Forty-five steep, rocky minutes later, with my thighs and calves screaming for relief, I reached my 87th summit. The mountaintop consisted of a small plateau, entirely ringed by trees, with a wooden summit sign and several large, flat rocks. I sat down on a sunny stone to eat my lunch, but soon began shivering from the freezing wind that shook the surrounding trees. I put my jacket on, but it didn't fully block the chill.

Clouds blew in to block the sun, and the cold drove me off the summit with my lunch half-eaten and my fingers burning. I descended along the far side of a loop trail that would take me back to the bus stop. I debated stopping to retrieve my hat and gloves from Blue, but hoped the mountain would block the wind at lower altitudes. The route was steep, but wooden trail supports created "stairs" that made this side of the trail much easier than the one I used on the ascent. In some places, wooden handrails lined the route. I made good time and, as I hoped, the wind soon disappeared.

At which point, it began to snow.

Unlike my previous mountain snowfalls, which began with a few white flakes that gradually built in density, the snow on Mount Amagi went from zero to blizzard in 90 seconds flat. I stopped to cover Blue and retrieve my gloves but didn't bother with a hat. The unruly curls that covered my head provided plenty of warmth, even in the snow.

As I hiked downward through the storm, the snow changed into tiny, lightweight hailstones about the size and shape of the pieces that make up styrofoam. It didn't hurt, but it did explain the unusual drifts I'd seen on the ascent.

I reached the trailhead an hour before the bus was due. A sign at the bus stop asked, politely but firmly, that hikers not board the bus in muddy shoes, so I walked across the road and washed the mud from my boots at a faucet built expressly for that purpose. Afterward, I joined a line of shivering hikers waiting in the snow.

Fifteen minutes before the scheduled departure time, the bus arrived, but the driver refused to let anyone on board. He pulled away and parked the bus, its engine running, up the hill just out of sight. Thirteen long, cold minutes later, the bus returned. The doors swung open, releasing a wave of heat that boded well for the one-hour trip to Ito. I climbed aboard and found a seat as the welcome heat began to seep into my freezing bones. My shivering stopped five minutes later.

Within seven, I was sound asleep.

60

THE LONGEST ROPEWAY IN JAPAN

March 22–23, 2019

After my return from Mount Amagi, I visited Dr. K., who performed a biopsy on the lump in my chest. The results would not return for another week, so I packed my bags and traveled three hours south by train for back-to-back climbs in mountainous Mie and Gifu Prefectures.

Mie, once called Iga, was the historical home of the Iga *ryu*, one of Japan's most famous ninja clans—as well as the home of my fictitious ninja detective, Hattori Hiro. I had traveled to Iga-Ueno and the surrounding area several times, researching my novels, and wanted to make at least one climb in Mie because of its connection to my books. When I learned that the prefecture was also home to Japan's longest ropeway, at Mount Gozaisho (御在所岳) (1,212 meters), the mountain seemed like a perfect fit.

My bus arrived at 11:15 a.m., but the gondolas were sold out until noon—the first time I had visited a ropeway ride so popular that tickets sold out hours in advance. I bought a seat on the 12:00 run and took a place in line. My chest ached from the biopsy, which made it hard to put my fears about the possible results aside.

I tried to distract myself by subtly watching the family in front of me—mom, dad, older sister and younger brother. They laughed and joked with one another, clearly excited about the gondola ride. I thought about the way my own small family did things together when my brother and I were young. Despite the intervening years, the divorces, and the deaths, it still made me happy to remember Saturday morning bicycle rides to the donut shop and Sunday dinners at the Mexican restaurant our family loved. I wondered what the children standing in front of me would eventually become and do. I would never know, but I silently wished them well.

The small red gondolas of the Gozaisho Ropeway carry up to eight passengers and take 15 minutes to travel from the base of the mountain to the upper station, where hiking trails and a "sightseeing lift" continue to the summit. None of the four other people who boarded the gondola with me were dressed for hiking. As the car climbed slowly up the cable, a woman stood up to take pictures of the view. The gondola began to swing.

I love gondolas and ride them every chance I get, but given the extreme height and length of the cable at Gozaisho, I felt safer when the woman sat back down and the car stopped wobbling.

At the upper station, I was hungry, so I stopped for lunch at the Ropeway Cafe. The long, rectangular restaurant had windows on three walls, giving every table an impressive view of the surrounding mountains. Everything on the menu looked delicious. I chose a hamburger steak with demi-glace that also came with salad, vegetables, rice, and a mountain-shaped citrus jelly for dessert.

My window seat looked down on a sledding hill below the restaurant window. It was the final day of the sledding season, and although the snow appeared man-made (the rest of the mountain was completely brown), nobody seemed to mind. I ate slowly, savoring the food, the mountain view, and the laughter of children playing in the snow.

After lunch, I bought a ticket for the sightseeing lift, a single-rider chairlift that operates year-round. The windy, eight-minute ride carried me past the ski slopes—dry and brown—to an upper station about 20 yards from the summit marker.

Couples in street clothes walked around the little summit park, enjoying the 360-degree views of the Suzuka mountain range, which serves as the border between Mie and Shiga Prefectures. After taking the obligatory selfie with the summit marker, I started hiking down the ski slope in search of the trail that connected Mount Gozaisho with neighboring Mount Kunimi (国見岳) (1,180 meters). It felt strange to walk down the steep, smooth slope. I half expected someone to call out and stop me, although no signs declared it closed. The mountainside was covered in grass so short and groomed that, but for its dead brown color and radical angle, it could have doubled for a golfing green.

I reached the bottom of the ski slope without incident but couldn't find the trail. YAMAP indicated the route ran down what appeared to be a river of rocks that descended sharply down the center of a narrow gully in the direction of Mount Kunimi. Alpine shrubs and leggy trees grew on either side of the rockfall. I saw no flashes of paint or tape and no signs to mark the trail, but the gully went in the right direction and the stones looked stable, so I started down.

I jumped from stone to stone, more hopping than hiking and having tremendous fun.

Halfway to the bottom, I passed a hiker in his 60s, who was heading upward toward Gozaisho's summit. He didn't seem surprised to see me, which suggested—despite the lack of other evidence—that this really was the proper route.

A river ran past the base of the gully, and as I crossed it I saw flashes of pink tape on the opposite bank. It marked a path, unseen from above, that curled upward through the trees on Mount Kunimi. I had found the trail.

Most of the route up Mount Kunimi wove through leggy trees, along a rocky trail with muddy patches left by recently melted snow. Fifteen minutes below the summit, I emerged from the forest into a sandy clearing. To my right, a gap between Mount Kunimi and Mount Gozaisho revealed a stunning view of Nagoya City, 50 kilometers away.

Directly ahead, on the far side of the clearing, the trail ended at a sheer stone cliff 10 meters high, and continued along a stone ledge halfway up the face, which curled around the cliff and disappeared into the trees on the far side. A length of knotted climbing rope hung down the face as an aid for climbers.

I crossed the clearing and laid a hand on the sun-warmed stone. It felt alive beneath my palm. I grasped the rope, well aware that this obstacle would have turned me back a year ago. But I was not that timid person anymore.

I climbed to the narrow ledge and walked along it to the place where the trail curved around the cliff. From there, three more large boulders— each about waist-high—stood between me and the top of the cliffs, where the earthen path continued toward the summit.

A grove of stunted, leggy trees covered the top of Mount Kunimi, which I reached at 1:28 p.m., about half an hour before I needed to turn back if I wanted to catch the final gondola down from Mount Gozaisho.

My original plan had called for hiking to another nearby peak as well, but on the north face of Mount Kunimi I encountered an enormous snow field, 30 meters long and over a meter deep. A crust of ice covered the snow. I felt confident I could descend it and return—if I had time. The summit beckoned me from across a narrow valley as I tried to remember how much wiggle room I'd built into my turn-around time.

In the end, I decided it was not enough. On a clear trail, I might have reached the summit and returned in time, but with the snow it simply wasn't possible. The hike had gone too well, and I'd enjoyed it far too much, to spoil it with a frantic race to catch the gondola. There would be other hikes, and other mountains.

I retraced my steps over Mount Kunimi, used the climbing rope to descend the cliff at the sandy clearing, and hiked down through the forest to the valley that separated Kunimi from Mount Gozaisho. At the river near the base of the rocky gully, I met a Japanese hiker who asked where I was going.

I indicated the narrow gully. "Up Mount Gozaisho."

"That way?" He looked impressed. "Wow. That way is difficult."

"There's an easier way?"

He gestured in the opposite direction. Sure enough, a narrow trail led up the north face of Gozaisho, through the trees. "It goes directly to the ropeway."

Since I'd already been to the summit of Mount Gozaisho, I felt no need to hike the longer trail back up to the sightseeing lift. I thanked the hiker and took the trail he recommended.

Halfway up, I passed a frozen river that had just begun to thaw. Fast-moving water flowed beneath the ice and six-inch icicles hung along the banks. Slanted beams of afternoon sun transformed the icicles to prisms that cast tiny rainbows on the ground.

I stopped to enjoy the river and take photographs, feeling glad that I'd turned back with time to spare. Before my mountain year, I was always rushed, always running late. Now, I was consciously giving myself the time to savor every precious day.

As I rode the gondola down from Mount Gozaisho, I thought about the many changes in my life—and, more importantly, in me—this year. I had experienced a true rebirth, and had grown from a wobbly, frightened child into the kind of woman who scaled boulders, forded rivers, and sought out new, exciting adventures like riding the longest ropeway in Japan and visiting sacred waterfalls—like the one I was headed to next, at Mount Yōrō in neighboring Gifu Prefecture.

I no longer had to wonder who I would become when the climbs were through. I had my answer. I was still me—and still imperfect—but I was braver, stronger, and more confident than I had ever been before.

61

OF GOURDS AND WATERFALLS

March 24, 2019

An ancient Japanese legend tells of a filial young woodcutter who lived near the base of Mount Yōrō (養老山) (859 meters) in Gifu Prefecture. In the woods one afternoon, he discovered a spring that flowed with sake instead of water. He scooped some into the dried-out gourd he used as a drinking flask and carried it home to his aging father. The miraculous liquid cured the elderly man of all his ailments and even turned his white hair black again. The story spread, and many people traveled to Yōrō to drink from the miraculous healing spring.

In 717 the Japanese Empress Gensho visited Yōrō and declared the water from its springs (which apparently no longer flowed with sake) to be a fountain of youth that could restore health and vitality. To this day, visitors come to Yōrō from across Japan to drink from its springs and experience sacred Yōrō Falls, which appears on the official list of the top 100 waterfalls in Japan.

My train arrived at Yōrō Station early on a sunny morning warm enough for hiking in short sleeves. The trailhead in Yōrō Park was only two kilometers from the station, so I chose to save the fare and go on foot.

I walked up a quiet asphalt road past lines of budding cherry trees as the sunlight changed from the orange glow of dawn to the gold of morning. Just before I reached the park, I passed a metal fence with an enormous sign reading "YOROLAND" in colorful three-foot letters. The amusement park beyond the fence contained a selection of carnival-style rides in bright primary colors, from an elevated monorail to a Ferris wheel, wildly spinning "teacups," and a tilt-a-whirl.

The ride designs and signage looked like throwbacks to the 1970s (or earlier), but the rides themselves looked fresh and well maintained. I wanted to go inside, but the mountains called, so I kept walking into Yōrō Park.

Two paths led through the forested park to Yōrō Falls, with a river between them and a row of traditional wooden shops along one side. Half a kilometer below the falls, the shops came to an end and the paths converged by means of a wooden bridge, past which only a single, forested trail continued to the waterfall.

Unlike most major waterfalls in Japan, Yōrō Falls was not loud enough to hear from a distance, so it surprised me when I rounded the final curve and the falls came into view.

A bridal veil of water cascaded 32 meters down a rocky face and splashed into a sacred pool. From the pool, the water tumbled down large rocks and over smaller drops before settling into a channel, where it became the Yōrō River.

I climbed to the edge of the sacred pool and watched the water flowing down the damp stone face. Refreshing mist dampened my cheeks, and although I didn't know if the water of Yōrō Falls could cure my body, I had no doubt that waterfalls were healing to my soul.

At 10 a.m. I started up a set of stairs behind the falls that led to the trailhead of Mount Yōrō. As I crossed the parking lot beside the trail, an attendant asked me to sign the trail register. I wrote down the required information, including an estimated return time of 2:30 p.m.

The trail pulled no punches; it began with a series of steep, narrow switchbacks that continued all the way to the top of Mount Sampo (723 meters), my first summit of the day. In places, the path measured less than half a meter wide. I stopped to take pictures along the trail, as much as to rest my burning legs as to preserve my memories of the forest, which changed little for the first half hour. Halfway up the mountain, deciduous trees gave way to pines, and drifts of snow appeared along the trail. The snow disappeared again as I approached the top of Mount Sampo, whose forested summit opened onto a cliff with a spectacular view of Gifu Prefecture, far below.

After a short break to admire the view, I followed another trail along the forested ridge that connected Mount Sampo with Mount Ogura (841 meters). Recently melted snow had turned the trail into a sucking mire of black mud several inches deep. Streaky boot prints in the mud revealed where previous hikers slipped and, in a couple of places, even fell. I picked my way along a narrow, grassy ridge beside the trail. It was slippery, too, but I trusted it more than the muddy path.

The trail led to a flight of more than 60 earthen steps—all covered in slippery mud—that led upward to the summit of Mount Ogura. Small logs reinforced the ends of the steps, preventing slides. They, too, were dangerously slick, so I avoided stepping on them when I could.

I squished slowly up the mountain, laughing at the strange sensation of gloppy mud beneath my feet and marveling at how much of it clung to the soles of my hiking boots. Halfway up the stairs, I passed a college-aged couple descending the sticky mess in sneakers that had been white that morning but never would be again. My language skills weren't good enough to understand precisely what the woman was saying to her male companion, but I strongly suspected it would take more than a new pair of shoes to salvage their relationship.

The summit of Mount Ogura featured a small park with a gazebo, numerous benches, and some picnic tables, all of which were full when I arrived. The ground was not quite as muddy on the mountaintop but not dry enough for a picnic. I decided to eat on the summit of Mount Yōrō instead.

The far side of Mount Ogura got more sunlight during daylight hours. As a result, the trail was squishy underfoot, but the mud wasn't deep enough to pose a hazard, except for a few puddles that were easily avoided. The air smelled faintly fetid, and felt humid due to the water that evaporated from the mud. The trees along the trail had started setting leaves as spring broke through in earnest.

One last snowbank hugged the steep slope near the summit of Mount Yōrō, on a stretch of trail that seemed to get no sun. Just beyond it, a narrow path wound sharply upward to the heavily forested mountaintop. I ascended slowly, testing the trail's stability before I trusted it with my weight. Birds sang, and I could hear the muted laughter of people on the summit.

The tiny mountaintop was crowded with trees and a hiking group composed of retirees and their school-aged grandchildren. Even when the hikers left, there were no benches, and the muddy ground was even less hospitable for picnics than the top of Mount Ogura. I spent less than three minutes on the summit before I headed down—surprising the hiking group, which I passed a little way below the summit.

"Sugoi!" one of the older women cheered, *"you're really fast!"*

The glow of her compliment fueled my pace back over Mount Ogura and Mount Sampo. I did feel fast, and strong, and I loved that the mountains made me feel that way. I signed the trailhead register at 1:10 p.m., 80 minutes ahead of my morning estimate. The early arrival gave me time for a second trip to the waterfall, where the cooling spray felt even more refreshing than it had before the sweaty climb.

With 92 summits now behind me, and the end of my journey finally in sight, I decided to add one last active volcano to my 100 Summits list—and I knew exactly which one to choose. As I finally ate my overdue lunch, I made plans to pay a visit to Godzilla.

62

LEARNING TO RUN
March 30, 2019

The volcanic island of Izu Ōshima rises from the sea 120 kilometers south of Tokyo. Measuring only 50 kilometers in circumference, and with a permanent population below 8,000, Ōshima (whose name means "big island") is the largest island in the Izu Archipelago. The island is known for its native camellias and for Mount Mihara (三原山) (758 meters), a feisty volcano that gained worldwide fame when Godzilla was lured into its erupting crater at the end of the 1984 feature film *Godzilla Returns*. The real Mount Mihara erupted two years later, prompting an evacuation of its residents and jokes that the movie was so bad, the volcano erupted in protest.

At 8 a.m. on Saturday March 30, I joined a line of roller bag–wielding weekend warriors at Tokyo's Takeshiba Ferry Terminal and prepared to board a high-speed jetfoil ferry for the 90-minute ride to Ōshima. Ferries dock at one of two ports on the island based on current weather, with the port of the day chosen the morning of departure. That choice also determines the island's bus routes for the day (which start and end at the port du jour).

I crossed my fingers for Motomachi, the closest port to the Mount Mihara trailhead and my inn. If the ferry landed there, it would save me several hours of travel time, which I would need if I hoped to climb both Mount Mihara and neighboring Mount Kushigata (櫛形山) (671 meters).

Fifteen minutes before boarding, fortune smiled. We would dock at Motomachi Port.

Aboard the ferry, I found my preassigned place among the rows of airline-style seats that packed the two-story interior. The jet engines powered up with a muted whine as announcements in English, Mandarin, and Japanese reminded all passengers to "fasten your seatbelt as required by law, and remain seated until the liftoff operation is complete." The crew walked through the cabin to ensure compliance.

Unlike other ferries I had ridden, in Japan and elsewhere, jetfoils have no observation rooms or open decks. The boats are actually hovercrafts, which travel just above the water's surface at an average cruising speed of 80 kph, so passengers have to remain in their seats (except for brief trips to the bathroom or the vending machines) for the entire ride.

I'd like to say I enjoyed the trip, but I fell asleep before we even cleared the breakwater at Tokyo harbor.

I did, however, enjoy the nap immensely.

I woke as the ferry "splashed down" to dock at Motomachi Port. The overcast sky and choppy, dark gray sea looked nothing like the brilliant blues in the tourist videos, but the ominous weather added to the allure of the volcano rising just beyond the shore. I dawdled on the pier, taking pictures and taking in the view, and I reached the bus stop three minutes after the bus left for the Mount Mihara trailhead. The next one wouldn't leave for more than an hour, so I hopped in a taxi for a 15-minute ride up a scenic, winding skyline road that got me to the trailhead 30 minutes before the bus I'd missed was scheduled to arrive. On the way, the driver pointed out a new Memorial Park being built to commemorate Mount Mihara's 1986 eruption and the pure white *yamazakura* (mountain cherry) trees growing wild on the mountainside, which were at their fluffy peak. The large white blossoms looked like giant popcorn kernels hanging from the branches.

The cherry blossoms filled my heart with joy. I had waited so long to see them in full bloom. It felt as if all my dreams were coming true.

The Mount Mihara trailhead sits at the edge of a wide plateau. The summit cone rises from the center of the open space, a flat-topped pyramid of dark volcanic rock. The route to the summit begins along a broad, paved path that winds slowly upward across the plateau through lava fields created by the mountain's regular eruptions. At the base of the cone, the trail grows steeper (though still wide and paved) as it winds upward toward the crater rim.

My trail guide described the walk to the crater as a one-hour hike, but the overcast weather kept the temperature comfortably cool, and I covered the distance in only 30 minutes. Even so, with the last bus back to Motomachi Port departing the trailhead at 2 p.m., it didn't look like I'd have time to climb Mount Kushigata also, especially if I circumambulated the crater rim of Mount Mihara, which I'd been looking forward to.

The famous volcano was the more important climb, and I wanted time to enjoy it properly, so I jettisoned the plan for Kushigata. I could always return when the current climbs were through, and from what I had seen of Ōshima so far, I planned to do so.

From an overlook on the crater rim, I looked down on the trails of cooled magma that had overflowed the crater like a pair of enormous crab claws reaching for the trailhead and Motomachi Port. Before beginning my hike around the crater, I stopped at Mihara Jinja, a Shintō shrine dedicated to honoring—and pacifying—the volcano. Lava flows surround the wooden shrine, which has survived a number of eruptions.

Afterward, I hiked around the massive crater on a rocky, unpaved trail that passed numerous smoking fumaroles. An ocean breeze blew away all but a hint of the fumaroles' distinctive odor and added a salty tang to the cool air.

Far below, slate-colored swells rose high in the dark gray sea.

I stopped at several points to gaze down into the rocky crater. I saw no evidence of Godzilla, but a dozen fumaroles rose up like the breath of dragons sleeping underneath the reddish stones. By noon I had walked three-quarters of the way around the crater rim and reached the place where the branch trail to Mount Kushigata curved away down Mount Mihara's flank.

According to the YAMAP trail times, which generally matched my pace, I could not descend Mihara, climb to the summit of Kushigata, and return back over Mihara to the bus stop before 2 p.m., but I had made the hike from the trailhead in half the standard time. By that measure, an ascent of Kushigata *might* be possible, if I hurried.

I didn't want to push myself and fail, but I would never know if I didn't try.

Descending the trail of scree down the back of Mount Mihara took much longer than I planned, and by the time I reached the lava field that separated Mihara from Mount Kushigata, I suspected the second summit wouldn't happen after all. But as I checked YAMAP to confirm the trail times, I noticed another trail that crossed the wide plateau at a lower elevation than the one that led to the trailhead bus. The app identified the lower trailhead as "Mihara Onsen," which struck me as the kind of place a bus should stop.

A quick cross-check of the Ōshima Island website confirmed my theory. The bus stopped at the *onsen* on its way back from the trailhead, at 2:15. Better yet, if I took the trail to Mihara Onsen, I wouldn't have to climb back up and over Mount Mihara to catch the bus.

That, in turn, meant I could climb Mount Kushigata after all, but I had no time to waste.

From its base, Mount Kushigata looked more like a moonscape than an earthly mountain. The roughly conical massif of charcoal-colored volcanic tuff appeared entirely devoid of life. Not a single blade of grass grew anywhere on its barren slopes. The trail consisted of a faintly trodden path, one meter wide, that ran directly up the mountainside. My calves began to burn within five minutes of beginning the ascent. I strained against gravity and time, pushing hard to reach the summit before my turn-around time. The volcanic scree beneath my boots sounded as if I was walking on shards of pottery.

The wind blew past, but it held no scent at all.

At 12:45 p.m. I reached the top of mountain number 94. Mount Mihara rose up to the south, blocking my view of the ocean. To the north, Ōshima's lava fields stretched as far as I could see. I suspected on a sunny day the ocean might be visible in the distance, but that afternoon I saw only mist and clouds on the horizon.

I began my descent, boots sinking into the scree with every step. I hurried downward, letting gravity increase my pace.

Without conscious thought, I started running. Wind whipped through my hair. I whooped and laughed, surprised—more accurately, shocked—at how good it felt to run.

I had not run on level ground in years, let alone on scree-covered mountainsides. And yet, that day, something inside me could not help but run.

After about a hundred yards I slowed to a walk to catch my breath, but the instant I recovered, I ran again. It felt even easier and more natural the second time. And the third.

When I reached the bus stop at Mihara Onsen—three minutes before the bus arrived—I realized I had hiked more than 10 kilometers, though I felt as if I'd barely hiked at all.

The change I experienced in the mountains happened incrementally, as a waterfall changes rock, and the effects were just as permanent. As I ran down Mount Kushigata, I made yet another break with the life I knew before, and embraced my freedom to live the life I wanted. The life the mountains had taught me how to live.

63

CHICHIBU FIVE

April 6, 2019

With the end in sight, and my friend Laura VanArendonk Baugh arriving from the United States the following week, I decided to make a daylong traverse through Chichibu Tama Kai National Park, northwest of Tokyo.

I headed home after calligraphy class on the evening of Saturday, April 6, and packed a bag for the two-hour trip to Seibu-Chichibu Station, where I planned to spend the night before the climb. Japanese trains run late on weekends, so I headed out the door at 7:55 p.m., confident that I had plenty of time to reach my destination. At the bus stop, I researched the route and learned, to my dismay, that only three more trains departed for Seibu-Chichibu that night—one of them at 8 p.m.—and the station where I had to catch the train was almost an hour away.

The second of the three remaining trains required me to transfer between train lines halfway to my destination. If I missed the two-minute connection, I'd be stuck in the middle of nowhere for the night.

Not good.

The last, and only viable, train was an express with all-reserved seating. As I headed for the station, I hoped it wasn't entirely sold out.

When the last express train of the night pulled out at 9:30 p.m., I was aboard in a window seat. The lights of Tokyo sped by, glittering like jewels in the night. Later, as the train rolled through the darkness of the countryside, I reviewed my hiking plan. I had chosen a set of mountains that, while popular as hiking destinations, weren't particularly famous. After spending a year on some of the country's best-known peaks, I wanted to see how "ordinary" Japanese mountains compared with their lionized counterparts.

Were famous mountains truly better, or merely better known?

Before leaving Seibu-Chichibu Station, I confirmed the bus stop and departure time. For once, there were no surprises.

The 7:19 a.m. bus for Matsueda departed right on time, with me as the only passenger. As it left the city, it rolled past hillsides covered with blooming cherry trees. Pale pink and ivory blossoms filled the branches, and the delicate flowers had begun to fall. Each time a wind blew through the trees, blizzards of petals swirled through the air like snow.

In Japan, *sakura* (cherry blossoms) symbolize the fragility, beauty, and brevity of life. My original *hyakumeizan* plan had called for me to finish the climbs in early summer—still more than a month away. Now, I was even happier those plans had changed. It seemed far more appropriate to finish my journey—this phase of it, at least—as the cherry blossoms finished theirs.

"Matsueda" was a bus stop on a curving, two-lane forest road with nothing *but* the bus stop for at least two kilometers in both directions. I never did figure out exactly why the bus stopped there, as it was equally far from the trailhead and the city, but I had too much distance to cover that day to waste time looking for an answer.

The temperature hovered around four degrees Celsius (40 Fahrenheit) as I walked along the shoulder of the road. Hazy sunlight filtered through feeble clouds that looked like they'd burn off by noon. The narrow, twisting mountain road was precisely the type that draws motorcyclists in the United States—and I'd barely been walking for three minutes when the first sport bikes zoomed by.

In the 45 minutes before I reached the trailhead, I saw two dozen more motorcycles and four sports cars—including a yellow Lamborghini and an electric-blue McLaren Spider. What I didn't see was hikers. (I later learned most people began the hike from a public parking lot that isn't accessible by public transportation.) I felt much safer when I traded the ersatz speedway for the trail, an earthen path that switchbacked upward through a forest of pines. The trees measured up to a meter in diameter and more than 30 meters tall. They were barren of branches to a height of 15 meters, but their heavy canopies shaded the forest floor.

Songbirds flitted from branch to branch and filled the air with chirps and calls more varied and more numerous than I had heard on other mountains. Crows held lively debates among the trees.

It took almost an hour to reach the summit of Mount Takekawa (武川岳) (1,051 meters), which looked out over rows of hazy blue mountains receding to the horizon.

The trail to neighboring Mount Maetakekawa (前武川岳) (1,003 meters) was steep and narrow. It descended along a dusty path studded with rocks the size of footballs and then along a narrow saddle that sat between the peaks before ascending again to a summit that offered no view of anything but leafless trees.

I stopped for a snack and discovered that a half-eaten package of glazed cashews had come open in my hiking pants, filling my pocket with sugar crystals and bits of crushed cashew. I did my best to clean them out, but the pocket was a sticky mess. I fed the cashews to a crow and retraced my steps to the summit of Mount Takekawa, where I descended another rocky trail toward a ridge that would eventually take me to neighboring Mount Tsutaiwa (蔦石山) (1,004 meters).

The ridge trail felt like a path through a living tunnel. Small pines and maples grew close together. Their branches mingled overhead. Sunshine filtered through, spotting the trail with golden polka dots of light.

At the end of the ridge, the final push to the summit of Mount Tsutaiwa rose up a steep slope covered in a thick carpet of dead pine needles and maple leaves. I couldn't actually see the trail, and tested each step carefully before trusting it with my weight.

On the jagged stony outcrop at the summit, I spent only a couple of minutes enjoying the view of Mount Takekawa before beginning yet another hour of up-and-down hiking on steep, forested slopes toward the summit of Mount Yake (焼山) (850 meters), whose name translates "grilled mountain."

Just before I reached the mountaintop, a bright orange butterfly flew down from a tree and fluttered up the trail as if leading me to the peak. It even landed on the summit marker before flying down to rest in a patch of sun on the small plateau.

"Grilled Mountain" sounded like an appropriate place to stop for lunch, so I found a spot with an excellent view of neighboring Mount Buko, a mountain famous for its limestone quarries, which I looked at as I ate a simple lunch of an orange, nuts, and crispy cheese bread.

Fifteen minutes later, I began the descent from Mount Yake, along a narrow path that led almost straight down, without any rocks to serve as stairs and with only a few skinny trees to offer handholds. Months before, I would have turned back without even attempting it. That afternoon, I saw it as an interesting puzzle, which I solved one enjoyable step at a time.

At the base of the slope, the trail leveled out along yet another ridge, where I caught my first glimpse of Mount Futago . . . and burst out laughing.

The trail map indicated Mount Futago (二子山) had two peaks. They measured 870 and 882 meters high but shared a single name, which meant they counted as a single mountain. The trail map had *not* prepared me for the fact that Futago's rounded summits looked exactly like a pair of breasts.

How strangely appropriate.

Three hundred sixty-one days after my final chemotherapy treatment, I hiked toward Mount Futago—technically mountain number 99, since I could only count the twin peaks once—and thought about how radically my life had changed in (slightly) less than a single year.

When I received my breast cancer diagnosis, I was terrified of everything and didn't think my life would ever truly change. One year later, I had climbed mountains on all four of Japan's primary islands, in all eight of its major regions, and in more than half of its 47 prefectures. I had slept in temples, eaten regional specialties, and walked 100 kilometers along an ancient pilgrim route. My permanent address was now in Tokyo.

The life that once seemed as distant as a mountain peak was now a low-hanging fruit I held in my hands, and I planned to savor every bite.

The climb up Mount Futago involved a mixture of hiking and bouldering. As I made my way up the rocky face, the sun disappeared. Dark clouds moved in.

But I no longer minded a little rain.

I reached the first of Mount Futago's summits at 12:45, and the second at exactly 1 p.m. The rain stopped just in time for me to begin the last descent—the steepest and most exciting of the day.

Instead of a normal trail, the route down Mount Futago was delineated by nylon climbing ropes tied to the trees in a zigzag pattern at waist height. One set of ropes ran down each side of the trail, which was about a meter wide. The mountain itself was far too steep to descend unaided, and climbing up would have been almost as hard.

The slippery, packed earth slope made a slow descent impossible. I bounded downward, letting the nylon ropes slide through my hands. The speed felt natural and fun, as it had on Mount Mihara. I reached the bottom far too quickly and almost wished I could climb back up and run back down again.

From the base of Mount Futago, the trail meandered through the forest beside a stream that dropped through several waterfalls. The scents of mosses, pine, and new growth filled the air. At the edge of the forest, the path continued through a tunnel underneath the railroad tracks.

Six hours after leaving the bus at Matsudaira, I reached my destination: a station surrounded by cherry trees in bloom. Their blossoms swirled down on the breeze like pink and white confetti, as if the trees themselves were celebrating the near-completion of my 100 Summits quest.

On the train ride home, I planned the logistics for my final climb, which would take place after Laura arrived the following week. I was looking forward to her visit and happy that she would share my final summit.

After spending most of the year climbing alone, I wanted to finish my journey in the company of friends.

STATION 9: YOU'RE HIRED
MOUNTAIN TOTAL: 99

I eventually heard back from the company that was looking for an English-language editor in Tokyo.

They offered me the job, and I accepted it.

One week later, a major English-language travel website also offered me a position as a part-time travel writer.

I accepted that one, too, and officially retired from the practice of law.

When I finished my climbs, I would transition seamlessly to a life of writing, editing, and traveling around Japan—with time to continue my calligraphy studies too.

In less than a year, I had gone from stressed-out cancer patient shackled by a life of fear to full-time writer, editor, and adventurer.

The dream had come true before I reached my 100th peak.

64

100 SUMMITS . . . PLUS ONE MORE

April 12–14, 2019

In an unofficial sense, I completed my 100 Summits project not only within a year but before the one-year anniversary of my final cancer treatment: April 10, 2019. Not only would the "twin peaks" of Mount Futago put me across that line, if I counted them separately, but if I had renumbered the climbs to include the extra summits I reached during my early *hyakumeizan* climbs, the summit total sat at 106.

However, my close friend Laura VanArendonk Baugh—an author of fantasy novels set in Japan—had planned a visit to coincide with my final hike, and it meant a lot to me to make the last official climb with her. This journey deserved a better end than duplicated summits and renumbered peaks. In fact, I had an elaborate plan to end the 100 Summits project with a series of meaningful, celebratory climbs in the places I loved most.

On the morning of April 13, we rode the *shinkansen* to Kyoto. As we passed Mt. Fuji, who rose majestically into a cloudless sky of eggshell blue, I didn't feel she was "my" mountain. Instead, I felt that I belonged to her, and I looked forward to seeing her often in the years to come.

From Kyoto, Laura and I headed slightly farther south, to begin our climbs with a celebratory ascent of Mount Inari. We stopped for a lunch of *inari-zushi* and ginger drinks at the mountainside restaurant where I had eaten with Team Fuji almost exactly nine months before. Afterward, we continued to the summit (number-100-that-didn't-count-because-I-had-already-climbed-it-with-Team-Fuji).

Laura and I descended from Mount Inari and returned to Kyoto, where we visited the geisha houses of Gion, the historical shopping streets of *ninenzaka* and *sannenzaka*, and, as darkness fell, the ruins of the Rashomon, an ancient gate that inspired a famous short story and a classic Kurosawa film.

From the gate, we walked to nearby Tōji, one of Kyoto's oldest Buddhist temples, for the final night of the annual cherry blossom illumination. As we walked through rows of blooming *sakura*, the delicate blossoms brightly lit against the darkened sky, I reflected on my climbing year. I had not set a mountaineering record. In the end, I had climbed only 23 of Fukada's famous peaks—but that just meant I still had mountains left to climb. I had achieved every one of the larger goals: to break away from fear, to find true, lasting happiness, to change my life completely— and to climb 100 mountains in a year.

The following morning, Laura and I headed south to Nara.

In 710 Nara became the first permanent capital of Japan, and many foundational aspects of Japanese culture had their start in the ancient city. It seemed appropriate to end my climbs where so much Japanese history began, so despite its modest stature, I had chosen sacred Mount Wakakusa (若草山) (342 meters) for my 100th climb.

The mountain stands adjacent to even more sacred Mount Mikasa (which is a different mountain, although online sources sometimes erroneously conflate the two) where, during the eighth century, a deity appeared on a white deer in response to prayers for protection of Nara City. Mount Mikasa remains off-limits to people to this day, but Mount Wakakusa had a hiking trail.

Laura and I paid the nominal entrance fee at the tiny booth beside the trailhead and started up a set of stairs that curled around the mountain's lower slope. Clouds gathered overhead, and we increased our speed, hoping to reach the top before it rained.

The stairs ended halfway up, and we continued up a steep trail covered in grass so short it looked like the world's most treacherous putting green. The air smelled of dry grass and approaching rain. At the top of the hill, the trail ran past another ticket booth, where we had to show our admission tickets to gain access to the final section of the trail. Ten minutes later we reached the mountaintop, under the watchful eyes of a sassy crow and a herd of Nara's famous deer.

On the summit, we took pictures and enjoyed the view of Nara City spread out far below. I didn't know what I expected to feel when I reached the top of that final mountain, though I was deeply happy to have Laura with me, even if I suddenly burst into tears. But I didn't cry. Or scream. Or even shout in victory. Laura took some goofy photos of me touching the summit marker and the moment passed in understated, yet entirely appropriate, normalcy. Appropriate, because the 100th summit was more a portal than a finish line. Like a torii, it marked the opening to another space, the beginning of another life (even though, in many ways, I was already living it).

Nearby, the crow strutted around the mountaintop like an emperor surveying his domain. His presence made me think of all the other crows that had crossed my path, and guided me, during my travels in Japan. At every crucial point, the crows had been there, a reminder that, like Emperor Jimmu, I was guided both by my own choices and by a higher power I did not control.

Later that afternoon, Laura and I took a train to Wakayama Prefecture and rode the brand-new cable car to the Koyasan Plateau. We arrived in the midst of a storm, and hurried to the 1,100-year-old temple where we planned to stay the night. Rain drummed on the roof as we feasted on *shojin ryori* in a private room with tatami floors and masterful calligraphy displayed in an alcove on the wall. I savored every bite of the celebratory feast, from slivers of crispy-fried wild onion to creamy *gomadofu* (sesame tofu) and a bowl of udon in savory broth cooked at the table over a tiny fire.

The following morning, Laura and I walked to Ōkunoin beneath a cloudless sky. The world seemed freshly washed and new. At Kōbō Daishi's tomb I lit candles and incense for my father, and for Annamaria's husband David, and offered prayers of gratitude for the safe completion of my 100 Summits journey—even though we had two mountains left to climb.

From the tomb, we followed a winding path through the forest to the *Nyonin-Michi* (Women's Pilgrimage Route), and then along a steeper section of forested trail to the summit of Manisan (摩尼山) (1,004 meters), the Koyasan Sanzan peak I had planned to climb with Annamaria several months before, and my second "100th summit" of the weekend.

A Buddhist altar sat on the forested mountaintop, and the spicy scent of pine trees filled the air. Sunlight speckled the ground beneath the trees. I listened to the breeze rustling the trees and felt an overwhelming sense of joy and peace, but a hint of sorrow too.

The mountains had become a way of life for me. They were my friends, my mentors, my cathedrals. I would keep climbing, but no longer as a primary vocation.

On our way back to Tokyo, Laura and I made an overnight stop in Osaka for one final climb: 5-meter Tenpozan (天保山)—the smallest mountain in Japan. The artificial massif was created during the dredging of Osaka harbor during the 19th century. We arrived after dark but decided to risk the dangers of a nocturnal ascent and soon established a base camp near the giant glowing Ferris wheel adjacent to Mount Tenpo Park. After several false starts, we located the stairs at the base of the mountain. Seconds later, we reached the summit marker and the official end of the 100 Summits project, which now included ascents of both the highest and lowest mountains in Japan.

Laura and I returned to Tokyo, where we spent another week visiting and traveling together. When she left, I was sorry to see her go, but it was time for both of us to return to real life—which, for me, meant a new life as a full-time, permanent resident of Tokyo. I would write, edit, and study calligraphy during the week, travel around Japan on weekends, and return to the mountains several times each month to watch the seasons change and experience the beauty of the wild, natural places that had healed my body and my soul.

I had come to the mountains wondering if it was truly possible to change my life, and I had the answer: an unqualified YES!

And now it was time to live it.

Because the first 100 summits are behind me, but my journey and the climb go on.

APPENDIX
The 100 Summits

#	Date	Mountain	Height (m)	Prefecture (Region)
1	May 20, 2018	Mount Akagi (Akagiyama)*	1,828	Gunma (Kantō)
2	May 27	Daibosatsu*	2,057	Yamanashi (Chubu)
3	June 1	Mount Iwaki*	1,625	Aomori (Tōhōku)
4	June 2	Mount Hakkōda (Ōdake)*	1,585	Aomori (Tōhōku)
		i. Akakuradake	1,548	Aomori (Tōhōku)
		ii. Idodake	1,550	Aomori (Tōhōku)
5	June 4	Mount Hachimantai*	1,613	Iwate (Tōhōku)
6	June 5	Mount Zaō (Kumanodake)*	1,841	Yamagata (Tōhōku)
		i. Jizōdake	1,736	Yamagata (Tōhōku)
7	June 14	Mount Nasu (Sanbonyari)*	1,917	Tochigi (Kantō)

		i. Chausu	1,915	Tochigi (Kantō)
8	June 15	Mount Bandai*	1,816	Fukushima (Tōhōku)
9	June 20	Mount Ibuki*	1,377	Shiga (Kansai)
10	June 21	Mount Ōmine* / Mitarai Gorge	1,719	Nara (Kansai)
11	June 22	Mount Odaigahara*	1,695	Nara (Kansai)
12	June 24	Mount Kurumayama*	1,925	Nagano (Chubu)
13	July 1	Mount Daisen*	1,709	Tottori (Chugoku)
14	July 3	Mount Hiei	848	Kyoto (Kansai)
15	July 3	Bentendake (Mount Benten)	984	Wakayama (Kansai)
16	July 13	Mount Takao	599	Tokyo (Kantō)
17	July 16	Mount Inari	230	Kyoto (Kansai)
18	July 19–20	Mount Fuji	3,776	Shizuoka (Chubu)
19	August 7	Shiroyama (Mount Shiro)	562	Kanagawa (Kantō)
20	August 14	Mount Asama	196	Kanagawa (Kantō)
21	August 14	Mount Gongen	245	Kanagawa (Kantō)
22	August 14	Mount Kobo	235	Kanagawa (Kantō)
	August 14	Mount Azuma	125	Kanagawa (Kantō)
23	September 10	Mount Yōtei*	1,898	Hokkaido (Hokkaido)
24	September 11	Mount Tokachi*	2,077	Hokkaido (Hokkaido)
25	September 14	Mount Tomuraushi*	2,141	Hokkaido (Hokkaido)
26	September 16	Mount Meakan*	1,499	Hokkaido (Hokkaido)
27	September 17	Mount Shari*	1,547	Hokkaido (Hokkaido)

28	September 19	Mount Rausu*	1,600	Hokkaido (Hokkaido)
29	September 21	Asahidake*	2,291	Hokkaido (Hokkaido)
30	September 23	Pon Yama	444	Hokkaido (Hokkaido)
31	September 28	Yoryusan	1,009	Wakayama (Kansai)
32	October 7	Iino-yama	442	Ehime (Shikoku)
33	October 8	Ishizuchi*	1,982	Ehime (Shikoku)
34	October 22	Takanosu	833	Kanagawa (Kantō)
35	October 22	Sengen	802	Kanagawa (Kantō)
36	October 22	Komagatake	1,356	Kanagawa (Kantō)
37	October 24	Daimonji	467	Kyoto (Kansai)
38	November 12	Hiuchiishiyama	989	Kanagawa (Kantō)
39	November 12	Myojingatake	1,169	Kanagawa (Kantō)
40	November 12	Myojogatake	924	Kanagawa (Kantō)
41	November 15	Mitake	929	Tokyo (Kantō)
42	November 15	Okunoin	1,077	Tokyo (Kantō)
43	November 15	Nabewari	1,082	Tokyo (Kantō)
44	November 25	Tsurugi	371	Wakayama (Kansai)
45	November 25	Meshimori	341	Wakayama (Kansai)
	November 24–30	Kumano Kodo Nakahechi	99 (km)	Wakayama (Kansai)
46	December 19	Byobu	948	Kanagawa (Kantō)
47	December 20	Marudake	1,154	Kanagawa (Kantō)
48	December 20	Nagaosan	1,144	Kanagawa (Kantō)
49	December 20	Kintoki	1,212	Kanagawa (Kantō)
50	December 31	Tsukuba*	877	Ibaraki (Kantō)

51	January 10, 2019	Nokogiriyama	330	Chiba (Kantō)
52	January 14	Ōyama	1,252	Kanagawa (Kantō)
53	January 15	Hakusan	284	Kanagawa (Kantō)
54	January 15	Sakurayama	280	Kanagawa (Kantō)
55	January 20	Tenjosan	1,140	Yamanashi (Chubu)
56	January 20	Shimoyama	1,302	Yamanashi (Chubu)
57	January 20	Kinashiyama	1,732	Yamanashi (Chubu)
58	January 21	Haneko	930	Yamanashi (Chubu)
59	January 21	Ashiwada	1,535	Yamanashi (Chubu)
60	January 21	Danwayama	1,233	Yamanashi (Chubu)
61	January 28	Homanzan	829	Fukuoka (Kyushu)
62	January 28	Bucchosan	869	Fukuoka (Kyushu)
63	January 30	Tsurumidake	1,375	Oita (Kyushu)
64	February 10	Asoyama	794	Saitama (Kantō)
65	February 10	Hinodeyama	902	Tokyo (Kantō)
66	February 13	Ishiwariyama	1,412	Yamanashi (Chubu)
67	February 13	Ichinosunanosawa-noatama	1,318	Yamanashi (Chubu)
68	February 13	Hiraoyama	1,290	Yamanashi (Chubu)
69	February 13	Okuboyama	1,267	Yamanashi (Chubu)
70	February 13	Imoyama	1,280	Yamanashi (Chubu)

71	February 13	Ohirayama	1,296	Yamanashi (Chubu)
72	February 13	Iimoriyama	1,191	Yamanashi (Chubu)
73	February 13	Nagaikeyama	1,178	Yamanashi (Chubu)
74	February 13	Odeyama	1,102	Yamanashi (Chubu)
75	February 14	Teppouginoatama/ Myojin	1,291	Yamanashi (Chubu)
76	February 14	Mikuniyama	1,343	Yamanashi (Chubu)
77	February 23	Harunasan	1,449	Gunma (Chubu)
78	February 24	Gyodosan	442	Tochigi (Kantō)
79	February 24	Oiwasan	417	Tochigi (Kantō)
80	February 24	Ryogaisan (×2)	251 (×2)	Tochigi (Kantō)
	February 24	Kagamiyama	160	Tochigi (Kantō)
81	March 10	Ougiyama	1,138	Yamanashi (Chubu)
82	March 10	Okuboyama	1,109	Yamanashi (Chubu)
83		Kanbanokashira	818	Yamanashi (Chubu)
84		Nagaomine	803	Yamanashi (Chubu)
85		Momokurasan	1,003	Yamanashi (Chubu)
86		Banjirodake	1,295	Shizuoka (Chubu)
87		Mount Amagi (Banzaburodake)*	1,406	Shizuoka (Chubu)
88	March 23	Gozaishoyama	1,212	Mie (Kansai)

89	March 23	Kunimidake	1,180	Mie (Kansai)
90	March 23	Sampozan	723	Gifu (Chubu)
91	March 23	Ogurayama	841	Gifu (Chubu)
92	March 24	Yōrōsan	859	Gifu (Chubu)
93	March 30	Miharayama	758	Tokyo (Kantō)
94	March 30	Kushigatayama	671	Tokyo (Kantō)
95	April 6	Takekawadake	1,051	Saitama (Kantō)
96	April 6	Maetakekawadake	1,003	Saitama (Kantō)
97	April 6	Tsutaiwayama	1,004	Saitama (Kantō)
98	April 6	Yakeyama	850	Saitama (Kantō)
99	April 6	Futagoyama	870 882	Saitama (Kantō)
100	April 13	Wakakusayama	342	Nara (Kansai)
101	April 14	Manisan	1,004	Wakayama (Kansai)
102	April 14	Tempozan	5	Osaka (Kansai)

* Denotes an official *hyakumeizan* peak